Apple Training Series
iLife '08

Michael E. Cohen / Jeff Bollow / Richard Harrington

Apple
Certified

Apple Training Series: iLife '08
Michael E. Cohen, Jeff Bollow, Richard Harrington
Copyright © 2008 by Peachpit Press

Published by Peachpit Press. For information on Peachpit Press books, contact:

Peachpit Press
1249 Eighth Street
Berkeley, CA 94710
(510) 524-2178
Fax: (510) 524-2221
http://www.peachpit.com
To report errors, please send a note to errata@peachpit.com
Peachpit Press is a division of Pearson Education

Contributing Authors, Previous Edition: Michael Rubin, Mary Plummer
Apple Series Editor: Serena Herr
Project Editor: Stephen Nathans-Kelly
Production Coordinator: Laurie Stewart, Happenstance Type-O-Rama
Technical Editor: Charlie Miller
Technical Reviewers: K.D. Gulko, Stephen Kanter, Ben Balser
Copy Editor and Proofer: Dave Awl
Compositor: Chris Gillespie, Happenstance Type-O-Rama
Media Producer: Eric Geoffroy
Indexer: Jack Lewis
Cover Illustration: Kent Oberheu
Cover Production: Happenstance Type-O-Rama

ISBN 13: 978-0-321-50267-4
ISBN 10: 0-321-50267-1
9 8 7 6 5 4 3 2
Printed and bound in the United States of America

Contents at a Glance

Table of Contents

Going Public

Getting Started

Welcome to the official Apple training course for the iLife '08 suite of products: iPhoto, iMovie, iWeb, GarageBand, and iDVD. You don't need to have any special background to get started, other than having a Mac (and perhaps a healthy curiosity about what you can do with it).

Learning iLife really means learning to live digitally; you're not so much learning to use new software as learning how to integrate your Mac comfortably into your home, school, and work. The iLife tools are only part of the picture—and this book is not so much a training manual as it is a way to show you how to enrich your world by weaving digital audio, photos, videos, and the web into many aspects of your life.

So instead of teaching you all the geeky details of these hip tools, we concentrate in this book on how real people really use them. We may even skip entire areas of functionality, all with an eye toward having fun, achieving quick success, and forming a foundation of confidence on which you can build.

What iLife Does for You

There was a time when your photographs were in one part of your house; your music collection somewhere else; VHS videotapes scattered around the television; and, if you have a camcorder, Hi-8 (or some such format) cassettes in a box. Each medium was tricky to keep organized.

But when all your media is digital—in the form of digital snapshots, digital audio (CDs, MP3s, and so on), and digital video (DVDs and DV cassettes)—keeping them organized is pretty easy, sharing content is streamlined, and using the material interchangeably between formats is both simple and kind of fun.

A Macintosh is designed to sit at the heart of your digital home. It's just a computer, but now it's finely tuned to make managing and combining all this content effortless. Better than that, Apple provides—free on all Macs—software that orchestrates the commingling of all this content. iLife is a family of products made up of applications designed to stand alone but also tuned to work together in remarkable ways.

What iLife teaches you is *media literacy:* the ability to communicate in a variety of powerful ways, different from speaking or writing or even doing page design. Making professional-quality videos, podcasts, and websites, and being able to combine picture and sound effectively, is a skill that can be applied throughout your life. Once you have it, you'll be stunned by how often you use it, whether for personal pleasure or commercial advantage.

It's too simplistic to say that iPhoto is the picture software and iMovie is the video software. iPhoto handles the organization of your pictures, true, but once your images are there, using them in slideshows and videos and on the web is very easy. You can't build a box around each component of iLife. So rather than focus on each product in turn, this book helps you create real-world projects, which sometimes involves dipping into several applications in a single lesson. Face it, learning software is seldom fun. But making movies or podcasts, promoting your business, or building a creative report for school can be. You'll end up learning the software along the way.

The Methodology

This book moves through lessons by progressively increasing the complexity of the media you're using. You start by managing still images alone, then move to publishing still images, turning still images into moving *(dynamic)* images, and exploring the possibilities of video.

With digital content and the five core iLife applications (iPhoto, iMovie, iWeb, Garageband, and iDVD), you can create everything from photobooks to DVDs, podcasts, dynamic websites, and polished movies.

Above all, these lessons are meant to be practical—not esoteric projects to show off the software, but real-life projects for real-life people with time constraints, well-worn equipment, and concerns about budget. The lessons cover four general areas: still images, movies, music, and publishing.

Section 1: Working with Photos

▶   In Lessons 1 through 4, you'll work with still images. You'll learn how to import images from your digital camera; how to organize, search, keyword, edit, and archive your pictures; and how to share your pictures in slideshows, cards, picture books, calendars, and on a web gallery.

Section 2: Creating Simple Movies

▶   In Lessons 5 through 10, you'll work mostly with video—though you'll also combine still photos, music, special effects, graphics, and titles in iMovie. You'll learn to shoot video creatively and edit to maximum effect; add narration to your videos; mix sound with picture; and finish your movie by fine-tuning color, contrast, and audio.

Section 3: Composing and Arranging Music

▶   In Lessons 11 through 13, you'll build a simple, original score for the movie you just made in Section 2. Then you'll record and produce a sophisticated podcast, and create original music with GarageBand.

Section 4: Going Public

▶   In Lessons 14 and 15, you'll put it all together, using iWeb, iPhoto, iMovie, and GarageBand together to build a website with dynamic content, and create and publish blogs, web albums, and podcasts. Finally, in Lesson 16, you'll use iDVD to build a DVD menu for your movie project.

A Word About the Lesson Content

Often, training materials are professionally created—using actors and complicated productions with multiple cameras, lights, microphones, tripods, and a crew. The resulting material is of high quality but bears little similarity to the kind of projects you will be working on.

To make this training as real-world and practical as possible, virtually all the media used in this book was made in precisely the way you would make your own videos. With the exception of the American Diabetes Association's Tour de Cure footage (which was shot professionally), the quality of the shots (for better or worse) is comparable to what you can get with typical consumer equipment, and the sophistication of the projects is precisely what you can achieve using the iLife tools, with settings (and challenges) you will commonly encounter yourself.

We tried to make sure the events depicted here were recorded in the way you are being taught to work. Ideally, this will give you clear and realistic expectations about what you can do with your newfound skills.

System Requirements

This book is written for iLife '08, which comes free with any new Macintosh computer. If you have an older version of iLife, you will need to upgrade to the current iLife version to follow along with every lesson. The upgrade can be purchased online at www.apple.com and is available from any store that sells Apple software.

Before you begin the lessons in this book, you should have a working knowledge of your Mac and its operating system. You don't need to be an expert, but you do need to know how to use the mouse and standard menus and commands, and how to open, save, and close files. You should have a working understanding of how OS X helps organize files on your computer, and you should also be comfortable opening applications (from the Dock or at least the Applications folder). If you need to review any of these techniques, see the printed or online documentation that came with your computer.

For a list of the minimum system requirements for iLife, please refer to the Apple website at: www.apple.com/ilife/systemrequirements.html.

Copying the iLife Lesson Files

The *Apple Training Series: iLife '08* DVD-ROM includes folders containing the lesson files used in this course. Each lesson has its own folder, and you should copy these folders to your hard drive to use the files for the lessons. Note that several lessons use the files from a previous lesson; in those cases, the lesson folder contains a simple text file indicating there are no new media files for that lesson.

To install the iLife Lesson files:

1   Insert the *ATS iLife08* DVD into your DVD drive.

2   Drag the iLife08_Book_Files folder from the DVD onto your desktop.

    This will copy the folder to your hard drive. Inside this folder is the Lessons folder, which contains all of the files you'll use for this book. Eject the disc.

About the Apple Training Series

Apple Training Series: iLife '08 is part of the official training series for Apple applications, developed by experts in the field and certified by Apple, Inc. The lessons are designed to let you learn at your own pace. Although each lesson provides step-by-step instructions for creating specific projects, there's room for exploration and experimentation. However, if you follow the book from start to finish, or at least complete the lessons in each section consecutively, you will build on what you learned in previous lessons.

For those who prefer to learn in an instructor-led setting, Apple also offers training courses at Apple Authorized Training Centers worldwide in Mac OS X, Mac OS X Server, and Apple's Pro applications. These courses are taught by Apple Certified Trainers, and balance concepts and lectures with hands-on labs and exercises. Apple Authorized Training Centers have been carefully selected and have met Apple's highest standards in all areas, including facilities, instructors, course delivery, and infrastructure. The goal of the program is to offer Apple customers, from beginners to the most seasoned professionals, the highest-quality training experience.

To learn more about Apple Training and Certification, or to find an Authorized Training Center near you, go to www.apple.com/training.

Resources

Apple Training Series: iLife '08 is not intended to be a comprehensive reference manual, nor does it replace the documentation that comes with the applications. Rather, the book is designed to be used in conjunction with other comprehensive reference guides. These resources include:

- ▶ Companion Peachpit website: as iLife '08 is updated, Peachpit may choose to update lessons or post additional exercises as necessary on this book's companion webpage. Please check www.peachpit.com/title/0321502671 for revised lessons.

- ▶ Apple's website: www.apple.com.

- ▶ *Apple Training Series: iWork '08,* by Richard Harrington, is an excellent companion to this book. Learn how to use iLife applications with iWork to create first-class presentations, slideshows, newsletters, publications, and spreadsheets.

- ▶ *Apple Training Series: Garageband 3*, by Mary Plummer. Written for GarageBand 3, this wonderful training book offers a comprehensive introduction to creating and recording music on a Mac.

- ▶ *The Macintosh iLife,* by Jim Heid (Peachpit Press), an accessible and popular reference guide for the iLife products.

- ▶ *The Little Digital Video Book,* by Michael Rubin (Peachpit Press), a concise resource on how to make your videos have more impact and look professional. While the book is not about the iLife software specifically, it expands on many of the concepts touched on in the lessons on shooting and editing video.

- ▶ *Making Fantastic Short Films*, from Embryo Films. This award-winning course module and DVD shows primary and secondary schools how to make short films in the classroom. www.MakingFantasticShortFilms.com/update

Working with Photos

1

Lesson Files	iLife08_Book_Files > Lessons > Lesson01 > L1_Five_photo_events
Media	This lesson takes approximately 45 minutes to complete.
Goals	Learn basic photographic terms and techniques
	See how to connect a camera to your Mac
	Import pictures and video from a camera into iPhoto
	Import picture files into iPhoto

Getting Pictures into iPhoto

When iPhoto was first introduced, it was described as the digital version of the shoebox where you store all your photos.

iPhoto is a pretty amazing shoebox. It lets you store thousands upon thousands of photos, and helps you organize them into memorable events and special collections. It gives you the tools to improve the color and quality of your photos. It offers you ways to order high-quality photo prints, or photo greeting cards, or books, or calendars. It also lets you create and play photo slideshows, or upload your photos to the web for your friends and family or the whole world to see.

But before you can do all these wonderful things, you have to get your photos *into* the shoebox.

That's what this lesson is about.

Shooting Pictures

Digital cameras come in all shapes and sizes, from disposable point-and-shoot pocket-size cameras to image-stabilizing, multi-sensored, super-high-resolution professional cameras that can cost as much as an automobile. But no matter how simple or how refined the camera, they all have the same job: to capture an instant of light and freeze it in a rectangular frame.

Even the best camera can take a mediocre picture, and even a mediocre camera can take a good one. When it comes to taking a good picture, what's more important than the camera is the photographer behind it.

Getting the Right Shot

Digital cameras have two profound advantages over traditional film cameras—you don't have to pay for the film, and you don't have to wait for the film to be developed.

Make the most of these advantages: Don't wait for the perfect shot. Instead, take a lot of pictures. Doing so costs nothing, and it may very well be that one of your shots will be the perfect shot, or at least something close to it. Keep the good ones, and throw away the rest.

Next, remember that a camera's sole job is to capture light. If there's more light behind the subject of your picture than on the subject itself, your camera will capture that background light, leaving your subject in darkness.

Backlit subject

Although iPhoto has a tool for bringing out the detail on a backlit subject, that tool can only do so much. Try to have the light source behind you, rather than behind your subject. If that's not possible, use the camera's flash if it has one—most cameras do.

TIP ▶ When you use a flash, don't position the camera directly in front of the subject. For example, if you take a picture of a person wearing glasses and you shoot from directly in front of the subject, the light of the flash will reflect directly back into the camera from the subject's glasses. Similarly, if there's a window or other reflective surface directly behind the subject, the flash will reflect off the surface back to the camera. Instead, when using a flash place the camera at an angle to the subject and to any reflective surfaces.

A third piece of advice: Exploit the frame.

Each photo you take consists of a view, contained in a frame, of a much larger scene. The first step in exploiting the frame is making sure that everything you want in the picture is within the frame. The next step is arranging the items framed in your picture in a pleasing or interesting way; this is called *composing* the shot. For example, a shot taken at an angle can often produce a more interesting composition than a shot taken straight on.

You can sometimes find natural opportunities that help you compose a shot: For example, you may be able to include a window, a door, or a tree in the frame to help focus attention on the subject or to present it in an interesting way.

Many photographers use the "rule of thirds" when they compose shots. That is, they imagine lines dividing the frame equally into three parts, either horizontally or vertically, and then place the subject on or near one of those lines. This technique puts the subject of the shot slightly above or below, or to the left or right of, the frame's center.

Also keep in mind that sometimes it's okay for part of your subject to fall outside of the frame. Using a close shot that omits part of the subject can add visual interest as well.

Grasping the Technical Details

Three factors combine to affect the quality of the image your camera produces: resolution, exposure, and aperture.

Resolution

Each digital picture consists of thousands of individual colored dots, called *pixels* (short for *picture elements*). The number of pixels that make up the picture is known as the picture's *resolution*. The more pixels, the more detail in the picture; the fewer pixels, the more fuzzy or ragged the picture looks.

Digital cameras are often rated by how many millions of pixels (*megapixels*) they can provide. Two or three megapixels is sufficient to produce attractive snapshots and more than sufficient for pictures on a web page. More megapixels are required for the high-quality full-page pictures that you might want to use in a print publication. However, the more megapixels your camera provides, the more storage space each picture takes up in the camera's memory and on your Mac's hard disk.

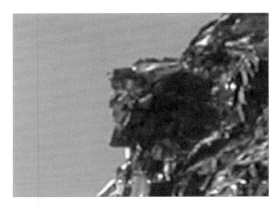

Low-resolution picture

Although the maximum resolution is determined by your camera's optics and can't be changed, some cameras allow you to reduce the resolution of your shots to conserve storage space.

Exposure

To capture a picture, your camera briefly opens a shutter to allow the light that makes up the picture to enter the camera. This length of time is called the *exposure*, and is usually measured in fractions of a second. The longer the exposure, the more light is captured, but the greater the chance that a small movement of the camera or your picture's subject will cause the image to appear blurred.

Long exposures are useful when shooting in low light, but such pictures require a steady hand (or the use of a tripod) and a stationary subject. Short exposures are usually required for action shots, such as capturing a shot of a batter swinging at a pitch, but short exposures require a lot of light to illuminate the subject. Many digital cameras can artificially boost their sensitivity to light, compensating for short exposures in poor light; however, such pictures can often contain electronic "noise" created by the boost in sensitivity.

Picture taken in low light shows noise

Aperture

How wide the camera's shutter opens when you take a picture is called its *aperture* setting. The wider the aperture, the more light that can enter the camera when the shutter opens. The amount of light that a picture captures, then, is controlled by both the exposure and the aperture settings. A wide aperture with a short exposure lets in the same amount of light as a long exposure and a narrow aperture.

The aperture, however, also controls *depth of field*, the distance between the closest and most distant objects in the picture that are in focus. A narrow aperture gives a wide depth of field, whereas a wide aperture produces a more narrow depth of field.

When it comes to aperture and exposure settings, digital cameras usually set aperture and exposure automatically. However, many cameras also let you adjust these settings manually for greater control in special situations. If your camera allows you to adjust these settings, experiment with them to learn how each affects the quality of your pictures.

Connecting Your Camera to iPhoto

Once you've shot some pictures, you need to move them from your camera into iPhoto on your Mac. Connecting a camera is a simple process that actually takes more time to describe than it does to perform. iPhoto is designed to work with the vast majority of digital cameras, including mobile phone cameras like the one in the iPhone, without any other software required.

Preparing iPhoto to Import from a Camera

Setting up iPhoto to import images from your camera simply means telling it that you want to use iPhoto whenever you connect a digital camera to your Mac. How you tell it to do this depends on whether or not iPhoto has ever been run on your Mac before.

To set a new, unused copy of iPhoto so that it opens whenever a digital camera is connected, follow these steps:

1   Open iPhoto.

A dialog appears that asks whether you want to use iPhoto when you connect a digital camera.

2   Click Yes.

From now on, your Mac will open iPhoto whenever a digital camera is connected to it.

> **NOTE** ▶ This setting causes iPhoto to open automatically when a digital camera is connected. Even if you click No in this dialog, iPhoto will still detect a connected camera when iPhoto is running, but it won't open automatically when you connect a camera to your Mac.

If the copy of iPhoto on your Mac has previously been opened, you won't see the dialog when you open the application. However, it is still easy to set iPhoto to open automatically when you connect a digital camera. Follow these steps:

1   Open iPhoto.

2   Choose iPhoto > Preferences.

3   Click the General button in the Preferences toolbar.

4   At the bottom of the window, choose iPhoto from the "Connecting camera opens:" menu.

5   Close the window.

Unless you change this preference, your Mac will open iPhoto whenever you connect your digital camera.

Making the Connection

To connect your digital camera to your Mac, you need the cable that came with your camera and a free USB port on your Mac. It's also a good idea to consult the manual that came with the camera for the exact steps you should follow as you set your camera up for downloading images to a computer. In most cases, though, those steps should be as follows:

1   Turn off your camera and set it in display mode.

Typically, digital cameras have two main modes: a display, or playback, mode, that you use to view pictures you've already taken on the camera's screen, and a photography mode, that you use when taking pictures with the camera. Some cameras have three modes: automatic photography, manual photography, and display; or photography, display, and video. Others may have no modes at all and automatically set themselves properly when connected to your Mac, such as the camera in an iPhone.

2 Connect the cable that came with the camera to its connector on the camera.

3 Connect the other end of the camera's cable to a free USB port on your Mac.

4 Turn the camera on.

That's it. iPhoto automatically opens and is ready to import the pictures stored in your camera.

TIP To avoid problems, make sure that your camera is fully charged, or is connected to an external power source, before you connect it to your Mac. You don't want your camera to turn off because of low power while it's in the middle of downloading pictures into iPhoto.

Importing Pictures from a Camera or Card

When you connect a camera to your Mac, iPhoto lists the camera in its source list at the left of the iPhoto window under the Devices heading. It also displays small versions of the photos (called *thumbnails*) currently stored in the camera in the main viewing area on the right.

To import all the camera's photos, do the following:

1   Click the Import All button in the lower-right corner of the iPhoto window.

A dialog appears, asking you if you want to keep the original photos in the camera after you import them.

2   In the dialog, click either Delete Originals or Keep Originals.

iPhoto imports the pictures, displaying each picture as it imports it.

3   When the import finishes, turn off your camera and disconnect it from your Mac.

The pictures are added to your iPhoto library.

TIP ▶ If you've chosen to Keep Originals when you import, you can protect yourself from accidentally importing the same pictures again the next time you connect your camera by selecting the "Hide photos already imported" checkbox in the lower-left corner of the iPhoto viewing pane.

☐ Hide photos already imported

Importing Selected Pictures

As you may have noticed, iPhoto gives you the option of importing either all of the pictures in your camera or just a selected group of pictures. Here's how you can import a subset of the pictures in your camera:

1   Connect your camera to your Mac and turn the camera on.

If iPhoto isn't open, it opens automatically.

2   In iPhoto's viewing pane, click the first photo you want to import.

3   To select a range of pictures, hold down the Shift key and click the last photo you want to import; to select individual pictures, hold down the Command key as you click the pictures you want to import.

Shift-clicking selects the first and last pictures you clicked and all the pictures in between. Command-clicking adds each picture you click to the selection. The selected pictures have a yellow outline.

4   Click the Import Selected button in the lower-right corner of the main iPhoto window.

| Import Selected | Import All... |

5   In the sheet that appears, click either Delete Originals or Keep Originals.

> **NOTE** ▸ If the camera appears on your desktop when you connect it, you must eject the camera in the Finder before turning it off and disconnecting.

6   When the import finishes, turn off your camera and disconnect it from your Mac.

Importing Pictures from a Memory Card

Most digital cameras store their pictures on a removable memory card. You can purchase additional memory cards for your camera in order to increase the camera's picture capacity. Additional memory cards also can come in very handy when you're taking a lot of pictures out in the field: Simply put an empty card in your camera when the card you've been using becomes full.

If you purchase a card reader that's compatible with your camera's memory card and connect the card reader to your Mac, you can import the pictures directly from the card using the card reader instead of having to connect your camera. This is useful when you want to conserve your camera's battery charge, or if you have several memory cards on hand from which you want to import pictures. Most card readers connect to a USB port on your Mac, much like a camera does.

To import pictures into iPhoto from a memory card, follow these steps:

1 Connect your card reader to your Mac.

2 If iPhoto doesn't open automatically, open the application.

3 Insert the memory card into the card reader.

The card appears in iPhoto's source list under Devices just as a camera does. Note, though, that the Mac also mounts the card on your desktop just as it does an external hard drive or a thumb drive, and that the card in the source list has an eject button next to it. Unlike most cameras, you must explicitly eject the card from your Mac before removing the card from the reader.

NOTE ▶ Your Mac may treat some cameras as removable memory devices rather than as cameras, and will mount them on the desktop as disk volumes. If so, refer to the section later in this lesson about importing pictures from memory cards.

4 Import the pictures from the card using either of iPhoto's Import buttons just as you would when importing pictures from a camera.

You can import all the pictures on the card or selected pictures, and you can choose either to keep or to delete originals after you import.

5 When you finish importing, click the eject button beside the card in iPhoto's source list and wait for the card to vanish from the list.

6 Remove the card from the card reader.

Importing Video from a Camera

Many digital cameras, including some mobile phone cameras, also have the ability to take digital motion video. Such video is often captured at a lower resolution and always at a lower frame rate than the video produced by digital video cameras, and usually of shorter duration due to capacity constraints. As you'll see later in this book, iMovie can use the digital video that you import into iPhoto from your camera quite readily.

When you connect a camera or memory card that contains digital video to your Mac, iPhoto can import it into the iPhoto library just as it does still pictures.

1   Connect your camera to your Mac and turn the camera on.

iPhoto starts up if it's not already running, and displays the items you can import in its viewing pane. Video thumbnails have a small white camera icon in their lower-left corners.

2   Either select the video you want to import and click Import Selected, or click Import All to import everything in the camera, including any video items.

3   In the sheet that appears, click either Keep Originals or Delete Originals.

iPhoto adds the items it imports, including any video items, to the iPhoto library. Videos in the library display the same camera icon on their thumbnails that they did in the viewing pane when you imported them.

Importing Picture Files

iPhoto can import image files in a variety of formats, which makes it useful for storing and arranging images other than those that come from your camera. For example, you can import photos sent via email from friends or family, images from web pages, and images that you've created with other programs on your Mac.

In this exercise, you'll import the images you will use in the following chapters from the DVD that accompanies this book. If you haven't already copied the iLife08_Book_Files to your hard drive, please refer to the Getting Started chapter to do so now.

1   Open iPhoto if it's not already open.

The viewing pane displays the pictures in the iPhoto library.

2   In iLife08_Book_Files > Lessons, open the Lesson01 folder, and drag the entire folder **L1_five_photo_events** and release it on the viewing area.

iPhoto imports all of the image files in the folder, including images in any subfolders, into the iPhoto library. When it finishes importing, iPhoto shows you the pictures in the last folder that it imported.

3   In the iPhoto window's source list, click Events.

The photos in the four subfolders inside of the folder you dragged appear as four Event thumbnails in the viewing pane.

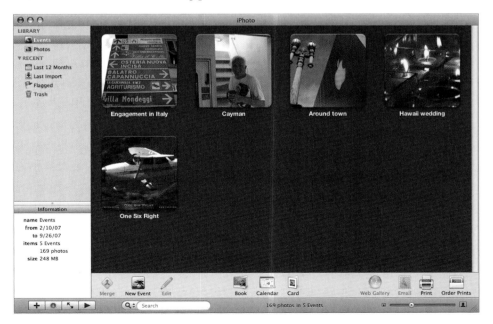

Although it may look as though there are only five photos in the iPhoto library, each of the Event thumbnails actually represents a collection of images. In the next lesson you'll learn more about Events, including what they are, how to label them, and how to combine and divide them.

Lesson Review

1.   What is the rule of thirds and how will it improve your pictures?

2.   What is the *aperture* and how does it affect an image?

3.   What is *resolution*?

4.   How can you control whether or not iPhoto opens automatically when you attach a camera to your Mac?

5.   How do you import selected pictures from a camera rather than all of them?

6.   How can you tell if an item to be imported from your camera is a video rather than a still image?

7.   Name one reason to use a card reader when importing photos instead of connecting the camera.

8.   How can you import image files into iPhoto?

Answers

1.   The rule of thirds helps improve a photo's composition by positioning the photo's subject a third of the way from the sides, top, or bottom of the photo rather than in the direct center.

2.   The aperture is how wide the lens is open when you take a picture. A wider aperture lets more light in, allowing a picture to be taken in lower-light situations, but it also reduces the distance between the nearest and farthest objects that can remain in focus.

3.   Resolution is the number of pixels that make up an image. The more pixels, the more detail the photo can display.

4.   Open iPhoto's preferences and choose iPhoto from the "Connecting camera opens" menu on the General pane of the Preferences window.

5. In the iPhoto viewing pane that shows the camera's contents, Shift-click to select a contiguous group of photos, or Command-click to select a non-contiguous group of photos, then click Import Selected at the bottom-right of the viewing pane.

6. Video thumbnails have a small white video camera icon in their lower-left corners.

7. To conserve the camera's battery power; or, because you have several memory cards from which you'd like to import photos.

8. Drag the images, or the folders that contain the images, into the iPhoto window's viewing pane.

2

Lesson Files	No additional files
Time	This lesson takes approximately 60 minutes to complete.
Goals	Learn how to view photos in iPhoto
	Understand and manage iPhoto Events
	Create an album
	Hide and discard photos
	Add descriptions to photos and Events
	Find a photo in your library

Arranging Your Pictures

As you've seen, it's very easy to add pictures to iPhoto. In fact, it's so easy that very quickly you'll find your picture library growing by leaps and bounds.

When you have only a few dozen pictures, finding the picture you want is simple. When you have a few hundred pictures, sorting through them becomes more difficult. When you have thousands of pictures—which is not uncommon when you have a digital camera—managing them all becomes a real challenge.

It would be a real challenge, that is, if you didn't have iPhoto's array of labeling, organizing, and searching tools at your disposal.

This lesson shows you how you can use iPhoto to manage your picture library easily, no matter how big it gets.

Viewing Pictures

As soon as you have some pictures in your iPhoto library, the first thing you'll want to do is to see them. iPhoto provides many ways to view your pictures.

Viewing Events

At the end of Lesson 1, you had imported a group of folders containing pictures into iPhoto, and, as a final step, you clicked Events in iPhoto's source list in order to see the folders you imported.

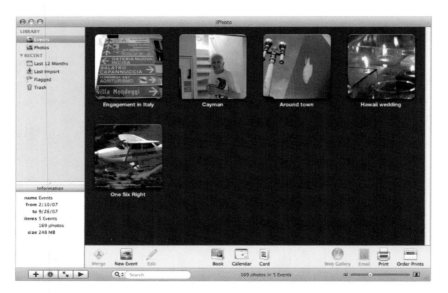

In iPhoto, an Event starts out as a group of photos taken at a particular time, such as all the photos taken on the same day. For example, if your camera contains photos taken over the course of a week or a month, iPhoto will group the photos into several Events when it imports them. Later in this lesson you'll see how you can move photos from one Event to another, how you can merge Events, and how you can split one Event into two or more Events.

You can create Events in iPhoto to serve whatever organizational purpose you wish. For example, if you take a bunch of pictures while on a hike with your friends, you can split those pictures into several Events: one that contains photos of scenic views, one that contains photos of your fellow hikers, and so on.

When you view the Events in your iPhoto library, iPhoto uses a thumbnail of one of the pictures in the Event to represent all the pictures contained in that Event. iPhoto refers to this thumbnail as the Event's *key photo*. You can adjust how big the Event key photos appear in iPhoto's viewing pane:

1 Click Events if something else is selected in iPhoto's source list.

2 Drag the magnifying slider at the bottom right of the iPhoto window to the left to make the key photos smaller, and drag it to the right to make them larger.

Skimming Events

Smaller key photos let you see more Events in the iPhoto viewing pane at one time; larger key photos provide more detail so you can more easily recognize them.

Large key photos become particularly useful when you want to *skim* the contents of an Event quickly. Skimming an Event shows you the Event's contents without actually opening the Event up. Because all of the Events remain displayed in the viewing pane, you can get a look at the contents of several events quickly and easily.

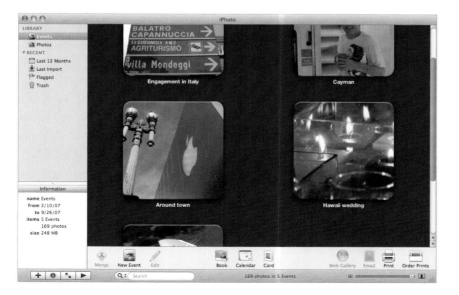

To locate an Event key photo by skimming and display it in iPhoto's viewing pane, do the following:

1   Move your pointer horizontally over the Event key photo.

As the pointer moves from one side of the key photo area to the other, the area displays the different pictures contained in the Event, one by one. iPhoto also displays the Event's date and the number of pictures it contains.

2   Double-click the Event.

3   Use the scroll bars at the right of the viewing pane to see more pictures if they don't all fit.

TIP You can change what iPhoto does when you double-click a key photo. Choose iPhoto > Preferences, click Events in the Preferences window's toolbar, and click "Magnifies photo." When you set this preference, double-clicking the key photo magnifies the picture that's currently displayed as you skim the Event. This preference also causes a Show Photos button to appear at the bottom of the key photo when your pointer is over the Event. To open the Event, simply click the Show Photos button.

Navigating the Viewing Pane

When a single Event is open, a bar at the top of the viewing pane provides the name and the date of the Event you're viewing. The bar also provides Event navigation controls, which you can manipulate as follows:

1   Click the right arrow to fill the viewing pane with the contents of the next Event in your iPhoto library.

2   Click the left arrow to view the contents of the previous Event in the library.

3   Click the All Events button to view all of the Event key photos in the viewing pane again.

Getting a Closer Look

When an Event is open and you see a picture that you want to examine more closely, you can quickly expand it to fill the viewing pane without using the magnifying slider at the bottom of the window:

1   Double-click the picture to expand it.

2   Click the picture again to shrink it back down.

Browsing Your Entire Photo Library

You're not limited to seeing the contents of just individual Events or to seeing just the key photos that represent all of the Events in your library, either. Here's how to make more photos viewable:

1   Click Photos in the iPhoto source list.

All the pictures in your library appear in the viewing pane. Unless your library contains only a few pictures, however, they won't all fit in the viewing pane.

2   Use the scroll bars at the right of the viewing pane to see more pictures.

3   If Event titles are not visible, choose View > Show Event Titles.

When Event titles are visible you can hide or show the pictures that belong to individual Events by using the disclosure triangle to the left of an Event's title.

4   Click the disclosure triangle to the left of an Event's title to hide its pictures. Click it again to reveal the pictures.

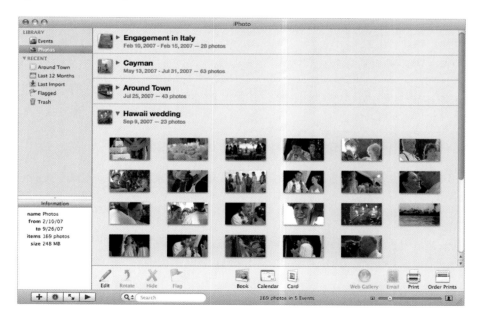

TIP   Hold down Command when you click the disclosure triangle to collapse or expand all of the Events in the viewing pane at once.

5   Slide the magnifying slider at the bottom-right of the window to shrink or enlarge the pictures shown in the viewing pane.

TIP ▶ Clicking any of the first three items under the Recent heading in the source list shows you specific Events and photos quickly. The item at the top of the list displays the Event you most recently opened. The item below it displays all the photos you have recently imported regardless of the Event to which they belong; the default is to show the photos imported over the last twelve months but you can change the duration using iPhoto's preferences. The third item shows you the Event, or group of Events, that you most recently imported.

Organizing Your Events

As the number of Events in your library increases, you probably will discover that the Event's key photo and date may not provide you with enough information to help you remember what the Event contains or why you created it. Giving an Event a title and providing it with a short description easily solves those problems.

Untitled Events have a date beneath their key photos when iPhoto displays them in the viewing pane. When you put your pointer over an untitled Event, iPhoto informs you of the Event's lack of a title.

Choosing Meaningful Event Titles

Even if an Event has a title, it may not be a particularly good one. For example, one of the Events you imported in Lesson 1 is titled Around Town. That title is not very descriptive because it doesn't tell us *which* town. We'll change it.

The steps you follow to give an untitled Event a title or to change an Event's title are identical:

1   In the source list, click Events.

2   Locate the Event titled Around Town in the iPhoto viewing pane.

3   Click the Event's title.

The title changes to an editable field. For an untitled Event, the field is empty; for an Event that has a title, the title is selected in the field.

4   Type the new title, *Around San Francisco*, and then press Return.

The new title appears below the Event.

Adding Event Descriptions

Giving Events meaningful titles helps you quickly identify them when you view their key photos in the viewing pane. Sometimes, though, a title doesn't provide enough information, especially when you make use of iPhoto's search abilities, which you'll learn about later in this lesson. For example, Around San Francisco doesn't tell you that the Event includes a photo of Lombard Street. That's where Event descriptions come in.

To provide a more detailed description of an Event, use the Information pane that optionally appears at the bottom of iPhoto's source list.

1   If the Information pane isn't showing, in the segmented button at the bottom-left of the window, click the second button from the left.

2   Adjust the size of the pane by dragging the dimpled separator bar above the title Information up or down.

3   Click in the description area at the bottom of the pane.

4   Type the description shown below.

5   Click anywhere outside of the description area to set your changes.

TIP You can provide an Event with a title and description at the time you import images from a camera or a card. Fill out the two fields that appear at the bottom of the viewing pane before you click one of the Import buttons.

| From: 9/9/07 | Event Name: | |
| To: 9/9/07 | Description: | |

☐ Autosplit events after importing
☐ Hide photos already imported   Import Selected   Import All...

Selecting a Key Photo

Ordinarily, iPhoto uses the first picture in an Event as the Event's key photo. If the key photo is not a good representation of the Event's contents, however, you can change it to one that's more suitable.

1   Open the Around San Francisco Event.

2   Click to select one of the Event's pictures, such as one of the cable car pictures.

3   Choose Events > Make Key Photo.

4   Click All Events. The Event in the viewing pane now shows the picture you selected.

  You can use the spacebar to quickly assign a Key Photo.

Splitting Events

iPhoto automatically creates Events when you import pictures, based on when the pictures were created. Sometimes, though, you'll find that the pictures in one iPhoto Event actually represent two or more real events. For example, if you take some pictures at a birthday party in the morning and then take some pictures at a soccer game in the afternoon, iPhoto may put the pictures in the same Event when you import them from your camera. If that happens, you need to split that one Event into two Events.

You may also wish to split an event to organize the pictures along thematic lines. For example, the Around San Francisco Event contains a number of pictures of signs. We can separate those pictures out into their own event.

1   Open the Around San Francisco Event.

2   At the bottom-right of the window, drag the magnifying slider to the right so that you can see more detail in each of the Event's pictures.

3   Click the first picture you find that contains a sign.

4   Scrolling through the viewing pane as necessary, Command-click each subsequent picture you see that contains a sign.

    iPhoto adds the individual pictures to your selection.

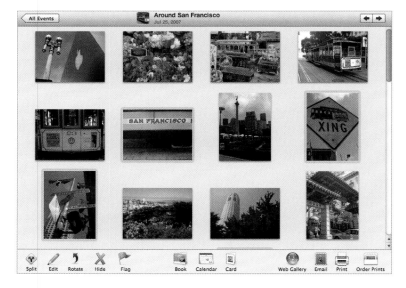

5   At the bottom-left of the viewing pane, click Split.

iPhoto creates a new untitled Event that contains the pictures you selected, removing them from the other Event.

6   Drag the magnifying slider to the left so that you can see both Events in the viewing pane.

7   Double-click the untitled Event's title and change it to *Signs of San Francisco.*

8   Click All Events.

The new Event appears in the viewing pane.

Merging Events

Just as iPhoto may sometimes import pictures that belong to two or more real events into one iPhoto Event, it may also break pictures that belong to one real event into two or more iPhoto Events. For example, you may have taken pictures on a two-day skiing trip that seem to belong to a single Event, but which iPhoto imports into two Events, one for each day of the trip. Or, you may have previously split an Event into several Events and have subsequently changed your mind. Fortunately, merging Events is even easier than splitting them.

Now that we've gone to all the trouble to split the Around San Francisco Event in two, let's put those two Events back together again:

1   Click the Around San Francisco Event.

2   Command-click the Signs of San Francisco Event.

3   Choose Events > Merge Events.

A sheet appears asking you to confirm the merger.

Do you want to merge these Events?

All photos in the selected Events will be moved into one Event.

☐ Don't Ask Again

Cancel   Merge

4   Click Merge.

TIP ▶ You can also merge Events by dragging one Event on top of another in the viewing pane.

Moving Pictures Between Events

You may find occasions when you already have two or more Events, but find that one Event contains some pictures that really belong in another Event. Here's one way to rearrange your pictures:

1   Click an Event.

2   Command-click another Event.

3   Double-click one of the Events you selected.

Both events open in the viewing pane.

4   Drag the pictures you want to move from one Event to the other.

5   Click All Events.

iPhoto shows all the Events in the viewing pane.

Reordering Events

iPhoto displays Events in iPhoto's viewing pane in the order in which you imported them, but you can change the order. Changing the order is useful when you need to work with two or more Events that are widely separated in the viewing pane, or if you want to see them organized by their titles or their dates.

Here's how to rearrange the display order of one or more Events manually:

1 Click an Event.

2 Optionally, Command-click one or more other Events.

3 Drag one of the selected Events to where you want them displayed.

As you drag, the other Events in the viewing pane move out of the way to make room for the Events you're dragging.

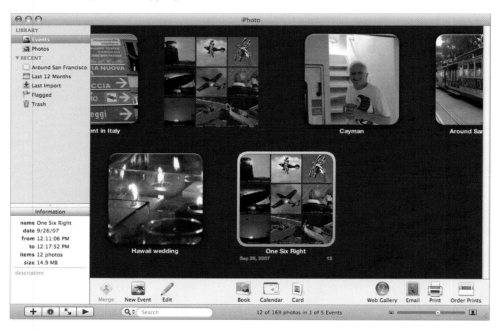

4 Release the mouse button when the Events are positioned where you want them.

TIP Make sure not to drop the Events on top of another Event because that will merge them rather than move them.

TIP You can also arrange the order in which Events are displayed by choosing an option from the View > Sort Events submenu.

```
Titles              ⇧⌘T
Rating              ⇧⌘R
Keywords            ⇧⌘K

Event Titles        ⇧⌘F
Hidden Photos       ⇧⌘H

Sort Events         ▶    By Date
                         By Keyword
Show in Toolbar     ▶    By Title
                         By Rating
Full Screen         ⌥⌘F  ✓ Manually
Always Show Toolbar
Thumbnails          ▶    Ascending
                         ✓ Descending

                         Reset Manual Sort
```

Building Picture Albums

Events are a great way of sorting the pictures in your iPhoto library into manageable and useful containers, but they have one important limitation: A picture can be only be stored in one Event at a time. You saw this limitation earlier when you temporarily made a Signs of San Francisco Event and had to remove all pictures of signs from the Around San Francisco event to do so.

It would be nice if you could have an Around San Francisco Event that would contain *all* of the pictures taken during that trip, and another container that would contain just pictures that depicted signs. Although you can't do that with Events, iPhoto offers you another organizing feature to meet that need: *albums*.

Albums are something like playlists in iTunes. Just as you can put the same song into as many iTunes playlists as you like, you can put the same picture into as many iPhoto albums as you like. And, just as removing a song from an iTunes playlist doesn't remove the song from your iTunes music library, removing a picture from an iPhoto album doesn't remove it from your iPhoto library.

Making an Album from an Event

To see how this works, let's re-create our Signs of San Francisco Event as an album:

1 Open the Around San Francisco Event, and use the magnify slider at the bottom of the window so you can see picture details more clearly.

2   Click the first picture you can see that has a sign in it.

3   Command-click two more pictures that depict signs.

You don't have to select all the pictures that depict signs right now.

4   Choose File > New Album From Selection.

A sheet appears that offers to create a new album containing the selected pictures for you, and that gives you the option of giving the album a name.

5   Type *Signs of San Francisco* in the Name field and click Create.

An Albums heading appears in the source list and under it is the new Signs of San Francisco album.

6   Click the album to see its contents in the viewing pane.

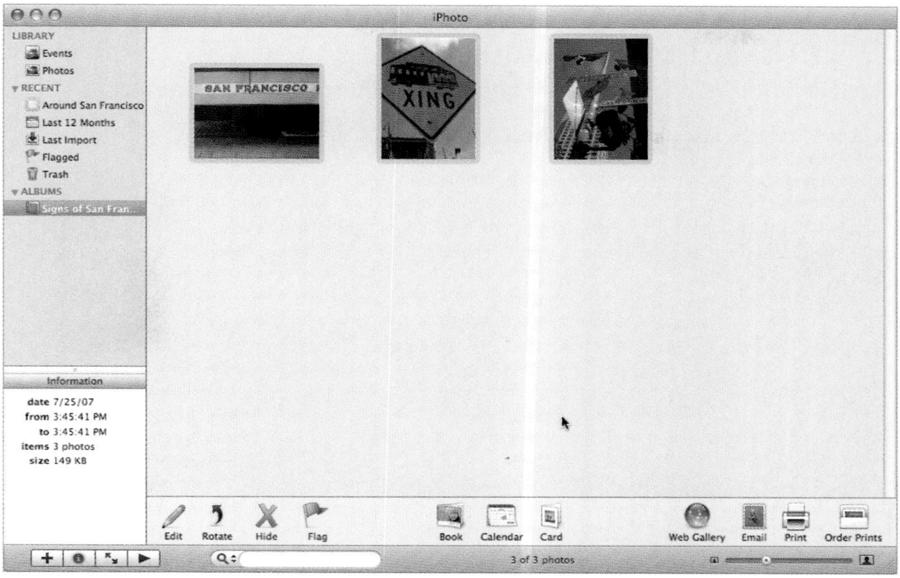

7   In the source list, under the Recent heading, click Around San Francisco to see the Event and to verify that the pictures placed in the new album haven't been removed from the Event.

Adding Pictures to an Album

Once you've created an album you can both add pictures to it and remove pictures from it freely, because any changes you make to the album won't affect the contents of your iPhoto library.

Let's add the remaining pictures of signs to the Signs of San Francisco album:

1   Scroll through the Around San Francisco Event until you find another picture of a sign, and then click that picture.

2   Find another picture of a sign in the Event and Command-click it, repeating the process until you have selected the remaining sign pictures.

3   Drag one of the selected pictures toward the album in the source list.

As you drag, a transparent image of the picture follows your pointer with a number on the image telling you how many pictures you're dragging. All of the selected pictures are included in the drag. A black line frames the album when the pointer is over it.

4 Drop the pictures on the album.

5 Click the album to see its contents in the viewing pane.

Removing Pictures from an Album

If adding pictures to an album is easy, removing pictures from an album is even easier:

1 Click a picture to select it.

If you like, you can Shift-click or Command-click pictures to add them to your selection.

2 Press Delete.

If you prefer to use menus, you can choose Photos > Delete From Album instead.

> **TIP** If you change your mind, or if you delete the wrong pictures, you can choose Edit > Undo Delete From Album before you make any other changes.

Sorting Photos in an Album

Just as you can with Events, you can arrange the order in which the pictures in an album appear. Albums, as you'll discover in a later lesson, can serve as the basis for several types of projects, such as slideshows and picture books, so being able to put an album's pictures in an appropriate order is essential.

For example, you might want to make the order of the pictures in the Signs of San Francisco album to reflect the order in which the pictures were actually taken. iPhoto provides a menu command to do just that:

1   In the source list, click the Signs of San Francisco album.

2   Choose View > Sort Photos > By Date.

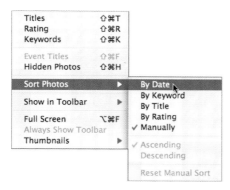

Arranging Photos by Content

On the other hand, if you're a big fan of bookstores you may want the picture of the bookstore window to appear right after the first picture in the album. You can do that with a simple drag:

1   Click the picture of the bookstore window and drag it up to the right of the first picture in the album.

As you drag, a transparent version of the picture follows your pointer. Notice that the image displays a red circle indicating the number of pictures being dragged. As this suggests, you can drag more than one picture at a time. Also notice that as your pointer reaches its destination, a black vertical line appears to the right of the first picture in the album. This shows you where the picture you're dragging will appear when you release the mouse button.

2   Release the mouse button.

The bookstore picture appears in its new position in the album.

Creating Selections of Pictures with Albums

Albums are such an easy and powerful way to create selections of pictures from your iPhoto library that you'll want to make and use them a lot. Often, you may want to make one or more albums before you actually choose the pictures to put into them. For example, the Cayman Event contains both pictures taken underwater and pictures taken on the boat.

You can make albums for each of these types of pictures before you actually pick out the individual pictures from the Event themselves. Here's how:

1   Click a gray area of the viewing pane to make sure that nothing is selected.

2   At the bottom-left of the window, click the + button on the far left of the multi-segmented button.

The same sheet appears that you previously saw when you made an album from selected pictures.

3 Type *Cayman diving* in the Name field and then click Create.

The Cayman diving album appears at the bottom of the Albums section in the source list.

4 Repeat steps 2 and 3, this time naming the new album *Cayman boat pictures*.

You now have two new albums into which you can put pictures.

Organizing Your Albums with Folders

As your collection of albums grows, you'll find you'll want to organize them. One way to do that is to put related albums into folders, like this:

1 Choose File > New Folder.

An untitled folder appears at the top of the album section in the source list. The name of the new folder is conveniently selected so that you can rename it.

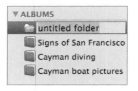

2   Type *Cayman albums* and press Return.

3   Click the Cayman boat pictures album to select it.

4   Command-click the Cayman diving album to select it as well.

5   Drag the selected albums to the new folder.

The folder is framed with a dark line when your pointer is over it.

6   Release the mouse button.

The albums are now in the folder.

Reordering Albums

You can rearrange the order of albums in the source list and of albums in a folder, too. For example, the Cayman boat pictures album should come before the Cayman diving album if you want the albums in the folder arranged alphabetically. A quick drag takes care of that:

1 Click a blank area of the source list to deselect the albums, then drag the Cayman boat pictures album to just above the Cayman diving album.

As you drag, a horizontal black line appears to show you where the album will end up when you release the mouse button.

2 Release the mouse button.

The albums in the folder are now in correct alphabetical order.

TIP ▶ For extra credit, and to prepare for a lesson later in this book, go ahead and look through the Cayman Event and put any diving pictures and boat pictures you see into their respective albums.

Hiding and Discarding Pictures

Not every picture is a gem, nor even a presentable pebble. When you import pictures into an Event, it's common to end up with some that you really don't want to look at. They may be too blurry, or obscured by your hand or because a passerby stepped into the frame at exactly the wrong moment. You can, of course, discard the image, but iPhoto also has several features you can use to save your eyes from beholding an unattractive or unusable image without deleting it.

Hiding Unwanted Pictures

This easiest way to preserve your aesthetic vision is to conceal these pictures from view. For example, the Hawaiian Wedding Event contains two pictures of a young girl on the dance floor. One of those pictures is blurred because the camera was jostled just as the picture was taken. Although you could discard the picture, you might not be ready to take that step, so you can hide it instead:

1   Open the Hawaiian Wedding Event and drag the magnification slider at the bottom-right of the window far enough to the right to see picture details.

2   Scroll through the Event until you find the blurred picture.

The flawed picture looks like the one below. (If you have the Information pane showing, the title of the picture is DS004.)

3   Click the picture to select it.

4   At the left side of the toolbar at the bottom of the viewing pane, click Hide.

The picture disappears. Your eyes have been saved.

TIP ▸ When an Event contains some hidden pictures, iPhoto lets you know about it when you peruse the Event in the viewing pane by putting a message in the Event's title bar. This message is, in fact, a button, even though it doesn't look like one; click it to make the hidden picture appear in the viewing pane.

Click the message in the Event's title bar to hide or show hidden photos.

NOTE ▸ When hidden pictures are showing, iPhoto clearly marks them so that you know they're pictures you've chosen to hide.

Unhiding Pictures

If you can hide pictures, it stands to reason that you can unhide them:

1   Click the hidden picture that you've made visible.

The Hide button on the toolbar changes.

2   Click Unhide.

The hidden picture marker goes away, and the Unhide toolbar button again becomes the Hide button.

Discarding Pictures

If you really don't want the picture hanging around anymore, hidden or not, you can discard it. Here's one way to do that:

1   Drag the picture over the Trash icon in the source list.

2   When the Trash is framed by a black line, release the mouse button.

> **TIP** ▶ Even easier, though, is to click the picture in an Event to select it, and then press Delete. That also moves the picture to iPhoto's Trash.

Restoring a Discarded Picture to Your Library

Putting a picture in iPhoto's Trash removes it from the Event to which it belongs and from all albums into which you've placed it. Like the Mac's own Trash, however, you have to empty the iPhoto Trash to completely discard the picture. Until you do, you can always restore the picture to your library:

1   In the source list, click Trash.

The pictures in the Trash appear in the viewing pane.

2   Click the picture you want to restore.

3   Choose Photos > Restore to iPhoto Library.

Show Photo Info	⌘I
Adjust Date and Time...	
Batch Change...	⇧⌘B
Rotate Clockwise	⌥⌘R
Rotate Counter Clockwise	⌘R
My Rating	▶
Flag Photo	⌘.
Hide Photo	⌘L
Duplicate	⌘D
Restore to Photo Library	⌘⌫
Revert to Original	

> **NOTE** ▶ To actually empty the iPhoto Trash and discard unwanted pictures forever, choose iPhoto > Empty Trash. But remember, once you do that, they're gone for good.

Describing Your Pictures

When you import pictures into your iPhoto library, iPhoto gives each picture a title based on the picture's file name. Even the pictures from digital cameras have file names, assigned by the camera automatically; these names are usually something like IMG_0673.JPG. Such names might be useful to the camera's tiny digital brain, perhaps, but they're probably not very useful to you.

Changing the Title of a Picture in an Album

You can change the title of any picture to something more meaningful. To see how to do this, you'll change the title of one of the pictures in the Signs of San Francisco album:

1 Click the Signs of San Francisco album in the source list.

You can change the titles of pictures whether they're in an Event or an album. The name will stick, regardless.

2 Choose View > Titles or press Command-Shift-T.

The titles assigned by iPhoto appear below each picture.

3 Click the title beneath the picture of the bookstore window.

The title becomes editable.

4 Type *Bookstore window* and press Return.

Rating Your Pictures

In addition to titles, you may want to assign star ratings to your pictures so you can see at a glance which ones are your really exceptional pictures and which are your not-really-so-exceptional pictures. Ratings help you find the best (or worst) pictures in your library more quickly.

Let's assign star ratings to a few of the pictures in the Signs of San Francisco album:

1   Choose View > Ratings or press Command-Shift-R.

    Nothing much seems to change if you haven't rated any pictures yet. However, if your pointer is over a picture, you'll see five dots below the picture, indicating that the picture has no stars.

2   Choose Photos > My Rating.

    A submenu appears with star ratings.

Show Photo Info	⌘I			
Adjust Date and Time...				
Batch Change...	⇧⌘B			
Rotate Clockwise	⌥⌘R			
Rotate Counter Clockwise	⌘R			
My Rating	▶	None	⌘0	
Clear All Flags	⌥⌘.	★	⌘1	
Hide Photo	⌘L	★★	⌘2	
		★★★	⌘3	
Duplicate	⌘D	★★★★	⌘4	
Move to Trash	⌥⌘⌫	★★★★★	⌘5	
Revert to Original				

3   Choose the four-star rating from the submenu.

    The stars appear beneath the picture.

TIP You can also set ratings directly by clicking the rating beneath a picture.

4 Select the three pictures of street signs that follow the Bookstore window picture in the album and choose a two-star rating from the Photos > Rating submenu.

The selected pictures all display a two-star rating.

TIP You can sort the pictures by ratings in either an album or an Event by choosing View > Sort Pictures > Ratings.

Assigning Descriptions to Pictures

When you need more detailed information associated with a picture than a title or a rating provides, you can give the picture a description. You've already learned how to assign a description to an Event. The process of assigning a description to a picture is similar.

To see how to assign a description to a picture, you'll assign one to the Bookstore window picture:

1 Click the Bookstore window picture to select it.

2 If the Information pane is not visible, show it.

3 In the Description area of the pane, type *City Lights Bookstore window with a reflection.*

4 Click outside of the description area to set it.

Later, when you learn how to search your iPhoto library, you'll be able to find this picture by searching for any of the words or phrases in the description.

Assigning Keywords to Pictures

A common way to categorize items in a large collection, such as a picture library, is to assign *keywords* to them. Keywords are simple tags consisting of a word or two, such as *vacation* or *night shot*. You can assign several keywords to the same picture, allowing the picture to belong to several categories simultaneously.

Try this technique out on pictures in the Signs of San Francisco album:

1   Choose View > Keywords or press Command-Shift-K.

     An area for keywords now appears below each picture.

2   Choose Windows > Show Keywords.

     A Keywords window appears above the iPhoto window. It already has several keywords available, but you're going to add one that it doesn't have.

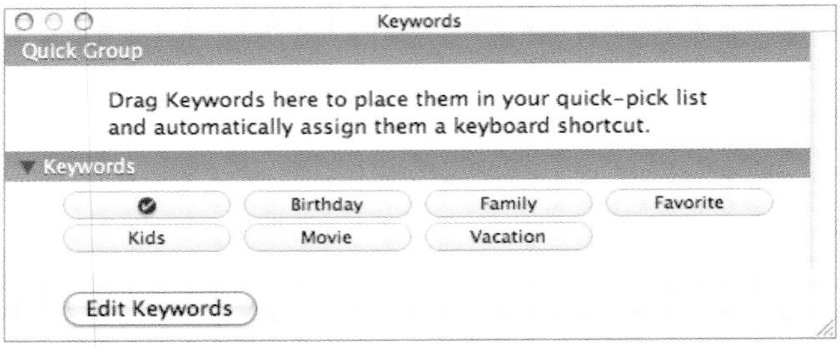

3   At the bottom-left of the Keywords window, click Edit Keywords.

     The window changes appearance to provide a scrolling list of keywords that you can edit.

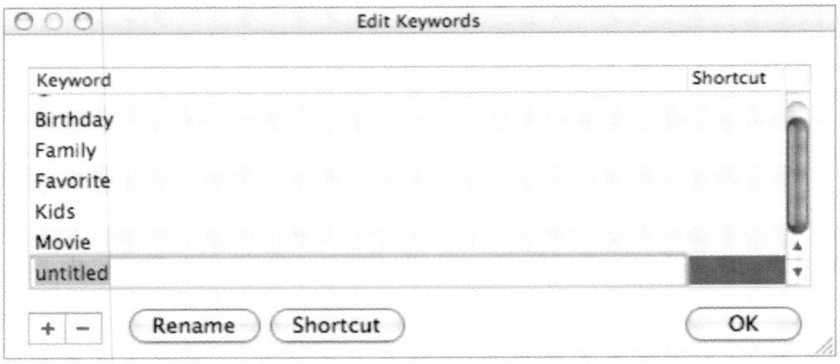

4   At the bottom-left of the window, click the + button.

A new entry appears at the bottom of the keywords list, with the keyword selected, ready for you to edit.

5   Type *Sightseeing* and then click OK.

The new keyword appears in the Quick Group section of the window. Notice that it has an *s* associated with it. iPhoto has assigned that letter as a keyboard shortcut so you can quickly assign that keyword to a picture selection by typing that letter when the Keywords window is open.

○ ○ ○		Keywords	
Quick Group			
Sightseeing Ⓢ			
▼ **Keywords**			
✓	Birthday	Family	Favorite
Kids	Movie		
(Edit Keywords)			

6   Press Command-A to select all the pictures in the album, then click the Sightseeing button in the Quick Group area.

The pictures all have the Sightseeing keyword assigned to them. You could, of course, have simply typed *s* to assign the keyword to the pictures.

Bookstore window
★★★★
Sightseeing

TIP ▶ You can remove a keyword by clicking its button in the Keywords window, or typing its shortcut, a second time.

Flagging Pictures in Your Library

Selecting the pictures that you want to work with is often hard to do because the pictures are scattered throughout your library. To help you overcome this difficulty, iPhoto provides a *flag* that you can assign to pictures. Flagged pictures appear in the special Flagged collection, which you can find under the Recent heading in the source list.

For example, suppose you want to do something with all of the pictures of the bride that are included in the Hawaiian Wedding Event, such as rate them or assign keywords to them. Flags help you build a temporary collection of these pictures.

1   Open the Hawaiian Wedding Event.

2   Select a picture that shows the bride.

3   Click the Flag button in the toolbar at the bottom of the viewing pane.

A flag appears on the picture.

4   Look through the pictures in the Event and flag each picture of the bride that you find.

5   In the source list, click Flagged.

All of the pictures that you flagged appear in the viewing pane. You can now do with them what you will, such as rate them, put them in an album, or move them to a new Event.

TIP To remove flags, simply select one or more flagged pictures and click the Unflag button in the viewing pane's toolbar.

Searching Your iPhoto Library

Much of the labeling and organizing work you've done up to this point is to help you overcome a basic problem that comes with having a large collection of pictures: finding the particular pictures you want in the heap of pictures you have. iPhoto's searching features offer yet another set of tools to cut that problem down to size.

Searching with Text

Once you've organized your pictures by giving them titles, keywords, or descriptions, you can search for them. For example, earlier in this lesson you used the word *reflection* in a description of a bookstore window. iPhoto can find that picture instantly:

1   Click Events in the source list so that all the Events appear in the viewing pane.

2   Click in the search field at the bottom of the iPhoto window.

3   Type the word *reflection*.

As you type, the viewing pane shows the pictures that match what you are typing. By the time you finish typing the word, only one picture is left in the viewing pane: the picture of the bookstore window.

NOTE ▸ A text search displays all the pictures that have titles, descriptions, or keywords that include text matching what you've typed. If any of the text in an Event's title or description matches, all the pictures in that Event are displayed as well.

Searching by Date

But you aren't just limited to text searches. The simple-looking search field can search for other things as well. When you click the magnifying glass icon to the left of the field, a pop-up menu appears from which you can select other ways to search your picture library.

Let's try searching for pictures by date:

1 Choose Date from the search field's pop-up menu.

   A calendar search window appears. The highlighted months are those that match pictures in the library.

2 Click July.

   The search field contains the range of dates in July, and the pictures that match those dates appear in the viewing pane.

3   In the calendar search window's upper-left corner, click the small triangle.

The calendar search window now shows the days in July. The highlighted days are those that have matching pictures.

NOTE ▶ On smaller monitors, depending on where the iPhoto window is positioned on your screen, you may see the date range on the bottom.

4   Click one of the highlighted days to see the pictures that match that date.

Searching by Keyword

Now try searching for pictures that have particular keywords associated with them.

1   Choose Keyword from the search field's pop-up menu.

A keyword search window appears.

2   In the keyword search window, click Sightseeing.

The pictures to which you applied the Sightseeing keyword appear in the viewing pane.

Searching by Rating

As you may have noticed, you can also search the photo library by the ratings you've given to pictures.

1   Choose Rating from the search field's pop-up menu.

The search field contains five small dots.

2   Click the second dot from the left.

Two stars appear in the field, and the pictures that have ratings of two or more stars appear in the viewing pane.

Using Smart Albums

The main drawback of iPhoto's search feature is that once you finish a search and move on to do something else, you have to start over from scratch if you want to perform the same search again. That's where iPhoto's *Smart Albums* come in.

A Smart Album, in essence, is a way to save a search in the form of an album. Unlike the albums you've already created, however, a Smart Album contains those pictures that match the search conditions you specify.

A Smart Album's search conditions can be considerably more complex than the searches you can perform with iPhoto's search field. The most important thing to remember about Smart Albums is that their contents can change dynamically as the contents of your iPhoto library change.

Let's create a Smart Album that contains only four-star-rated pictures from any Event that has a title or description with the words "*San Francisco*" in it:

1   Choose File > New Smart Album.

A sheet appears in which you can name the Smart Album and specify its search conditions. You can have several search conditions, and you can specify whether the Smart Album's contents can match any of them, or whether the contents must match all of them.

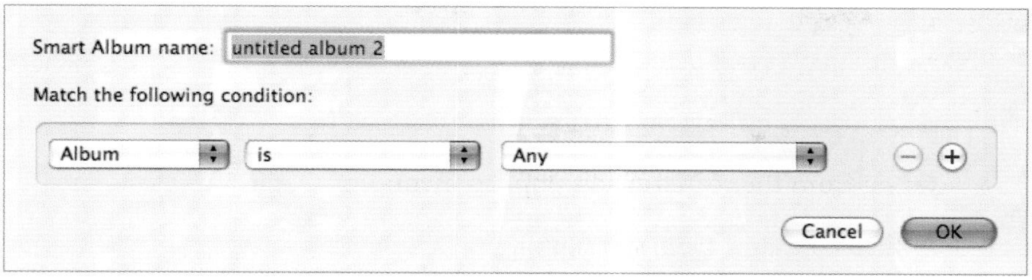

2   Type *Four-Star San Francisco Pictures* in the Smart Album name field at the top of the sheet.

3   Set the pop-up menus and fields on the line below so that the text reads *Event contains San Francisco*.

To do that, choose Events from the left-most menu, choose "contains" from the second menu, and type *San Francisco* in the field that appears to the right.

4   Add a new condition by clicking the + button.

5   In the new condition, choose "My Rating" from the left-most pop-up menu, "is" from the second pop-up menu, and then click in the field to the right to put four stars into it.

6   Set the pop-up menu that appears at the top of the sheet so that the text reads "Match all of the following conditions."

When you finish, the sheet should look like the one below.

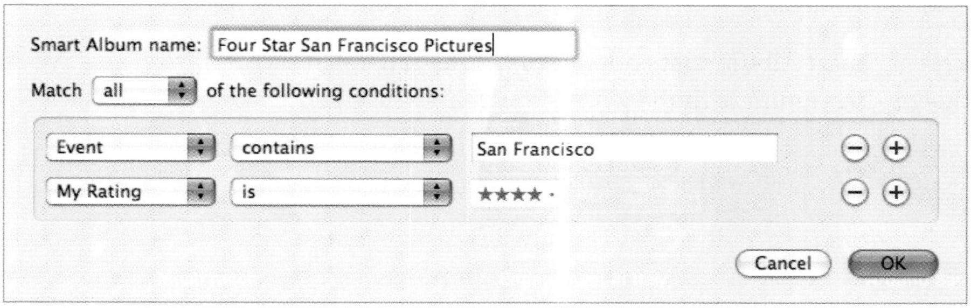

7   Click OK.

A new Smart Album appears in the source list. Select it, and the viewing pane shows the one picture that matches the conditions you specified.

If, at any time, you assign four stars to another picture in the Around San Francisco Event, that picture will automatically appear in the Smart Album.

Lesson Review

1. What is an Event?

2. What is a key photo?

3. How can you split an Event in two?

4. How can you see the pictures in more than one Event at a time?

5. How can you move a picture to a different Event?

6. How do you change an Event's title?

7. What is an album?

8. Describe two ways to rearrange the order of pictures in an album.

9. How can you see the pictures that you have hidden in an Event?

10. What is a keyword?

11. Name the four types of basic searches in iPhoto.

12. What is a Smart Album?

Answers

1. A collection a pictures taken around the same time.

2. The picture in the Event that represents the Event in the iPhoto viewing pane.

3. Open the Event, select the pictures in the Event that you want to put in a separate Event, and then click the Split button on the viewing pane's toolbar.

4. Click Photos in the source list, or select two or more Events in the viewing pane and then double-click one of them.

5. Open both Events and then drag the picture from one Event to the other.

6. In the viewing pane, click the Event's title and then type a new title.

7. A collection of pictures from one or more Events; the iPhoto equivalent of an iTunes playlist.

8. Drag the pictures into the order you want, or choose a sorting order from the View > Sort Photos submenu.

9. Open the Event and click the "Show hidden photos" message that appears at the top-right of the Event's title area in the viewing pane.

10. A word or short phrase that you can assign to one or more pictures to categorize them.

11. Text, Date, Keyword, and Rating.

12. An album that contains just the pictures matching the search conditions that you've specified.

3

Lesson Files   iLife08_Book_Files > Lessons > Lesson03 > L3_fixer-uppers

Time   This lesson takes approximately 60 minutes to complete.

Goals   Crop pictures

Rotate and straighten pictures

Touch up pictures

Adjust color and exposure

Apply effects

Lesson 3
Editing Your Pictures

"Picture perfect." You've probably heard that phrase before: It's used to describe anything that looks just right.

Most photographers know quite well, of course, that this phrase is misleading: Most pictures *aren't* perfect. But just because a picture isn't perfect doesn't mean you have to give up on it. iPhoto has a wide assortment of tools that you can use to bring your pictures closer to perfection. You'll get a chance to play with those tools in this lesson.

Prepare for the Lesson

To get ready for the lesson, you need to import some specially selected pictures into your iPhoto library that have the kinds of problems photographers—even the very best ones—run across all the time.

1   If iPhoto isn't open, open it.

2   Open the Lessons folder that you copied to your Mac from the enclosed DVD.

3   Open the Lesson03 folder and drag the **L3_fixer-uppers** folder inside onto the iPhoto window.

     iPhoto makes a new Event named L3_fixer-uppers that contains the pictures you'll work on in this lesson.

4   If the L3_fixer-uppers Event isn't open, click Last Import in the source list.

5   If the picture titles aren't visible, choose View > Titles.

     When you finish, the iPhoto window should look like the one below.

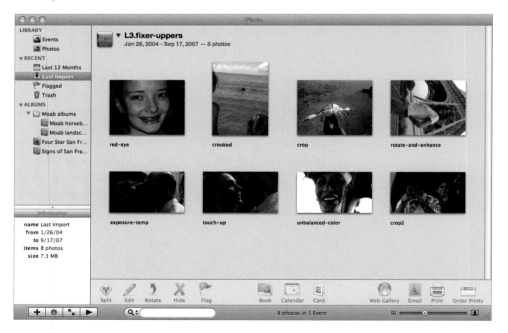

Cropping Pictures

Cropping is the act of trimming the edges of a picture. You may want to crop a picture for several reasons:

- ▶ To improve the picture's composition
- ▶ To change the picture's shape
- ▶ To remove unwanted elements from the picture
- ▶ To highlight an important detail in the picture

Among the pictures you just imported is one that you'll crop for both the first and the last of these reasons.

1 In the L3_fixer-uppers Event, click to select the picture of the crab.

The picture is titled "crop."

2 In the toolbar below the viewing pane, click the Edit button.

iPhoto's viewing pane becomes a picture editing pane. The picture expands to fill the pane, a collection of editing tools appear in the toolbar below the picture, and thumbnails of the pictures in the Event appear in a row above the picture. Now you'll crop the picture so that the crab fills the frame.

3   Click the Crop button in the editing toolbar.

A frame is superimposed on the picture, and a small, semi-transparent floating crop panel appears. A pop-up menu in the crop panel is labeled with the picture's current dimensions. You can drag the crop panel to move it anywhere you like on your screen.

NOTE ▶ The crop panel's pop-up menu offers several different choices for the cropping frame's aspect ratio; that is, the ratio between the frame's horizontal and vertical dimensions. Choosing a 2 x 3 aspect ratio, for example, produces a frame that is two units along one dimension and three units along the other: A three-inch-wide picture with this aspect ratio would have a height of two inches. Later in this lesson you'll learn how to change a picture's aspect ratio.

1680 × 1050 (Display)
✓ 2592 × 1944 (Original)
2 × 3
3 × 5
4 × 3 (DVD)
4 × 3 (Book)
4 × 6 (Postcard)
5 × 7 (L, 2L)
8 × 10
16 × 9 (HD)
16 × 20
20 × 30 (Poster)
Square
Custom…

Constrain as landscape
Constrain as portrait

4   Click the Constrain checkbox to select it.

When the Constrain checkbox is selected, changing the size of the cropping frame maintains the selected aspect ratio. When the picture's original dimensions are selected in the crop panel's menu and Constrain is selected as well, cropping the picture changes the picture's size but retains its shape.

5   Drag the upper-right corner of the cropping rectangle down and to the left.

Your pointer becomes a crosshair cursor. As you drag, the cropping frame changes size. It also displays thin guidelines that divide the frame into thirds both horizontally and vertically. These lines help you compose your cropped picture using the "rule of thirds" described in Lesson 1.

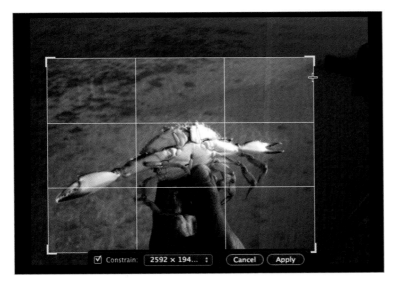

6   Click the center of the frame and drag it down.

When your pointer is inside the cropping frame, it becomes a hand cursor, and dragging slides the frame over the picture. You can also see the "rule of thirds" guidelines when you drag the frame over the picture.

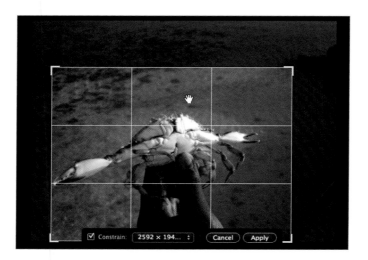

7   Continue adjusting the size and position of the cropping frame until the crab is just barely contained within the frame, and the crab's body is aligned with the top guide-line in the frame.

8   In the crop panel, click Apply.

The crop panel and the cropping frame go away and the cropped picture fills the edit-ing pane.

9 In the toolbar, click Done to save your changes and to see the iPhoto viewing pane again.

TIP If the iPhoto window seems too cramped for you when you're editing pictures, you can have iPhoto's editing view take over your entire screen. Click the double-arrow segment of the multi-segment button at the bottom-left of the iPhoto window to enter full-screen editing mode. The current picture takes over the entire screen. To see the editing tools, move your pointer to the bottom of the screen; to see the thumbnails of other pictures in the current Event, move your pointer to the top of the screen. To go back to the normal iPhoto window (and finish your editing session), click the X button that appears at the far right of the full-screen mode's editing toolbar.

iPhoto's full-screen editing view

Cropping a Video Frame

Next you'll crop a picture to create a portrait of a young guest at a wedding. The photo you'll start with is taken from the Hawaiian Wedding Event. It's not an ordinary photograph, however, but a single frame from the wedding video. Because the video is a high-definition video, the picture is wider than a normal photograph, and it shows some motion-blurring. Nonetheless, it can still be salvaged to produce an acceptable portrait.

NOTE ▶ To extract a single frame from a video clip to use as a still image, open iMovie and choose File > Save Frame. For more information, see Lesson 9.

1   Click the picture titled "crop2" to select it.

2   Click the Edit button in the viewing pane's toolbar.

3   Choose View > Thumbnails > Hide.

This command hides the row of picture thumbnails across the top of the editing pane so that you have more room in which to work.

4   In the editing toolbar, click Crop.

5   Choose "4 x 3 (Book)" from the crop panel's pop-up menu.

This choice produces a cropping frame that's taller than it is wide, which is more suitable for portraits. Choosing "4 x 3 (Book)" automatically selects the Constrain checkbox in the crop panel as well.

6 Adjust the cropping frame's size and position so that the top horizontal guideline in the frame is over the boy's eyes.

7   In the crop panel, click Apply.

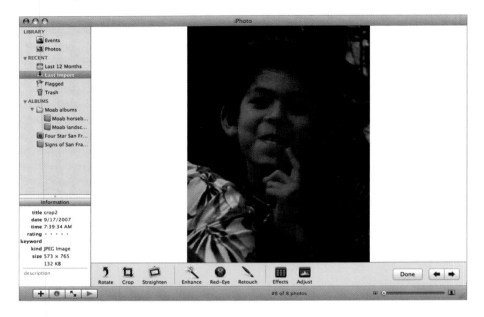

8   In the editing toolbar, click Done to save your changes.

> **TIP ▶** You can experiment freely to see what various settings in the floating crop window's pop-up menu do. After you click Apply to view your cropped image, choose Photos > Revert to Previous. The changes you've made will be discarded, leaving the original picture ready for you to experiment with a different crop.

Rotating and Straightening Pictures

Most cameras are designed to take photos with a landscape orientation: that is, photos that are wider than they are tall. People, on the other hand, are usually taller than they are wide. So, if you want to take portrait-style photos, or to photograph somebody standing, you have to turn the camera 90° clockwise or counter-clockwise in order to orient the picture properly.

However, unless your camera can detect its orientation and mark the photo with that information in a way that iPhoto can recognize, those pictures will end up sideways in iPhoto when you import them.

Changing a Picture's Orientation

Changing a picture's orientation is such a common thing to do that iPhoto makes that task very easy to accomplish, as you're about to see:

1 Click the photo titled "rotate-and-enhance" to select it.

2 In the viewing pane's toolbar, click Rotate.

By default, iPhoto's Rotate tool rotates the selected picture (or pictures—you can rotate more than one at a time) 90° counter-clockwise, which is what this particular picture needs. However, you can adjust iPhoto's preferences to set the Rotate tool to turn pictures clockwise instead. Or you can just press the Option key when clicking the tool: When the Option key is pressed, the Rotate tool reverses the direction in which it rotates pictures, and its button in the toolbar changes to show you the new direction in which it will rotate the picture.

NOTE ▶ Although, as you've just seen, you don't need to edit a picture in order to rotate it, iPhoto's editing toolbar also has a Rotate tool you can use. This is convenient when you want to make other changes to a picture in addition to adjusting its orientation.

Straightening Crooked Images

Even if a picture is rotated properly, it may not be quite on the level. It's easy to take a crooked picture; many otherwise perfect pictures suffer from this flaw.

You can straighten out such pictures with iPhoto's Straighten tool. The L3_fixer-uppers Event includes a tilted picture for you to untilt:

1   Click the picture titled "crooked" to select it.

2   Click the Edit button in the viewing pane's toolbar.

3   In the editing pane's toolbar, click the Straighten button.

The Straighten tool's panel appears over the editing pane, and a grid of yellow lines is superimposed on the picture.

4   Drag the slider in the Straighten panel to the left.

As you drag the slider, the picture begins to tilt in the direction that you're dragging.

5   Continue dragging until the horizon aligns with one of the horizontal grid lines.

6   Click the close button at the left side of the Straighten panel.

The grid lines and the panel disappear.

7   In the editing pane's toolbar, click Done.

> **NOTE ▶** When you straighten a picture, iPhoto must trim the picture's top, bottom, and sides in order to keep them straight as well. Take a close look at the picture you just straightened: The puffy cloud at the top-right has been cropped, and portions of the figures on the right and the left of the picture have been lopped off as well. The more a picture needs to be straightened, the more you'll lose from the edges of the image.

Touching Up Pictures

Cameras can be cruel. Not only can they reveal, in all-too-visible detail, every blemish, wrinkle, or scar on your face; they can even add new flaws—especially when the camera's flash is involved.

In this part of the lesson, you're going to undo some of the flaws that either nature or the camera has imposed.

The first flaw you'll tackle is the photographic phenomenon known as *red-eye*. When you take a picture using a flash attachment mounted directly on the camera, the light from the flash can travel directly into your subject's eyes, brightly illuminating the blood vessels at the back of the subject's eyeballs. The iPhoto red-eye tool can get the red out.

1 Click the picture titled "red-eye" to select it.

2 Click Edit in the viewing pane's toolbar.

3 Slide the magnifying slider at the bottom of the iPhoto window far enough to the right to allow you to see the eyes of the image in detail, adjusting the editing pane's scroll bars as needed to keep the eyes in view.

> **TIP** ▶ Pressing the spacebar turns your pointer into a hand cursor when it's over the editing pane. While the spacebar is down, you can drag the image around the editing pane to position it instead of using the scroll bars.

4 Click the Red-Eye button in the editing pane's toolbar.

A Red-Eye tool panel appears over the editing pane, with a pop-up Size menu that's set to Automatic. Your pointer becomes a crosshair cursor.

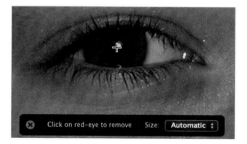

5 Place the pointer over one of the red pupils in the picture and click.

The red part of the pupil turns black.

6 Choose Manual from the Red-Eye tool panel's pop-up menu.

A slider appears beside the menu and the crosshair cursor changes to show a circle at the intersection of the crosshairs.

NOTE ▶ You use the Manual red-eye feature to adjust your pointer to match the size of the pupil you want to fix in those cases where the Automatic setting of the Red-Eye tool doesn't completely fix a particular red-eye. Usually, the Automatic setting is all you need.

7 Drag the panel's Size slider to the right until the circle in your pointer is about the same size as the remaining red pupil in the picture.

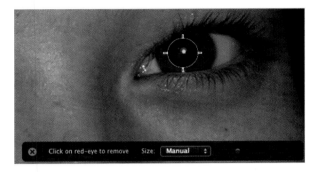

8 Place the pointer over the red pupil and click.

The part of the pupil inside the circle turns black.

9 In the editing pane's toolbar, click Done.

NOTE ▶ The Red-Eye tool eliminates the red component of *any* part of the picture on which you click, whether it is an eye or not. If you're curious, try clicking on red parts of any picture to see what it does. You can zoom in on the eye to make the editing area larger.

Retouching Your Pictures

Next, you'll engage in a different kind of touch-up: removing a few laugh-lines from the eyes of a bride using iPhoto's Retouch tool.

1   Click the picture titled "touch-up" to select it, and then click Edit in the viewing pane's toolbar.

2   Adjust the iPhoto window's magnifying slider and the editing pane's scroll bars so you can see the bride's right eye magnified in the editing pane. Notice the laugh-lines at the corner of the bride's eye.

3   Click the Retouch button in the editing pane's toolbar.

The Retouch tool panel appears and your pointer becomes an open circle.

4   Adjust the Retouch panel's slider so that the pointer becomes about twice as wide as one of the laugh-lines.

5   Drag the pointer along one of the laugh-lines, then release the mouse button. Repeat for each line by the eye.

As you drag, the pointer paints a light color over the laugh-line. When you release the mouse button, the light color and the laugh-line both vanish.

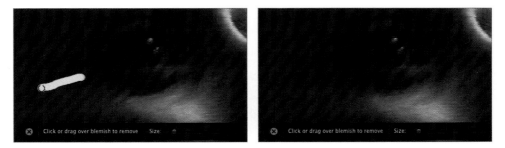

6   Optionally, retouch the creases in the bride's forehead.

7   Click Done.

NOTE ▶ The Retouch tool continuously calculates an average of the color and texture of the area surrounding the pointer as you drag and it applies that average to the area under the pointer. The result is usually a smooth blend that eliminates small flaws and blemishes. However, when you drag the tool over the edge of an object you'll often see strange smears and similar artifacts appear. Experiment with this tool on various parts of an image to see what it can and can't smooth.

Applying Adjustments and Effects

Your eye and your brain make a wonderful team: Your eye provides the image, and your brain processes it, compensating for things like poor illumination, tinted light, and obscuring haze. As the eye and brain work together, you end up seeing a much richer image than the one your eye started out with.

Your poor camera, on the other hand, doesn't have the power of your brain to adjust its images with the same subtlety or dexterity—the images it produces may not match in color or clarity what you remember seeing when you took them. iPhoto has several tools, however, to provide the image-processing capabilities that your camera lacks.

To see these tools in action, you'll start with a picture you've previously seen, and adjust it to improve its color and clarity. When this picture was taken, the weather was hazy, resulting in a photo with muted colors and dark areas that the haze made look more gray than black.

1   Select the picture titled "rotate-and-enhance" in the L3_fixer-uppers Event, and then click Edit in the viewing pane's toolbar.

2 In the editing pane's toolbar, click the Enhance button.

iPhoto uses predefined operations that adjust a picture's brightness and contrast and that intensify its colors. Often, clicking this tool is all you need to improve a drab-looking picture.

Using the Adjust Panel

Although the Enhance tool has done a pretty good job with this picture, the result isn't picture perfect: The enhancement has made the subject's face look a little too dark. A quick trip to iPhoto's Adjust panel can fix that.

1 In the editing pane's toolbar, click the Adjust button.

The Adjust panel appears. This panel has a variety of controls you can use to modify a picture's colors, brightness, and sharpness. You'll be using this panel a lot in the remainder of this lesson.

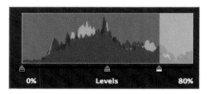

2   Near the top of the panel, drag the rightmost Levels slider to the left until the percentage number under it reaches 80%.

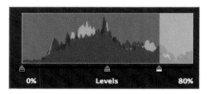

As the slider moves to the left, the lighter parts of the picture become even lighter, making areas that were almost white become white. At the 80% setting, the parts of the picture that were 80% as light as the very lightest parts of the picture now have the same level of lightness. The result is a brighter picture that still retains most of the dark shadows under the Eiffel Tower, but that lightens the subject's face.

3   Click Done.

> **TIP** ▶ If you completely mess up your picture while using the Adjust panel, click its Reset button. This resets all the sliders, leaving your picture as it was before you began tinkering. Either way, the original photo remains unchanged.

Adjusting Your Picture's Color Cast

The next problem you'll deal with is color cast. Your brain is pretty good at compensating for the color of the light that illuminates what you see: Put on a pair of sunglasses, for example, and in just a few minutes you adjust to the color shifts that the glasses impose.

Modern automatic cameras try to do the same thing, eliminating slight color variations in lighting to produce pictures with more accurate colors, but sometimes they just don't quite get it right. When that happens, a picture ends up with a color cast that is bluer, or greener, or redder, than it should be. The effect is most apparent in the white or gray areas of the picture, but it actually affects the entire image.

Here's how you adjust the color cast of a picture:

1   Select the picture titled "unbalanced-color" in the L3_fixer-uppers Event.

2   Click Edit in the viewing pane's toolbar.

This picture, taken near sunset in Hawaii, has a blue cast to it, caused when the camera tried to compensate for the orange tint of the setting sun's light. Your job is to restore the warm look of sunset to the picture.

3   Click Adjust to bring up the Adjust panel.

> **TIP** ▶ Although you could tweak the individual sliders that control the picture's saturation (how intense the colors are), the temperature (how warm/orange or cool/ blue the picture looks), or the tint (the balance between green and red in the picture), the Adjust panel provides a quick shortcut for adjusting color cast: the white point eyedropper.

4   Click the white point eyedropper in the Adjust panel.

The pointer becomes a small crosshair cursor and instructions for using it appear in a panel over the editing pane. The color of the place you click in the picture is used by iPhoto to calculate the other colors in the picture. It takes that color and treats it as a neutral white or gray color, and then moves the Saturation, Tint, and Temperature sliders in the panel to compensate.

5   Click the gray part of the subject's front tooth, as shown.

The picture becomes warmer looking.

6   Click Done.

> **NOTE** ► As long as the Color Cast tool is selected, you can click various parts of the picture to see how the color cast changes. Depending on where you click, you can see some startling results.

TIP ▶ When you're in the editing pane, you can always compare how your work has changed the picture from the original by pressing the Shift key. When the Shift key is down, iPhoto displays the picture as it was before you began making changes. This feature is very useful when you work with color casts, which often cause subtle changes that are hard to detect without a comparison.

Adjusting Exposure and Color Temperature

Next, you'll fix a picture that has a combination of problems: It's both under-exposed (the camera's shutter was not open for long enough) and it has a warmer color temperature than it should.

You can correct both problems in the Adjust panel:

1 Select the picture titled "exposure-temp" in the L3_fixer-uppers Event, and then click Edit in the viewing pane's toolbar.

2 Click Adjust.

3 Slide the Exposure slider to the right until the number at the right side of the slider is between 1.45 and 1.55.

   The picture becomes brighter, and the warm color cast is even more apparent.

NOTE ▶ Although you can't go back in time and increase the camera's shutter-speed or aperture, you can adjust the relationship between the darkest and the lightest part of the picture, and thus simulate a change in how the picture was exposed. The Exposure slider adjusts that relationship mathematically and it does a pretty good job—within limits, of course.

4   To correct the color temperature, move the Temperature slider slightly to the left until the number at the right side of the slider is about -15.0.

The color cast of the picture becomes cooler and looks more natural.

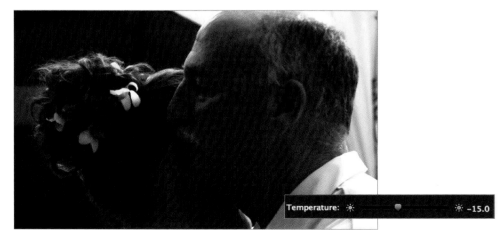

5   Click Done.

> **TIP** If you have a number of pictures with the same problem, you can use the Adjust panel's Copy and Paste buttons to copy the panel's settings from one picture and then paste them into another.

Using iPhoto's Effects Panel

Finally, now that you've done the hard work of fixing problems, it's time to play.

iPhoto includes an Effects panel that presents a number of interesting and amusing visual effects you can apply to pictures. Some effects can be applied multiple times to intensify what they do. Other effects act like switches: They're either on or off. You might want to apply effects, for example, to pictures that you plan to use for cards, or books, or calendars (you'll find out how to make these things with iPhoto in Lesson 4).

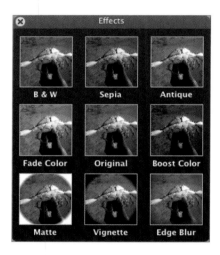

Rather than working through an exercise, you should simply pick a picture or two and try some effects out. Below you can see a few different effects that have been applied to the crab picture with which this lesson began. Have fun!

Black and white crab

Antique crab

Crab with color boosted four times

Crab with edges blurred seven times

Crab with matte applied five times

Lesson Review

1. What does "cropping" mean?
2. Give a reason for cropping a picture.
3. What is "red-eye?"
4. What is a common cause for crooked pictures?
5. What is color cast?
6. What iPhoto tool is used to correct color cast problems?
7. Where in a picture might the Retouch tool produce odd results?
8. Describe a side effect of using the Straighten tool.

Answers

1. "Cropping" is the act of trimming the edges from a picture.
2. There are several reasons to crop a picture: To improve the composition, to remove unwanted elements from the picture, to highlight a specific detail in the picture, and to change the picture's shape.
3. "Red-eye" is the glowing-eye effect created when the light from the camera's flash illuminates the blood vessels at the back of the photographic subject's eyes.
4. Crooked pictures are often caused by inadvertently tilting the camera when pressing the shutter button.
5. A color cast is a tinting of the picture created when the camera unsuccessfully compensates for the color of the light present when the picture was taken.
6. The white point eyedropper tool in the Adjust panel is used to correct color cast problems.

7. Using the Retouch tool along the edge of an object in a picture can cause odd artifacts and smears to appear.

8. The Straighten tool has the side effect of slightly cropping the picture.

4

Lesson Files   No additional files

Time   This lesson takes approximately 90 minutes to complete.

Goals   Back up pictures

Create a slideshow

Print pictures

Order prints

Create a greeting card

Create a picture book

Create a calendar

Share pictures over a network

Publish a Web Gallery

Publishing Your Pictures

Okay, you have a library full of pictures. You've titled them, rated them, sorted them into Events and albums, cropped some, color-corrected others, and retouched the ones that had it coming. Now what?

Why, you share them with the world, of course!

In this lesson you'll learn how to share your pictures in all sorts of ways: on disc, on your network, online, and on paper.

Archiving Your Pictures

The first way you'll learn to share your photos is with yourself: You're going to back up your iPhoto library.

iPhoto can easily and quickly burn your iPhoto library to a recordable CD or DVD. This is something you should do regularly. Recordable discs are cheap, but the time you've spent creating, arranging, and cleaning up your pictures isn't.

When you burn your library to a disc, iPhoto puts an iPhoto library on the disc that contains the albums, Events, and folders from your Mac's iPhoto library. What you're doing is taking a snapshot of your library at the moment you burn the disc.

You can use this snapshot to recover from mistakes—such as accidentally deleting the wrong Event—or to store pictures and albums that you don't want to throw away but no longer want cluttering up your iPhoto library.

Pull out a blank recordable disc and let's get started.

1   Open iPhoto and make sure that all the Events are showing.

    When iPhoto burns a library to disc, it copies only the items that are selected. In this activity, you're going to back up your entire iPhoto library, so if an Event is open, you should click All Events in the Event's title bar to make all of the Events visible in the viewing area. Similarly, if you're viewing an album's contents, click Events in the source list to make all Events visible.

2   When all the Events are visible, choose Edit > Select None to make sure that nothing is selected.

    TIP ▶ When you don't have anything selected, iPhoto's burn feature copies your entire library—but if you *do* have something selected, the burn feature copies only the items you have selected. You can use this behavior to your advantage: For example, if you're working with other people on a photo project, you can burn just the albums needed for the project to a disc, and then give the disc to your collaborators. They can use this disc directly with iPhoto on their own Macs; the pictures will be conveniently titled, rated, and arranged exactly as they were on your Mac.

3   Choose Share > Burn.

A sheet appears instructing you to insert a blank disc in your CD/DVD recorder. Note that iPhoto uses the hardware name of your Mac's recordable drive.

> **Please insert a blank disc.**
>
> Burn Disc In: MATSHITA DVD–R UJ–845
>
> Cancel   OK

4   Insert the recordable disc in your disc drive and click OK.

iPhoto takes a few moments inspecting the disc to make sure that it's recordable. Then the disc burning pane appears at the bottom of the iPhoto viewing area. The pane tells you how many items and how much data will be burned to the disc (in megabytes, abbreviated as MB); provides a graphical representation of how much of the disc's capacity the library will use; and presents a field in which you can give the disc a name other than the one iPhoto suggests. The suggested name is useful if the disc is going to be part of a series of regular backups, because it includes the date when you made the backup.

> Used: 287 MB   Name: iPhoto Library – 9/20/07
> Available: 391 MB   Items: 249 photos   Cancel   Burn

5   In the burning pane, click Burn.

The Burn Disc window appears, confirming what iPhoto is about to burn, and giving you another opportunity to cancel the burning process.

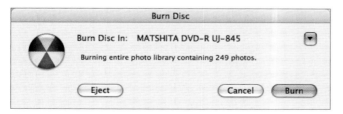

> **Burn Disc**
>
> Burn Disc In: MATSHITA DVD–R UJ–845
>
> Burning entire photo library containing 249 photos.
>
> Eject   Cancel   Burn

6   In the window, click Burn.

A progress sheet appears, and iPhoto begins burning the library to the disc. Depending on the size of the library and the speed of the disc burner, burning the disc could take anywhere from a few minutes to half an hour. After iPhoto finishes burning the disc, iPhoto verifies it, which takes additional time—though not, usually, as long as it takes to burn the disc.

Burning to the MATSHITA DVD-R UJ-845 drive

Writing track 1

Stop

When iPhoto finishes burning and verifying the disc, a Shares heading appears in the source list, with the disc that you just burned below it.

7 In the source list, click the newly burned disc's disclosure triangle to see its contents.

The disc contains a copy of your library's Events, along with copies of any albums and folders that the library includes. Although you can't change any of the disc's contents, you can use them for projects, export them, and even copy them back to your current iPhoto library.

8 Click the eject button beside the disc's name in the source list.

iPhoto ejects your disc from the drive.

9 Label the disc and put it in a safe place.

Making a Slideshow

If you hear the word "slideshow" and think of Uncle Leo once again hauling out his projector, screen, and the five hundred faded slides that show every mile of his road trip in 1976 to see the World's Largest Ball of String in Cawker City, Kansas, then you've never seen an iPhoto slideshow. Unlike Uncle Leo's version of after-dinner entertainment, iPhoto slideshows can both dance and sing, and they are *much* more fun to set up and view.

To see how to make an iPhoto slideshow from your own pictures, you'll start with the Signs of San Francisco album that you made in Lesson 2.

1 Click the Signs of San Francisco album in the source list.

2 In the multi-segment button below the source list, click the + segment at the left side of the button.

You can use this button to create a variety of items, as noted by the help tag that appears when you rest your pointer over the button.

3 In the sheet that appears, click the Slideshow button and then click Create.

A Slideshows heading appears in the source list, and the slideshow editing area opens in the iPhoto window.

4 In the toolbar at the bottom of the slideshow editing area, click Play.

The slideshow occupying the whole screen begins to play, accompanied by music. If you move your pointer, a controller appears over the slideshow. You can use the controller to pause the show, move manually among the slides, and rate, rotate, or discard the currently displayed slide.

5 Click the slideshow as it plays.

The slideshow ends.

As you've just seen, iPhoto can create a polished-looking slideshow quickly and easily without requiring you to do much work. You don't, however, have to accept the creative choices that iPhoto has made.

Next, you'll modify the playback settings for the slideshow that you've just created.

1   In the toolbar at the bottom of the slideshow editing area, click the Settings button.

A sheet appears with options for modifying the slideshow's appearance and playback behavior. Take a moment or two to look this sheet over. Among other things, you can specify how long to show each slide, what transition effect to use when changing slides, how long the transition takes, and whether or not to use the Ken Burns Effect to put the slides in motion.

NOTE ▶ The Ken Burns Effect is named for documentary filmmaker Ken Burns, who popularized the technique of moving a camera over a still image both to better tell the picture's story and to create visual interest.

2   Click the Repeat slideshow checkbox to deselect it, and then click Fit slideshow to music.

When you finish, the sheet should have the same settings as the one shown here.

Default Settings for the entire slideshow

Play each slide for   3   seconds

Transition: Dissolve

Speed: ———————

☐ Repeat slideshow
☐ Scale photos to fill screen
☑ Automatic Ken Burns Effect
☐ Show titles
☐ Show my ratings
☐ Show slideshow controls

◯ Repeat music during slideshow
   The music will repeat for as long as the slides play.

◉ Fit slideshow to music
   Slide durations will be adjusted to make the slides play for as long as
   the music plays.

Slideshow Format: Current Display

Cancel   OK

3 Click OK to close the sheet, then click the Music button in the slideshow editing area's toolbar.

A sheet appears with a list of songs from which you can choose to provide your slideshow with musical accompaniment. iPhoto provides a selection of music samples you can use, but you can also choose your slideshow music from your iTunes library or from any GarageBand compositions you may have. You can use the search field at the bottom of the sheet to find particular songs in your music collection, and you can preview the selected song by clicking the Play button in the sheet. However, for this exercise, you'll leave things as they are.

4 Click Cancel in the music sheet, and then click the Play button in the slideshow editing area's toolbar.

The slideshow plays using the settings you've applied. When the music ends, the slideshow ends.

You aren't limited to tinkering with the playback settings for the whole slideshow: You can also adjust the presentation of each slide individually. You can specify exactly how long each slide stays on screen, you can set where the Ken Burns Effect begins and ends for each slide, you can choose a transition effect and the transition duration on a slide-by-slide basis, and you can choose the order in which slides appear.

Let's get started customizing the slideshow:

1   With the first slide showing, click the Ken Burns Effect checkbox to select it.

Doing this allows you to set how the Ken Burns Effect behaves for the current slide.

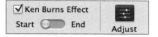

2   Drag the magnifying slider at the bottom right of the window toward the right to zoom in on the slide, then drag the slide in the editing area to the right until the beginning of the San Francisco sign on the slide is visible on the left side of the frame.

When the slide appears in the slideshow, it will first display the slide using the same magnification and position that you've just set.

3   At the bottom of the Ken Burns Effect control, slide the switch to the End position.

Putting the switch in this position lets you adjust where the Ken Burns motion effect ends for the current slide.

4   Magnify the slide as you did in step 2, but drag the slide so that the text in the right side of the slide is showing.

When this slide plays, your view of it will *pan* across the slide from left to right.

5   Click the Adjust button in the toolbar.

An Adjust This Slide Panel appears. You use this panel to control the slide's duration on screen, to set a different transition effect for the slide, and to set how long the transition takes.

6   Choose Reveal from the panel's Transition pop-up menu, move the Speed slider below it one notch to the left, and then click the left arrow in the round direction control beside the pop-up menu.

These settings will cause the picture to slide off-screen to the left, revealing the next slide beneath it as it moves.

7   In the toolbar, click the Preview button.

iPhoto animates the slide in the slideshow editing area to show the effect of your setting adjustments.

8   At the top of the slideshow editing area, drag the second slide (the one showing the bookstore window) to the right of the following slide.

Dragging a slide changes the order of slides in the slideshow.

9   At the top of the slideshow editing area, click the first slide again, and then click the Play button.

Selecting a slide starts the slideshow presentation from that slide. The slideshow begins playing, using the Ken Burns Effect and transition settings you've made on the first slide. The other slides use the default settings from the Settings sheet.

Once you've tweaked your slideshow to your satisfaction, you can export it as a QuickTime movie so you can share it among your circle of friends and admirers.

1   Choose File > Export.

A sheet appears in which you can name your slideshow movie, select a location in which to save it, and specify a size for the movie.

2   In the Save As field, type a name for your slideshow movie. By default, iPhoto saves movies to your Movies folder in your Home directory.

3   Choose a size from the sheet's "Movie size" pop-up menu.

You can choose from Small, Medium, and Large. The bigger the movie, the longer it will take to export and the more disk space it will take, but the more detail it will show when played.

4   Choose Export.

An Exporting Slideshow sheet appears, showing the progress of the export. While the export is taking place, you can't do anything else in iPhoto.

Exporting Slideshow...

Cancel

5   When the export finishes, switch to the Finder, open your Movies folder (or the folder in which you chose to save the movie), and double-click the slideshow movie you've just created.

The QuickTime Player application opens with your slideshow in it.

Congratulations! You have just made your first feature film. Fame and fortune await you.

Printing Pictures

There are a lot of different reasons you might want to print a picture. For example, it's just not convenient to share a picture by sticking your Mac to the refrigerator door with a magnet. iPhoto can produce very attractively formatted prints of your pictures, whether you need them for the refrigerator door or for the picture frame on your wall or desk.

To learn how iPhoto's printing feature works, you'll print a picture from the Hawaiian Wedding Event.

1   Open the Hawaiian Wedding Event and click to select the picture of the couple exchanging their wedding vows. The picture is titled DS023 and looks like this:

2   In the toolbar at the bottom of the viewing area, click the Print button.

A sheet appears with various printing layout controls and options. Along the left side of the sheet are several printing *themes*. Themes provide different layouts for printing; for example, the Contact Sheet theme is good for printing thumbnail pictures for an entire Event, so that you have a printed record of its contents. For this picture, the Standard theme, which is the default choice, is fine.

3   From the Printer pop-up menu, choose the printer you want to use, and from the Paper
Size pop-up menu, choose the size of the paper on which you want to print the picture.

The paper size choices available vary depending on the printer you choose. For this
picture, we chose an ink-jet printer and a 4-by-6-inch paper size.

NOTE ▶ If necessary, iPhoto crops the picture to fit the aspect ratio of the paper size
that you have chosen.

4   From the Presets pop-up menu, choose a preset appropriate for the kind of printer
and paper you're using.

Different types of printers offer different presets. For example, a laser printer might
offer only a single preset, whereas a color inkjet printer might offer several presets for
printing on regular paper and on different kinds of photo paper.

At this point, you could simply press the Print button and let iPhoto and your printer do
their work. However, you can further fine-tune the picture layout before you print it, and
that's what you'll do next.

1   In the printing sheet, click Customize.

The sheet retracts, and the viewing area is replaced by the printing layout area. Across
the top are thumbnails of the pictures you've selected to print (in this case, there's
only one). A toolbar with layout tools is at the bottom of the area.

2 Click the Layout button.

A pop-up menu appears, with a single choice: One. Different themes offer different choices on this menu.

3 In the pop-up layout menu, choose One and then choose the second item on the sub-menu that appears.

This choice lays the picture out in a landscape view with a caption below the picture.

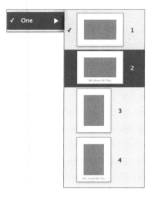

4 In the layout area, click the picture's caption and type *The Wedding Vows.*

When you click the caption that iPhoto provides, it's automatically selected so you can quickly change it.

> **TIP** ▶ Click the Settings button in the toolbar to see a sheet in which you can choose a font, style, and size for the caption.

5 Click the picture in the layout area.

A panel appears above the picture with controls that you can use to adjust the picture's size and position.

> **TIP** ▶ If iPhoto has cropped the picture to match the aspect ratio of the paper size you've chosen for printing, you can restore the full picture in the layout area: Control-click or right-click the picture and choose Fit Photo to Frame Size.

6 Drag the slider in the panel to magnify the picture, and drag the picture so that the couple is centered in the frame.

Try to adjust the picture layout so that it looks like the one here.

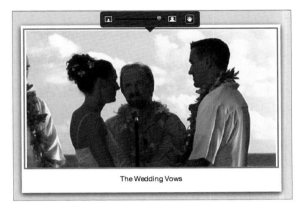

TIP ▶ Click the Adjust button in the toolbar to open a panel with a combination of adjustment and effects controls similar to the ones in the iPhoto editing area's Adjust and Effects panels. Use this panel, for example, if you need to make any temporary color or exposure setting changes before you print.

7 In the toolbar, click the Print button.

A Print window appears with standard printing controls.

8 Optional: In the Print window, click Print.

The picture prints using the printer you have chosen. When it finishes, the print layout area is still present so you can print again.

9 In the source list, click Events.

NOTE ▶ When you customize printing, a Printing project appears under the Recent heading in the source list. Until you choose something else to print, or click Cancel in the print layout area, you can click the Printing project to return to the print layout area and print more copies using that layout and to make additional layout changes.

Ordering Prints

You don't need a color printer, or even a printer at all, to get high-quality color prints. You can order professionally produced color prints of your pictures right from within iPhoto.

Here's how it works—but don't worry, it won't cost you any money; you'll cancel the operation before you actually order anything!

1   Open the Hawaiian Wedding Event and select the picture of the couple exchanging their wedding vows.

2   In the viewing area's toolbar, click the Order Prints button.

An Order Prints window appears. If you haven't previously ordered prints with your copy of iPhoto, the ordering options are disabled until you sign in.

At this point, instead of actually signing in or creating an account right now, click Cancel, and just read the following description of how the ordering process and the account creation process work.

If no one has ever ordered prints from your copy of iPhoto, the Order Prints window offers a Set Up Account button. Click this button to either sign in to your existing account or to create a new one. A Set Up Account window appears that provides for both possibilities.

When you click Create Account in the Set Up Account window, an Account Info window appears in which you go through the account creation steps. Among other things, you'll need to supply your email address (used to create the Apple ID that you use when you sign in to the account), your credit card number, its expiration date, and a shipping address. Once Apple has verified the credit card information you've supplied, your account is ready for you to use.

NOTE ▶ The Apple Account creation process uses a secure connection to protect your personal information.

If you already have an account, you enter your Apple ID and your password in the Set Up Account window to sign in. Once you've signed in, you use the Order Prints window to specify the number and size of the prints you want. You can also choose where to have the prints sent and how to have them shipped. When you click Buy Now, iPhoto uses your Internet connection to transfer the pictures to the print service and, within a few days, your prints arrive in the mail.

⊖ ⊖ ⊖		Order Prints		
Kodak Print Service			Quick Order 4 x 6's	

	4 x 6	$0.19 each	5
	5 x 7	0.99 each	2
	Wallet	1.79 for 4	0
⚠	8 x 10	3.99 each	0
⚠	16 x 20	17.99 each	0
⚠	20 x 30	22.99 each	0

Account: ▢@mac.com (1–Click® enabled)   Use a Coupon...

Ship To: Myself

Ship Via: Standard ($2.49)

Usually ships in 1–3 business days.

Sizes and availability are based on your United States billing address. Pricing is in US Dollars.

⚠ Low resolution may result in poor print quality.

Subtotal: $2.93
Tax (Estimated): 0.29
Shipping: 2.49

Order Total: $5.71

(?) (Account Info)   (Cancel) (Buy Now)

NOTE ▶ The Order Prints window places a yellow warning icon by any print sizes that may not look good at the picture's resolution—for example, a 2-megapixel image can't produce a good quality print in sizes larger than 8 by 10 inches.

Making a Greeting Card

Suppose you have a picture that would be perfect for a holiday card or a party invitation. You can use iPhoto to create such cards and have them professionally printed, just as you can with picture prints.

To learn how to make a card, you'll make a party invitation, using one of the pictures from the Hawaiian Wedding Event:

1   Open the Hawaiian Wedding Event and click to select the picture of the sunset.

If you can't find it, the picture is titled DS006 and looks like this:

2   In the toolbar at the bottom of the viewing area, click the Card button.

A sheet appears with various card themes. Along the left side of the sheet are different theme categories. At the right are samples of the available themes. Above the category list is a pop-up menu; from it you can choose whether to create a Greeting Card or a Postcard. A Greeting Card layout has the picture on the front and opens to reveal a message inside. A Postcard layout has the picture on the front and the message on the back. You'll use the Greeting Card setting for the invitation.

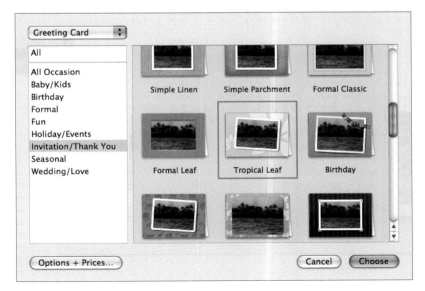

3   In the theme category list, choose Invitation/Thank You.

The theme samples area displays the samples that are suitable for invitations and thank-you notes.

4   Scroll through the theme samples until you find the Tropical Leaf sample, click it, and then click Choose.

The viewing area becomes a card layout area, with the outside and the inside of the card displayed, and a toolbar beneath it with tools similar to those in the printing layout area's toolbar. Also, a Projects heading appears in the source list, with an "untitled card" project beneath it.

5   In the source list, rename the card project *Beach Party Card*.

6   Click the picture on the face of the card and use the magnifying and positioning panel that appears to adjust the picture's appearance.

This panel should look familiar to you: It's the same one you saw in the printing layout area.

7   Optional: In the toolbar, click the Background button, and then choose a different background from the pop-up menu that appears.

Depending on the theme you choose, a card can offer both different backgrounds and different variations on its basic design (the latter of which you can choose by clicking the Design button on the toolbar). You can also change the card's orientation with the

Orientation pop-up menu in the toolbar, and, if that's not enough, you can choose an entirely different theme for the card by clicking the Theme button.

8 In the card's interior, click Insert Title and type a new title, then click "Insert your information here" and type the invitation's details.

You can type multiple lines of text by pressing Return in both the card's title and its information. You can see what we typed for the invitation here.

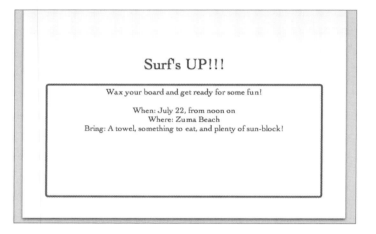

NOTE ► You can also adjust the font family, size, and typeface of the card's interior text by choosing Edit > Font > Show Fonts (or by pressing Command-T) and then selecting different settings in the standard Font window that appears.

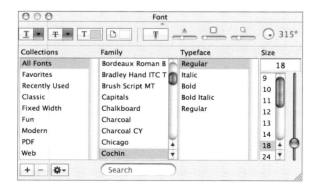

9 When your card looks the way you want it, click Buy.

An Order Card window appears, which is similar to the Order Prints window you saw earlier. If you have an Apple ID, you can order cards the same way you order prints.

10 Click Cancel in the Order Card window.

You didn't really want to buy this example card, did you?

TIP ▶ You can also choose File > Print instead of clicking the Buy button to print the card on your own printer. If you print your own card, though, remember that a card has two sides, so you may need to print the first page by itself, and then turn the paper over and put it back into the printer before you print the second page. Consult your printer manual for the best way to perform double-sided printing with your printer.

Creating a Calendar

Time is money—if you don't believe that, just walk into any bookstore and count how many picture calendars there are for sale! But you don't have to rely on the shrink-wrapped offerings that you find on the bookstore racks. Instead, you can use the pictures in your iPhoto library to make a custom-designed, professionally printed calendar that you can give to your friends or family—or hang on your own wall.

To see how you build a calendar in iPhoto, you'll use the promotional photos from the aviation film *One Six Right* that you imported in Lesson 1. (You can find out more about this film at http://www.onesixright.com.)

> **NOTE ▶** If you're wondering, the title of the film is aviation-speak for a runway that is oriented 160 degrees from magnetic north, and is on the right when you approach it on landing or take off.

You'll build the calendar in two steps: First, you'll set up the calendar's layout, and then you'll add the pictures to it, along with marking any special dates that should be on the calendar.

1   In the Events viewing area, click the One Six Right Event to select it, and then click the Calendar button on the viewing area's toolbar.

A sheet appears with a list of available calendar themes.

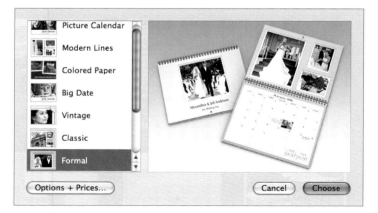

> **NOTE ▶** You don't have to select an Event to make a calendar. Any selection of individual pictures, or a selected album, can serve as the source for a calendar project.

2   Click the Formal theme and then click Choose.

Another sheet appears in which you specify the range of dates the calendar will cover, and, optionally, choose whether it shows holidays and events from your iCal calendars and birthdays from your Address Book contact lists. By default, the sheet offers a 12-month calendar with no holidays.

Start calendar on: January   2008

Months: 12

Show national holidays: None

Import iCal calendars:

☐ Show birthdays from Address Book

Cancel   OK

3   Choose United States from the "Show national holidays" pop-up menu (optional), and then click OK.

iPhoto adds the calendar item under the Projects heading in the source list, and presents a sheet explaining how to put pictures into the calendar.

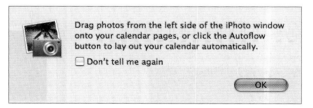

Drag photos from the left side of the iPhoto window onto your calendar pages, or click the Autoflow button to lay out your calendar automatically.

☐ Don't tell me again

OK

4   Click OK.

The viewing area is replaced with the calendar layout area. In the area is the cover of the calendar, waiting for a picture to be added to it and for you to supply a title and other text. A toolbar at the bottom of the calendar layout area contains tools much like those found in the card and printing layout areas. Along the left side of the area, a picture browser displays the pictures you selected.

5   Click the page button above the picture browser.

The picture browser becomes a page browser that shows reduced images of the calendar's pages. You can use this page browser to see the layout of individual calendar pages and to navigate to any calendar page quickly. If you scroll down the page browser, you'll notice that some pages have a placeholder for one picture, some have two, and so on. For this calendar, every page should have one picture.

6   Click the first page in the browser you see that has more than one picture placeholder.

The page appears in the layout area.

February 2008

7 Click the top of the page in the layout area, and then click the Layout button in the toolbar.

The Layout button produces a pop-up menu from which you can choose the number of picture placeholders on the selected calendar page and, for each number choice, a set of layouts.

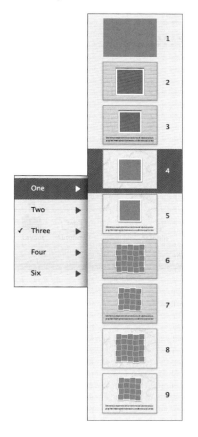

8 From the Layout pop-up, choose One > 4.

This produces a simple one picture layout for the calendar page.

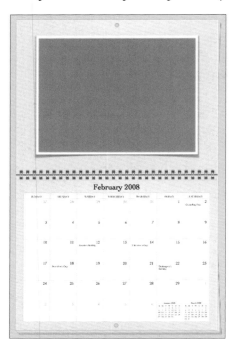

9 For each page in the calendar, repeat the previous two steps so that all the calendar pages have a single picture placeholder.

You are now ready to start putting pictures into the calendar and to add notes to specific dates.

1 Select the calendar cover from the page browser, and then click the picture button above the browser.

The cover appears in the layout area, and the page browser becomes a picture browser again.

2 Drag a picture from the picture browser to the calendar cover's picture placeholder in the layout area.

The picture you dropped appears on the calendar cover. You can click the picture to see a panel that you can use to magnify and reposition the picture on the page, just as you did when you laid out a card and a printing job.

TIP You can use the Adjust tool in the toolbar to make changes to the pictures used in the calendar. Adjustments and effects made with the calendar layout area's Adjust panel only affect the picture in the calendar.

3   Click the placeholder calendar title and delete the word *calendar* so it simply reads One Six Right, then click to select the placeholder subtitle and type *The Romance of Flight*.

When you click placeholder text on a calendar page, including the cover, iPhoto selects it so you can quickly replace it by typing something else.

NOTE ▶ iPhoto marks the pictures you've already used in the calendar by placing a checkmark on them in the picture browser. The checkmark, though, is just a reminder; you can use a picture more than once in a calendar if you like.

4   Click the Autoflow button in the toolbar.

iPhoto places the unused pictures in the picture browser into the calendar. When it finishes, every page but the last has a picture. There are twelve pictures in the Event you selected, but you need thirteen—one for each month and one for the cover.

5   Click the page button to switch to the page browser, select the final page, and then click the picture button to show the picture browser again.

6   Drag the picture you used for the calendar cover to fill the placeholder on the final calendar page.

7   In the layout area, click a calendar date.

A date panel appears in which you can type a note for that date. The note will appear on the printed calendar.

8   Type a note in the date panel, and then click the panel's close button.

9   Click the Buy button in the toolbar.

By this time, you should be able to guess what will appear: an Order Calendar window, similar to the windows you've already seen for ordering prints and cards.

10 Click Cancel to exit without ordering.

Assembling a Picture Book

If a picture is worth a thousand words, how many words is a book of pictures worth? Here's your chance to find out: iPhoto gives you the opportunity to use your pictures to make professionally printed picture books in a variety of sizes and designs.

The book you create, like iPhoto calendars, can be made from any selection of pictures you like. You'll start with the pictures in the Cayman diving album that you created in Lesson 1. You'll construct the book in stages, setting up the book's basic layout, adding the pictures to the book, adding some captions and fine-tuning the layout, and finally previewing it for printing.

1   In the source list, click the Cayman diving album to select it, and then click the Book button on the viewing area's toolbar.

A book themes selection sheet appears. The themes themselves appear in the list on the left, and an illustration appears on the right showing a book made using the currently selected theme. Above the theme list is the Book Type pop-up menu: The list of available themes depends on the type of book you select.

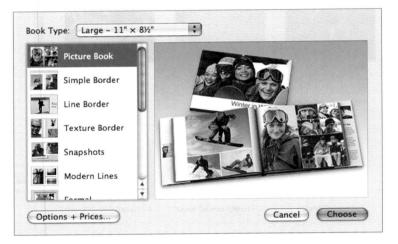

2   From the Book Type pop-up menu, in the Softcover section of the menu, choose Medium - 8″ x 6″.

You can create a hardcover book, a softcover book, or a wire-bound softcover book. Both kinds of softcover books are available in several sizes.

3   In the themes list, click Contemporary and then click Choose.

The viewing area becomes a book layout area, and a sheet appears explaining how to add pictures to the book. Also, your book project appears in the source list under the Projects heading. Like cards and calendars, you can return to your book project at any time by clicking it in the source list.

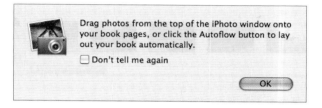

4   Click OK.

The sheet goes away, and your book is ready to be assembled.

Filling the Book

You probably notice quite a few similarities between the book layout area and the calendar layout area. The main part of the layout area displays the current page of the book on which you're working. The pictures that you can add to the book appear in a scrolling picture browser along the top of the layout area, much like the scrolling picture browser on the left side of the calendar layout area. You use the buttons at the left side of the browser to switch between the picture browser and the page browser, just like you could with the calendar's browser. The toolbar at the bottom of the layout area has many of the same tools as the calendar and the card layout toolbars as well.

Let's start putting your book together.

1   On the cover image in the layout area, click the title of the book and type a new title, then click the subtitle of the book and type a new subtitle.

When you click the default title and subtitle that iPhoto provides, the text is selected so that what you type immediately replaces it.

2   Drag a picture from the picture browser to the picture placeholder on the book's cover in the layout area.

The placeholder is highlighted when your pointer is over it, and when you release the mouse button the picture you dragged from the browser appears on the book's cover.

3   Click the page button at the left of the picture browser.

The picture browser becomes a page browser. You can scroll through the browser to see how your book lays out. Beneath each item in the page browser is a page number or page name.

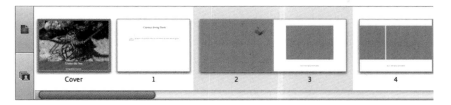

4   Click page 1 in the browser to show it in the main layout area, and then click and type to replace the placeholder text on the page as you did with the cover.

The placeholder text suggests the kind of information you can type, but those are only suggestions. You can type whatever your want, or even delete the text and leave the page blank if you prefer. It's your book!

5   In the toolbar, click the Autoflow button.

The pages shown in the page browser are now filled with pictures rather than place-holders. Notice, by the way, that the browser displays the pages in two-page *spreads*, so you can see what the left and right pages look like when you open the book to that place. This is helpful when previewing the book in the browser, but it is less conven-ient when you want to move individual pages around. You'll change the way the page browser displays pages next.

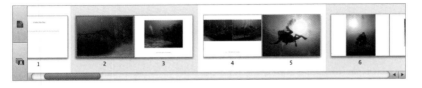

6   In the toolbar, click the right side of the multi-segment View button.

The page browser and book layout area now show the pages individually. The View button lets you switch the page browser between spreads and individual page views. You can still tell which pages are included in each spread by the browser's background shading, which groups the pages by spread.

7   In the page browser, drag a page to a new location in the browser, then release the mouse button.

As you drag, the pages in the browser move aside to make way for the page you're dragging. When you drop the page, the browser rearranges itself to show the new arrangement.

8   Click a page in the browser, and then click the picture on that page in the main layout area.

A magnification and positioning panel appears, like the ones you've seen for customized printing, greeting cards, and calendars. You can use the slider to zoom in on the picture, and the hand tool to adjust what part of the magnified picture is seen on the page.

NOTE ▶ iPhoto picture books are designed to use pictures that have a 4:3 aspect ratio, which is the most common aspect ratio for digital cameras. If your pictures have a different aspect ratio, you may want to crop them before using them in a book project.

Adding Captions and Fine-Tuning the Book's Layout

Although some pictures speak for themselves, others may need some assistance. Next you'll add captions and adjust the layout of individual pages.

1   In the page browser, click a page with a picture that completely fills it.

You'll change this page's layout so that it has room for a caption.

2   In the toolbar, click Layout, and then choose One > 4.

This page layout crops the picture horizontally and provides room for a caption beneath it.

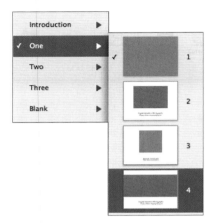

3 Click the caption placeholder beneath the picture and type a short caption.

You can add captions to any page in the book by choosing a layout with captions from the Layout tool's menu.

4 In the toolbar, click Settings.

A sheet appears, in which you can specify the typeface, style, and type size for various elements in the book: captions, cover text, subtitles, page numbers, and so on. You can also specify whether certain items (such as the Apple logo) appear in the book.

Cover Title:	Hoefler Text	Regular	22
Cover Subtitle:	Hoefler Text	Regular	12
Back Title:	Hoefler Text	Regular	11
Back Subtitle:	Hoefler Text	Regular	8
Headings:	Hoefler Text	Regular	20
Paragraphs:	Hoefler Text	Regular	11
Photo Captions:	Hoefler Text	Regular	10
Page Numbers:	Hoefler Text	Regular	10

☑ Include Apple logo
☑ Automatically enter photo information
☑ Double-sided pages
☑ Show page numbers

Restore Defaults   Cancel   OK

TIP If you've entered descriptions of your pictures in iPhoto's Information pane, those descriptions will be used for the pictures' captions in the book when you select the Settings sheet's "Automatically enter photo information" checkbox.

5 Choose 12 from the Photo Captions size pop-up menu, and then click OK.

The caption you just typed becomes larger.

6 In the toolbar, click Background and choose 3 from the pop-up menu.

This choice sets the background of the current page to a light gray, and displays the text on the page in a darker gray. You can change the background of any page in the book with the Background tool.

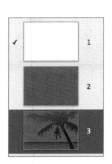

Previewing Your Book

Before you go to the trouble and expense of ordering a professionally printed copy of your book, you should go over it carefully and make sure it looks the way you want it. iPhoto provides two ways to preview your book: a slideshow, so you can see how the sequence of pictures in the book works, and a print preview, so you can get an idea of how it will look when printed.

You'll preview first using a slideshow:

1   In the page browser, click the book's cover.

    When you preview a book as a slideshow, the show begins with the currently selected page. For a complete preview, you want to begin with the cover.

2   In the multi-segment button at the bottom-left of the iPhoto window, click the arrow-shaped segment at the far right of the button.

    This is the Play Slideshow button. This button creates a quick slideshow of selected pictures.

NOTE ► Unlike the slideshow you created earlier, this quick slideshow is created on the fly and can't be saved or exported as a movie. However, it's a very convenient way to look through a collection of pictures (or, in this case, the pages of your book).

When you click the Play Slideshow button, a Slideshow window appears. It has two panes that you can switch between using the buttons at the top of the window. The Settings pane is where you set how long slides will stay on screen, what transition to use between slides, whether to repeat the show, and so forth. Use the Music pane to select music to accompany the slideshow.

3   In the Slideshow window's Settings pane, make sure that the "Shuffle slide order" checkbox is not selected.

To get an accurate preview of how the sequence of book pages plays out, you don't want to shuffle them.

4   At the top of the Slideshow window, click the Music button and deselect the "Play music during slideshow" checkbox.

The readers of your book won't have your music to listen to, anyway, and right now you want to focus on how the pictures relate to each other.

5   In the Slideshow window, click Play.

The slideshow begins, filling the screen and showing the pages of your book in sequence. You can stop the slideshow at any time by clicking the screen, and you can pause and resume playback by pressing the spacebar.

Next, you'll create a print preview of your book.

1   Choose File > Print.

A Print window appears. You can ignore the printer and the presets because you aren't actually going to print the book on paper.

2   At the bottom of the Print window, click Preview.

iPhoto processes your book for printing. This can take a few minutes, depending on the number of pages in your book. When it finishes processing, the Preview program opens and displays your book in print format.

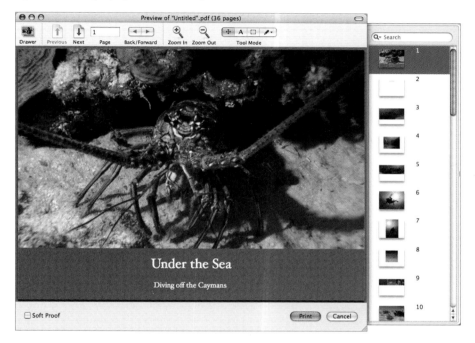

3   Look over your book by clicking the page thumbnails in the drawer on the right side of the Preview window.

4   When you finish looking your book over, choose Preview > Quit Preview.

All that's left to do now is to buy the book, a process which is quite similar to the way you buy greeting cards and calendars: Click the Buy Book button in the toolbar and complete your order in an Order Book window that looks a lot like the Order Calendar window and the Order Card window that you've already seen.

Of course, this is just an exercise, so you're not going to do that now—unless the book you've just made has really struck your fancy!

Sharing Your Pictures on Your Network

One simple and safe way to share your pictures uses the local network to which your Mac is probably already connected—such as a home network, a school network, or an office network. It's simple because it takes just a few clicks. It's safe because when you share your pictures over a local network, they are available for viewing only.

Let's try local network picture sharing with one of your albums:

1   Choose iPhoto > Preferences.

iPhoto's Preferences window opens.

2   In the window's toolbar, click the Sharing button.

The iPhoto Preferences window displays its Sharing pane.

3   Click the "Share my photos" checkbox.

You can share all the photos in your library, or just the pictures in albums that you select. In this context, the term *album* includes albums, smart albums, picture projects like slideshows or books, and the items that appear under the Recent heading in your iPhoto source list, such as flagged pictures, or the pictures that you most recently imported.

4   Click Share selected albums, and then scroll down the album list and click the Signs of San Francisco album.

5 Type a name for your shared pictures in the Shared name field.

This name identifies the pictures you share from your iPhoto library on the local network. Providing a name is important because more than one Mac at a time can share pictures on the same network, and the name you specify helps other iPhoto users tell which sets of shared pictures are which.

6 Click Require password, and then enter a password in the password field.

When you assign a password to your shared pictures, other iPhoto users on the network can still see that you are sharing pictures, but they won't be able to view the pictures unless they enter the password. Requiring a password, of course is optional; you probably won't want to bother with one on a home network, but you very well might when you share pictures on an office or a school network.

When you finish, the Sharing pane of the iPhoto Preferences window should look something like this:

7 Close the Preferences window.

Notice, by the way, that there is no OK button that you have to click: From the moment that you select the Share my photos checkbox, iPhoto begins sharing your pictures. As long as iPhoto is open, your pictures continue to be shared.

Viewing Shared Pictures on a Network

Now that you've shared some pictures on the network, let's set up iPhoto so you can view pictures that someone else has shared.

1 Choose iPhoto > Preferences.

2 Click the Sharing button in the Preferences window toolbar.

3 If the "Look for shared photos" checkbox is not selected, click it.

That's it; no other steps required. Whenever someone shares iPhoto pictures on your network, a Shares heading appears in your iPhoto source list, and below it are the names of the shared picture collections.

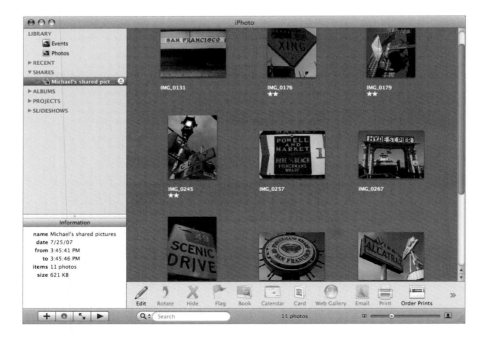

To see the shared pictures, click the shared name in the source list. The shared pictures appear in your iPhoto viewing area.

If the shared pictures are protected with a password, you have to enter the password to see them, of course.

NOTE ▶ Your pictures are shared "live"—that is, any changes you make, such as adding, deleting, or modifying the shared pictures in your copy of iPhoto, are immediately visible to anyone on the network who is viewing your shared pictures.

TIP ▶ Create a special album just for network picture-sharing purposes. Keep this album shared, and update it whenever you have any pictures you want to make available to others.

Publishing a Web Gallery

Sharing pictures on a local network, as you just saw, is quick and easy, but the world is much larger than your local network. If you want to share your pictures with a bigger audience, iPhoto and a .Mac account can make your pictures available worldwide.

NOTE ▶ A .Mac account costs $99 a year, and in addition to giving you iPhoto Web Galleries, it provides you with 10 gigabytes of online storage, email, software, and a bunch of other features. Most iLife applications can make use of a .Mac account. If you don't have a .Mac account and want to try it out, you can sign up for a free 60-day trial account. Otherwise, just read through this exercise to see how Web Galleries work.

As with most of the other picture-sharing features in iPhoto, you start off by selecting the items you want to share, and then choosing how you want to share them. For this trip into the world of Web Galleries, you'll share an international Event, Engagement in Italy:

1 Select the Engagement in Italy Event and then click the Web Gallery button in the iPhoto viewing area's toolbar.

You can also create a Web Gallery by choosing Share > Web Gallery, or by choosing File > New Album from Selection and then clicking Web Gallery in the sheet that appears. It's good to have choices.

NOTE ▶ If you don't have a .Mac account, or haven't signed into it on your Mac, iPhoto gives you a chance to rectify that problem.

When you create a Web Gallery from your selection, a sheet appears with options you can select to control who has access to the Web Gallery, how it appears, and what visitors to it can do. For example, by making a choice from the "Album Viewable by" pop-up menu, you can restrict who can see the gallery's pictures to yourself only, to everyone, or to one or more specific individuals. In this exercise, you'll share the pictures with the world.

Would you like to publish "Engagement in Italy" to your Web Gallery?

This will create an album in olorin4's Web Gallery on .Mac. The album can be viewed with Safari or any modern web browser.

Album Viewable by: [Everyone ⬍]

Options: ☑ Show photo titles
☐ Allow visitors to download photos
☐ Allow visitors to upload photos
☐ Allow photo uploading by email
☐ Show email address to visitors

(Cancel) (Publish)

2   In the sheet, click to select all of the checkboxes and then click Publish.

When you select "Allow photo uploading by email," the final checkbox, "Show email address to visitors," becomes available, so be sure to click it, too.

NOTE ▶ If you have an iPhone, be sure to check "Allow photo uploading by email." This option allows you to send photos to the gallery directly from your iPhone with a single tap. If you don't have an iPhone, you can add pictures to your gallery from any computer just by emailing the picture to your gallery's email address.

As soon as you click Publish, the pictures that belong to your new Web Gallery appear in the viewing area, and iPhoto begins uploading them to your .Mac account. A progress indicator appears in the viewing area's title bar. Also, a Web Gallery heading appears in the iPhoto source list with the name of the new gallery beneath it. A circular progress gauge appears beside the gallery's name in the source list so you can switch to some other activity in iPhoto and still keep tabs on the upload's progress.

When the upload is done, the Web Gallery's title bar changes. At the left is the address of the new gallery followed by a circular arrow link icon that you can click to view the gallery in your web browser. If you have chosen to allow email uploads to the gallery, the email address of the gallery appears at the right side of the title bar.

Engagement in Italy
http://gallery.mac.com/olorin4/100014 ↻   olorin4-pqf3@gallery.mac.com

3   Click the circular link icon to the right of the gallery's web address in the title bar.

Your web browser (typically Safari unless you've chosen a different default browser on your Mac) opens and displays the gallery.

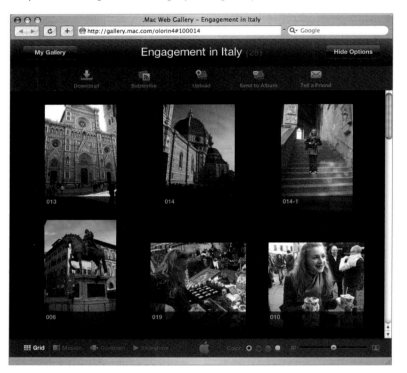

NOTE ► Like a locally shared album, a Web Gallery is live: Any changes you make to it are uploaded to the gallery. In addition, any pictures added to the gallery by other users (if you have allowed them to do so) are downloaded to your gallery in iPhoto. This means, for example, that you can post pictures to your Web Gallery with your iPhone while on a trip or while visiting friends, and have the pictures arrive on your Mac the next time you open iPhoto.

Viewing a Web Gallery

Unlike the local network-sharing feature in iPhoto, a Web Gallery can allow people to do more than just view your pictures, depending on the settings you chose when you created it.

The viewing options for the gallery appear in a strip at the bottom of the web browser window, and a set of additional options appears in a strip at the top.

NOTE ▶ You can hide the top set of options by clicking Hide Options at the top-right of the viewing area if you want more space in the browser window to view the pictures.

We'll take a look at the Web Gallery's viewing features first.

1   In the page's bottom strip, click the Mosaic button.

The view in the window changes to show an enlarged picture on the left, and a grid of thumbnails on the right. The Mosaic button is highlighted. You can click any picture in the mosaic on the right to expand the picture on the left.

2   Slide the magnifying slider at the right of the bottom strip in either direction.

The size of the pictures in the mosaic changes depending on the direction you drag the slider. The slider also controls the size of the thumbnails shown in the page's default Grid view.

3   Click the Carousel button in the bottom strip.

The view changes again to show an enlarged picture in the center flanked on either side by two other pictures. A scroll bar appears below the pictures, and the Carousel button is highlighted. You can scroll through the pictures much as you would scroll through album covers in iTunes by dragging the scroll bar control left or right.

4   Click the Slideshow button in the bottom strip.

The pictures appear, one by one, in a simple slideshow.

5   As the slideshow plays, click a picture.

The slideshow halts and a set of controls appears below the current picture. You can use the arrow buttons to move manually through the slideshow, click the download button on the left to copy the current picture to your computer, or click the information button on the right to see technical details about the picture.

NOTE ▶ These controls are available when you click a picture in Grid, Mosaic, or Carousel view as well.

6   Click the picture again.

The slideshow resumes.

7   At the top of the left window, click Back to Album, then click Grid in the bottom strip

NOTE ▶ You can click one of the Color buttons at the right of the bottom strip to change the background color of the Web Gallery from its default black.

Finally, let's look at the strip of options at the top of the gallery.

1   Click the Send to Album button.

A sheet appears, with instructions for contributing to the gallery by sending an email with an attached picture.

Send to Album

To upload to this album by mobile phone or email, send photos or movies to:

olorin4-pqf3@gallery.mac.com

OK

2 Click Cancel to dismiss the sheet, then click OK, and then click the Upload button.

Another sheet appears, with instructions for uploading a picture to the gallery from your computer. You supply your name, email or web page address, and a verification code (to keep automated systems from fraudulently uploading pictures to your gallery), and then click the Choose Files button to select files to upload.

3 Click Cancel to dismiss the sheet, and then click the Download button.

Another sheet appears telling you that you're about to download the entire gallery, which could take a while.

4   Click Cancel to dismiss the sheet, and then click the Tell a Friend button.

Once again, a sheet appears, with fields you can fill out to send a link to the gallery to anyone you like, along with a personal message. The sheet includes a security code like the upload sheet does to protect the gallery from automated abuse of this feature.

5   Click Cancel to dismiss the sheet, and then click the Subscribe button.

This time, a sheet doesn't appear in your web browser. Instead, a sheet appears in iPhoto, telling you that you're about to subscribe to the gallery. When you subscribe to someone else's Web Gallery, your copy of iPhoto receives a copy of every picture in the gallery, and when changes are made, those changes are reflected in your subscribed copy. You can control how often iPhoto checks for changes in the iPhoto Preferences window.

As you've just seen, with a copy of iPhoto and a .Mac account, you can become a one-person picture-publishing empire!

Now, close your web browser, quit iPhoto, and take a break. You deserve it.

Lesson Review

1.   How can you save a snapshot of your iPhoto library?

2.   What is the Ken Burns Effect?

3.   What is a theme?

4.   What is a layout?

5.   What do you need an Apple Account for?

6.   What does a yellow warning icon mean when you see it on a picture in a card, calendar page, or book page, or by a print size on a print order form?

7. What aspect ratio should pictures have in a book?

8. How can you preview how your picture book will look when printed, without order-ing it?

9. What happens when someone uploads a picture to your Web Gallery?

10. What do you need to enable in iPhoto to allow an iPhone to upload a picture to your Web Gallery?

Answers

1. Record a copy of it on a recordable CD or DVD by using the Burn command.

2. A technique, popularized by documentary filmmaker Ken Burns, that appears to put a still picture in motion by moving the viewpoint across the image.

3. A theme is a collection of visually related layouts for printing or display. When you create a greeting card, picture book, or calendar project, you begin by choosing a theme. You can change a project's theme at any time.

4. A layout is a particular arrangement of items on a page. For example, one page in a picture book may use a single-picture layout, and the next page may use a four-picture layout.

5. You need an Apple Account to buy professionally printed copies of picture prints, books, greeting cards, and calendars using iPhoto.

6. The yellow warning icon appears when a picture's resolution is too low for it to look good when it is printed professionally.

7. Picture books are designed to use pictures that have a 4:3 aspect ratio.

8. Choose File > Print and then click Preview in the print window to preview what your book will look like when printed. The same technique also works for previewing greeting cards and calendars.

9. iPhoto regularly checks the Web Gallery, and when it finds pictures that have been uploaded to the gallery, it copies that picture to your Mac's iPhoto library.

10. You need to enable email uploading for the Web Gallery before you can send pictures to it from your iPhone.

Creating Simple Movies

5

Lesson Files   iLife08_Book_Files > Lessons > Lesson05 > Start_project_5

iLife08_Book_Files > Lessons > Lesson05 > Finished_project_5

Time   This lesson takes approximately 30 minutes to complete.

Goals   Create a new iMovie project

Import movie files into Events, and organize Events in the Event Library

Understand the video skimming and selection tools

Assemble, trim, and reorder clips in your project

Learn how to add transitions to your movie

Learn how to crop footage to get the best framing

Learn how to add music to your background for a quick finish

Do it all in 30 minutes or less

Assembling a Simple Movie

So far, you've imported, organized, edited, and published photos. It's time now to make the leap to video. Thanks to iMovie '08's new approach to editing, that leap is more like a hop. Gone are the days when you had to master a complicated software program to create a polished movie. Editing video has just become as much fun as watching it.

In this lesson, you'll turn raw footage from a snowboarding vacation into a cool home movie that's worth sharing with the world. You'll tour the new iMovie '08 interface, import files, and discover the power of skimming clips. Then you'll drag clips into a project, add smooth transitions between clips, and add background music for a truly professional result. And best of all, you'll do it in about half an hour.

If you have prior experience with editing software, be aware that iMovie '08 introduces a whole new approach to video editing—one that dramatically simplifies the process, but can seem to go against the grain of what you already know. Rather than using the old time-line structure, iMovie '08 takes an "iPhoto approach" to video creation. Selecting clips is much like selecting text in a word processing program, and manipulating clips is much like manipulating photos. The result is strikingly good video in almost no time at all.

Opening iMovie

To make video editing as easy as working with photos, iMovie '08's interface has been redesigned and simplified. So even if you've used previous versions of iMovie, you'll benefit from taking a quick tour of the interface.

NOTE ▶ If you have a camcorder, make sure it's unplugged from your Mac before launching iMovie. When you attach a camera to your Mac (as we'll do in Lesson 7), iMovie will automatically recognize it and open the Import Video window. But for this exercise, we'll use the movie files on the DVD, so we don't want iMovie to see your camera just yet. For now, keep the camera off.

1 Open iMovie.

The easiest way to understand iMovie's interface is to think of the top half of the screen as your current movie project and the bottom half as your source material. The two halves are separated by the silver toolbar running through the middle.

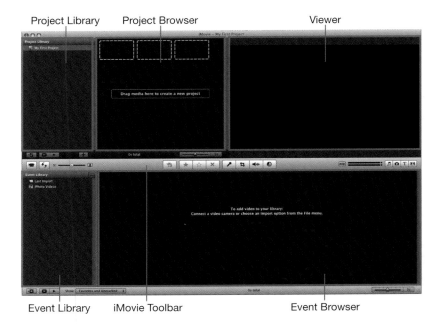

By default, the top half of the iMovie interface is where you'll find your current movie project areas:

▶ **The Project Library** lists your video projects. As you create new movie projects, this list will grow.

▶ **The Project Browser** shows your active project. The three dotted rectangles will be replaced by the clips of your movie when we start assembling it in a few minutes.

▶ **The Viewer** is where your video will play.

The bottom half of the iMovie interface is where you'll find your source material areas:

▶ **The Event Library** is where your raw video is stored when you import video or capture it from your camera.

▶ **The Event Browser** is where clips are displayed when you select an event in the Event Library.

Separating the two halves is the silver toolbar.

We'll learn more about the tools on the iMovie toolbar throughout the lesson. For now, let's make a movie.

Importing Clips into the Event Library

When you first open iMovie, it's already got a new project waiting for you, ready for you to add some footage. But let's create a new project to make sure we're on the same page.

When you're working with your own material, there are many different ways to bring it into iMovie, and we'll cover them in Lesson 7. But for the exercises in this book, you'll use the clips on the DVD.

1   Click the plus (+) sign at the bottom of the Project Library to create a new project.

2 Name your project *SnowTrip* and select Widescreen from the drop-down list.

Project Name:	SnowTrip
Aspect Ratio:	Widescreen (16:9)

Cancel   Create

3 Choose File > Import Movies.

The Import dialog opens.

4 In the Lesson05 folder, open **Start_project_5**.

You'll find 11 snowboarding clips in this folder.

5 Select the **Snowboarding_01.mov** clip and then Shift-click the **Snowboarding_11.mov** clip. This will select all the clips.

Clips		
	Name	Date Modified
	Snowboarding_01.mov	Yesterday, 10:31 AM
	Snowboarding_02.mov	Yesterday, 10:27 AM
	Snowboarding_03.mov	Yesterday, 10:27 AM
	Snowboarding_04.mov	Yesterday, 10:30 AM
	Snowboarding_05.mov	Yesterday, 10:31 AM
	Snowboarding_06.mov	Yesterday, 10:32 AM
	Snowboarding_07.mov	Yesterday, 10:29 AM
	Snowboarding_08.mov	Yesterday, 10:29 AM
	Snowboarding_09.mov	Yesterday, 10:30 AM
	Snowboarding_10.mov	Yesterday, 10:22 AM
	Snowboarding_11.mov	Yesterday, 10:28 AM

ELM, Mac HD, Drive 2, Desktop, jeff, Applications, Documents, Movies, Music, Pictures

Save to: Mac HD (154.2GB free)

○ Add to existing Event: No Existing Events
● Create new Event:

Import 1080i video as: Large – 960x540

This setting has no effect for DV, MPEG-2 or MPEG-4 video.
Selecting Large significantly reduces file size with little image quality loss.

● Copy files   1080i movies will be converted to Large (960x540) and
○ Move files   copied to the event. The original files will be left in place.

Cancel   Import

6 In the "Create new Event" input field, type *Snowboarding*, select Copy files, and click Import.

We'll take a closer look at the options available to you later. For now, use the default choices.

iMovie imports the files.

During the import, iMovie creates an Event called Snowboarding containing all your clips, and generates thumbnails you'll use for skimming.

Understanding Events

Events in iMovie work exactly the same way as they do in iPhoto. Events are simply groups of video files, organized by the year they were shot. To navigate to your files, do the following:

1   Click Event Library > iPhoto Videos.

The Event Library window opens.

2   Click the triangle next to the 2007 folder.

The folder expands, and all events within that year appear as thumbnails in the Event Browser to the right.

3 Click Snowboarding.

The Snowboarding clips will be displayed. To see only the clips within a single Event, select the Event's name in the Event Library.

Understanding the Event Browser

The Event Browser shows you thumbnails of the clips within the Event. The clips can be any length; iMovie shows the thumbnails in strips, using frames.

Thumbnail Frame

The number of frames that a thumbnail represents is determined by the setting on your zoom slider, at the bottom right corner of the Event Browser.

1 Move the zoom slider to the far left. Notice that the thumbnails expand until each frame in the clip's thumbnail represents a half second. Move the slider to the far right, and the entire clip is represented in the single frame.

The snowboarding clip is 7.5 seconds long. With the slider set at 5 seconds, there are two frames in the thumbnail. Set at 10 seconds, there is only one frame. Set at 2 seconds, there are four frames.

NOTE ▶ When you're finished experimenting, be sure to set the slider to 5s for the remainder of this lesson.

Understanding the slider will help you understand how to view clips in iMovie.

Skimming Video

Probably the coolest feature of iMovie '08 is *skimming*. It's a whole new way of looking through your footage that makes rummaging though your video archive not only quick, but more fun than ever before.

By moving your mouse, you can zip through hours of footage to find exactly the moments you're hunting for. Remember when Jack hit the snowball with his baseball bat? Skim your footage, and there it is.

Skimming is really the heart of the new iMovie, and everything we'll cover from this point forward builds on this concept.

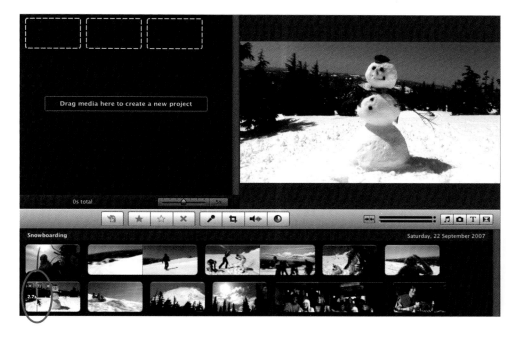

1   In the Event Browser, move your pointer from the left side of the snowman to the right side.

You'll notice two things.

▶   First, the video of the man jumping into the snowman is moving along in the Viewer at the speed you move your pointer across the clip.

▶   Second, a red vertical line, known as a *playhead*, is moving along the clip with your pointer in the Event Browser. The playhead represents the part of the clip being shown in the viewer (and in the background of the frame of the clip itself).

As you move the playhead, you are *skimming* your video.

2   Move your pointer to the left of the snowman and press the spacebar to play the clip.

As the clip is playing, you're no longer able to skim your video. To stop playing the clip, press the spacebar again, and you're ready to skim some more.

NOTE ▶   Skimming shows you exactly what's at the point of the playhead. Because you can move your pointer quickly or slowly, you can skim through your footage at whatever speed and in whatever direction you prefer.

TIP ▶   As you begin to skim through the video, you'll notice that the audio is skimming, too. This can be distracting to people around you, or even to your own train of thought. To turn off the audio while you're skimming, click the Audio Skimming toggle on the center toolbar.

As its name implies, the Audio Skimming toggle only affects skimming. You'll notice that when you play a clip, the audio still plays loud and clear.

Arranging Clips in a Project

Now comes the fun part.

You've got your clips ready, and you've skimmed through them. It's time to start piecing together a video.

Selecting Clips and Adding Them to the Project

Selecting the clips in your Event Browser is just as easy as importing and skimming them, and there are several ways to do it.

1   Click the first clip of the Snowboarding Event to select it.

A yellow selection border surrounds the entire clip, and the pointer becomes a hand when it's inside the selection area.

2   Hold the mouse button down anywhere within the yellow selection area, and drag the clip to the Project Browser.

3   Click the next clip.

You'll notice that iMovie doesn't select your whole clip. That's because its default selection length is 4 seconds.

4   Press Command-A to select the whole clip.

5   Click the Add Selection to Project button in the iMovie toolbar.

As with most tasks in iMovie, there is more than one way to move a clip into the project. Instead of dragging the clip, the Add Selection button can save time when you're working quickly.

6   Drag to select 2.1 seconds of the middle of the snowball fight clip.

As you drag your selection to the right, you'll notice the duration moving alongside you, also in yellow. This lets you know exactly how long your selection is.

7   Drag the top of the yellow selection box to the start of the clip.

If you look very closely, you'll notice that when you move the cursor over the top of the yellow selection box, two arrows pointing left and right appear over the hand cursor. This indicates that you're ready to slide the selection while keeping its duration.

TIP ▶ If you choose View > Play Selection, you can preview the selected part of the clip. Previewing your selection is a great way to ensure you're only taking the part of the clip you really want.

8 Add this clip to your Project by pressing the E key on your keyboard.

9 Now grab the left yellow selection handle, and drag it to the right, all the way to the end of the clip.

It will become the right handle when you're done with this move.

10 Drag the left selection handle to make this clip 4.5 seconds long, and then click the center of the clip to bring up the hand pointer, and drag the clip into your project.

11 Select the next snowball fight clip.

12 As you hold down the Shift key, click the last clip in the Event.

This selects all the remaining clips at once. Alternatively, you can Command-click to select individual clips.

13 Move the remaining clips into your Project using any of the methods you've learned.

NOTE ▶ When you add multiple clips to your Project simultaneously, iMovie suggests adding clips individually. This is a great tip, but for this lesson, just click Continue.

Reordering the Clips

No matter what type of movie project you're creating, the most effective videos follow the classic storytelling rule of "Beginning, Middle, End." Play back your project by clicking the Play Project from Beginning button at the bottom left of the Project area.

When you do, try to watch your video objectively. The first thing you'll notice is that it starts rather abruptly with the guys on the chairlift.

Generally, it's more effective to *establish* a scene with an opening shot that gives the audience some sense of where they are. It could be the outside (what the pros call an *exterior*) of a house, or any shot wide enough to set the scene. In this case, we'll use the shot of the mountain to establish Jackson Hole.

1   Select the clip of the mountain in the project, and drag it to the beginning of the project.

As you drag the clip, watch for the vertical green line, which lets you know where your clip will go if you release the mouse button. Make sure the green line is before the start of the first clip.

NOTE ► Be careful not to drop the clip on top of another clip. If you do so, the clip you're moving will split the other clip into two pieces and sandwich itself in the middle. We'll take a closer look at situations where you'll want to apply that technique later, but for now, just be sure to release the clip over the dark gray background in the Project area.

TIP ► If you accidentally drop a clip where you didn't intend to, simply Undo the mistake by pressing Command-Z or choosing Edit > Undo.

2   Drag the snowman to the fourth position.

Notice that the third clip is broken over two lines in your project, as indicated by the jagged edge on either side. Be sure to insert the snowman after the snowboarder.

3   Move the two clips inside the lodge to just after the mountain, and swap their order.

The guy eating the hot dog says "Yeah, it's gonna be a fun road trip", which is a great way to begin a story. By using the shot of the whole group next, we create a fun, festive tone for the movie.

4   Rearrange the rest of the clips until your project looks like this:

And that's what's called a *rough cut*. We've arranged the clips into the order we want them. Try playing the project back and see how it flows. Truth be told, we could probably fine-tune it a bit. And that's where Trimming comes in.

Trimming Clips

Trimming is where you start to get precise, and make your movie really work. The most effective videos are tightly edited, meaning the clips show only what's really needed to convey the message.

Let's tighten the snowball fight to make it a little more dynamic.

Notice that it currently starts with snowballs already flying. That's a bit random, and doesn't prepare the audience for what they're about to see. So let's start with the first guy throwing a snowball.

1   Select the last 1.7 seconds of the second snowball fight clip.

2   Choose Edit > Split Clip.

Now your clip has been split into two clips. Notice that they retain the same order as before.

NOTE ► If you make a selection in the middle of a clip, you'll divide that clip into three parts—the part in front of the selected area, the selected area, and the part after the selected area.

3   Move the selected clip so that it follows immediately after the snowman.

This sequence starts pretty well now, but it gets a little flat toward the end. Let's tidy up the second half of the snowball fight.

4   Select the first 1.6 seconds of the remaining part of the clip.

If you hold your Pointer over it, you should see that it's about 2.7 seconds long.

NOTE ▶ By default, iMovie shows clips in *time* duration rather than *frame-accurate* duration. NTSC video has about 30 frames per second (29.97, to be precise), and PAL video runs at 25 frames per second. So if you trim a clip at, say, 1.7 seconds, it's not frame-accurate. (In other words, that amount of time doesn't correspond to a precise number of frames.) This is why on your system, you may see this clip as being 2.6 seconds long, even if you followed these steps to the letter. We'll look at how to achieve frame-accurate edits in Lesson 8.

5 Choose Edit > Trim to Selection.

Everything outside of the selection is trimmed away.

And finally, let's get rid of the photographer directing the action in the next clip.

6 From the second clip in your project, select a 2.5 second chunk from the middle, starting just after the guy smiles and ending just before the mustard comes out of the bottle.

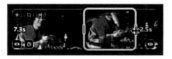

7 Press the Delete key to remove the selected part of the clip.

When you delete a section from the middle of a clip, the remaining parts on either side are separated into individual clips.

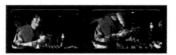

Cropping a Clip

Sometimes a shot just isn't framed very well. The main action is off to the side some-where, or the camera is showing too much of the surrounding area to make a shot effec-tive. Cropping a clip is the act of repositioning the frame to show only the part of the frame you want.

Cropping a clip can also be used for effect. In our group shot in the lodge, there's some extra space around the group, and it makes the shot feel very staged. If we crop in to the group, we can create a more spontaneous feel, and give the movie's setup a bit more energy.

1 Select the shot of the group in the lodge.

2 Choose the Crop tool from the iMovie toolbar.

3 Move the playhead to find a reference frame that shows the group clearly.

4 Select the green rectangle along the outer edge of the shot.

The cursor will change shape depending upon which edge you drag.

5   Drag the green rectangle inward to make it about 75% of its original size.

6   Drag the rectangle from its center, and position it just below the center of the frame.

7 Preview the crop by clicking the "Play clip" button.

If you don't like the preview, move the green rectangle into other positions and pre-view again until you find one you like.

NOTE ▶ By zooming in on this frame, we're changing the *resolution* of the clip to less than half its original. Because we're planning to post this on the Internet (and we started out with high-definition video), this resolution loss shouldn't affect the picture quality noticeably. But be aware that playing significantly cropped footage on a TV or a large monitor may show a loss in quality.

8 Click Done to apply the crop to this clip.

Now you have a well-framed shot to introduce the group and heighten the excitement.

Adding Clip Transitions

Sometimes, the jump from one clip to the next can be a little jarring, or a little too quick. A *transition* moves us fluidly from one clip to another, usually by blending the end of one clip with the beginning of the next clip in some way. And even the simplest of transitions can be dazzling. To apply a transition, do the following:

1 Click the Transitions button to open the Transitions Browser.

Take a moment to hold your pointer over each of the transitions to get a preview of what that transition looks like.

One transition you'll want to use frequently is the "Fade Through Black" transition. By simply adding it to the start and finish of your project, you will immediately give your movie a professional polish.

2   Drag "Fade Through Black" from the Transitions browser to the start of the project, before the first clip. Be sure the vertical green line appears before you release the mouse button.

3   Click the "Play Project from Beginning" button to see the transition effect.

4   Click the little square transition icon in front of the first clip to select the transition, and choose Edit > Set Duration.

5   Type *3* to change the duration to 3 seconds, and select "Applies only to selected transition."

```
Duration:          3.0  seconds
 ⦿ Applies only to selected transition
 ○ Applies to all transitions
                ( Cancel )   ( OK )
```

NOTE ▶ When you see the transition in your project, you'll notice it only goes to 1.3 seconds, even though you changed it to 3 seconds. Remember that transitions are limited by the length of the clips they are eliding. By adding this transition, we're actually covering some of the original clip with the fade. Because the original clip was only 2.7 seconds long, iMovie automatically adjusts the length of the transition to its maximum allowable size.

6   Add a 1-second Wipe Right after the group shot.

Since the snowboarder in the following clip is moving from the left side of the frame to the right, this transition will effectively "bring him into the shot."

7   Add a 2.2-second Fade Through Black at the end.

8   Add a 1-second Fade Through White before the snowman.

Adding Background Music

An interesting irony of film and video is that roughly 50 percent of what you see comes through your ears. Poor-quality video looks better with great sound, and great video actually looks worse with bad sound.

So it's no wonder that adding great background music to your video will do wonders to impress even the harshest critic. Fortunately, iMovie makes it as easy as dragging and dropping.

1   Click the Music button to open the Music Browser.

NOTE ▶ With the music browser, you have full access to your entire iTunes library, along with all your GarageBand songs and demos.

2 Navigate to iLife Sound Effects > Jingles.

3 Preview the tracks by selecting a song title and clicking the Play button.

4   Select the Half Dome Long.aif track, and drag it into the background of your Project area. Release the mouse button.

The background will turn green when the clip is ready to become background music.

NOTE ▶ Don't drop the music clip on any of the video clips themselves, or the music will attach to that clip. We'll get into iMovie's more advanced audio tools in Lesson 10.

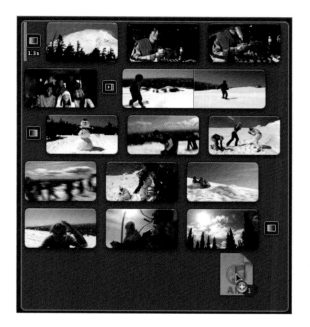

Try playing back your project now and notice the difference that music makes. iMovie automatically fades the start and end of your background music, so usually, you don't even have to worry about it.

With this track, though, the music starts and stops a little too abruptly, so let's manually adjust the fade in and fade out.

5   Select the green music track in the background of your project, and click the Adjust Audio button.

6 In the Audio Adjustments window, select the "Manual" radio button under "Fade In" and move the slider to 1.0s. Then select the "Manual" radio button under "Fade Out" and move the slider to 2.0s.

We'll look at the capabilities of the Audio Adjustments window in more detail in Lesson 10, but while we have it open, let's adjust the first and last clips with people in them. The dialogue in those two clips is drowned out by the music, and we need to hear them for the movie to make sense.

7 Keeping the Audio Adjustments window open, select the second clip in your project.

You'll notice as you move the cursor over the clip, an audio icon appears on the play-head line.

8 In the Audio Adjustments window, click "Normalize Clip Volume".

iMovie will automatically increase the volume in the clip to the same level as the music.

9 In the project area, scroll down to the clip on the chairlift, and repeat step 8.

10 Click Done to close the Audio Adjustments window.

Adding Titles

Your movie is looking and sounding pretty good now. But because this is a vacation video, it might help your friends and family to know where you went.

That's where Titles come in, and give a great polish to your project.

1   Click the Titles button to open the Titles Browser.

2   Drag the "Torn Edge - Black" title from the Titles browser to the center of the first clip in your project.

> **TIP** ▶ Make sure to drop the title on top of the first clip and not in front of or behind it. When you're holding the cursor at the correct position, the clip behind will have a blue shading over it.

> **TIP** ▶ If you drop a title before or after a clip, iMovie inserts a black background with the title on it. This is known as a *title card* and it's how movie credits are often done.

3   Click to select the title. Notice the duration is indicated as 1.3s or 1.3 seconds.

4   Place your pointer on the right edge of the title, and drag the right edge of the title to the right, until the duration readout changes to 3.8 seconds. Release the mouse button.

5 Move your pointer back to the middle of the Title. Hold down and slide the title to the right until the left edge is centered on the Mountain clip.

6 In the Viewer, change the large text to *2008 Senior Snow Trip* and the small text to *Jackson Hole, Wyoming*.

To adjust the fonts, click the Show Fonts button.

7 Click Done when you're finished.

8 Click the "Play Project full screen" button to play at full screen.

And there you have it. The fastest, simplest, most fun way to make a movie ever invented.

And you did it all in less than an hour. That's what iMovie is all about. And as you're about to discover, we've only just scratched the surface.

Lesson Review

1. By default, which area is on the top half of the iMovie interface?
2. What are Events?
3. What determines the number of frames in a thumbnail?
4. What is *skimming*?
5. How do you add clips to your project?
6. What does it mean to *trim* a clip?
7. Where must you drag your music clip for iMovie to recognize it as background music?
8. How can you add a title over black in the middle of your video?

Answers

1. Your Project area, which includes the Project Library and the Project Browser, is on the top half by default, as is the iMovie Viewer.
2. Events are groups of video clips.
3. The number of frames represented by a thumbnail is determined by the clip's length, and this can be adjusted using the zoom slider.
4. Skimming is moving the playhead across the clip, the results of which play in the Viewer window.
5. First, you select the clip (or part of a clip) in the Event Browser, and then do any one of the following: drag it to the Project area; click the Add Selection to Project button; or press the E key.
6. Trimming is the act of removing all but the selected area of a clip in your project.
7. You must be sure to drag the music clip to the gray background, which will then turn green, being careful to avoid dropping the music onto a video clip.
8. Simply drop a title between two clips.

6

Lesson Files | No additional files

Time | This lesson takes approximately 30 minutes to complete.

Goals | Learn how to share your movies in a variety of sizes and formats using iTunes

Understand how to send your movies to GarageBand, iDVD, and iWeb

Publish your movies to YouTube and your .Mac Web Gallery

Export to QuickTime

Sharing a Movie

In the previous lesson, you created your first movie, and probably had a great time doing it. This short lesson will look at various ways to share that movie with the world.

Over the past few years, personal video has exploded onto the scene. With iMovie, it's easier than ever to add your voice to the chorus. Whether you want to publish to YouTube right from the iMovie menu, or send your masterpiece to your iPod or Apple TV, iMovie makes sharing your projects as simple as making them.

Ironically, it's only *after* you've shared your movie with the world that you'll begin to see your projects differently—you'll see them through the eyes of an audience. As we'll discover in the coming lessons, that can forever change the way you approach your movie-making.

Using iTunes to Share a Movie on Your iPod, iPhone, or Apple TV

The increasing popularity of personal video has been pushed along by the growing number of gadgets and devices on which your movie can play. Unfortunately, each device tends to have its own preferred video size and format, which can complicate matters when it's time to share your video.

Thankfully, iMovie takes the hassle out of sharing to the most common video formats by offering standard sizes you can publish directly to iTunes.

1   Open the iMovie project you built in the previous lesson.

2   Choose Share > iTunes.

A dialog box opens asking you which size you would like to publish to. The icons help you identify your target media (iPod, iPhone, AppleTV, or computer playback), and the dots beneath each icon indicate which sizes are suitable for which medium. The numbers to the right indicate the video's Width x Height dimensions in pixels.

NOTE ▶ If your original media isn't large enough to render in any of these sizes, those size options will be grayed out.

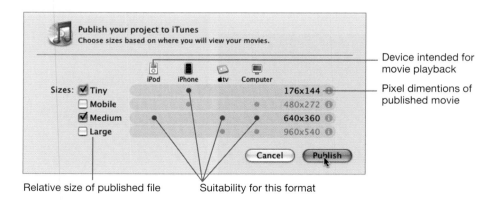

3   Select the "Tiny" and "Medium" options.

By selecting these two options, your movie will be viewable on all three of the Apple devices, as well as on full-size computers.

TIP Hold your pointer over the "i" at the far right of a size option, and information about that choice will pop up. Pay close attention to the last number: the file size. Longer movies with larger file sizes, particularly those created with HD footage, can quickly chew up your iPod or iPhone disk space. Experiment with different sizes and settings, and keep your audience and their technical limitations in mind.

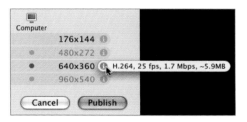

The pop-up shows you the compression format, frames per second, megabits per second, and the approximate size of the file you'll be creating.

4   Click Publish.

When iMovie has finished publishing your movie in the sizes and formats you've selected, iTunes will open automatically.

NOTE ▶ When your files have been published to iTunes, they can always be found in the Movies section of the iTunes Library.

TIP To delete a published movie from iTunes, Control-click (or right-click) the movie icon and choose Delete. Be sure to select Move to Trash, or you will only be removing the file from the iTunes Library, and not actually deleting the movie. Until you empty your Trash, you'll still have a copy on your hard drive, which can use up space unnecessarily.

After your project has been shared, iMovie lets you know at a glance where your movie is, and in which sizes you've rendered it.

Movie shared indicator   Rendered file sizes indicator

Once your movie is in iTunes, you're ready to share it to the device or medium of your choice.

NOTE ▶ When you make a change to your project, iMovie lets you know that the online version (or the version in iTunes) is outdated by adding little yellow caution icons.

Caution icon

Posting Your Movie on YouTube

YouTube has become a genuine Internet phenomenon, and one of the most exciting features of iMovie '08 is its seamless integration with the world's most popular video sharing service. Once you've set up your free YouTube account, posting movies from iMovie takes just a few clicks of the mouse.

Getting iMovie to Talk to YouTube

If this is your first time using this feature, you'll need to add your YouTube account to iMovie (and if you're new to YouTube, that means creating an account).

1   Choose Share > YouTube.

2   Click Add to add your YouTube account.

3   Click the Sign In button to sign in to YouTube.

4   If you don't already have a YouTube account, create one (or just sign in).

5 When you've successfully signed into your YouTube account, go back into iMovie and click Sign In again.

This will take you to a YouTube page asking you to give iMovie permission to upload files to your YouTube account.

6 Click Allow.

7 Back in iMovie, click Confirm Sign In, and then click Done.

TIP When bouncing back and forth between iMovie and the web browser, it's not uncommon to get a communication error. If you get one, don't worry. Simply click OK, and then Cancel. As long as you've successfully clicked "Allow" on the YouTube website to give iMovie permission to upload, simply repeat steps 1-6.

Uploading Your Movie

When your account is ready and set up in iMovie, the Share > YouTube dialog is where you determine how your movies will be categorized on the YouTube website.

1 Select "Travel & Places" from the Category menu.

2 Add a description to identify your clip.

3 Add search tags for your clip.

If anyone uses the YouTube search box to search for a keyword you've used in your tags, your clip will show up in the results page.

NOTE ▶ What you enter in each of these steps is subjective. How you categorize and identify your clips is determined by your personal preferences, and they're all optional. But the more detail you include, the easier it will be for YouTube visitors to find your movie.

TIP ▶ If you don't want to make your video available for public viewing, select "Make this movie private." Your movie will only be available to people on your YouTube Friends & Contacts list.

4 Select the size and click Next.

5 Agree to YouTube's terms, and click Publish.

YouTube provides you with a direct website address to access your movie, and provides you with options for letting friends or colleagues know about your movie.

Putting a Movie in Your .Mac Web Gallery

As you spend more time making movies, you'll soon develop an appreciation for the quality of the final product. That's where the .Mac Web Gallery comes in.

The .Mac Web Gallery is like a remote media center. You can upload much higher-quality movies at higher resolutions than you can with YouTube. Family and friends can easily view and download your movies to their computers, instead of having to burn and ship expensive DVDs. If nothing else, it's worth taking a look at, because you can try it free for 60 days.

1   Choose Share > .Mac Web Gallery.

If you don't already have an account, sign up for the free trial, much as you did in the YouTube section.

2   Give your project a title and description, and choose a size to publish.

The .Mac Web Gallery can offer your website visitors different sizes of the same video, and you can decide whether videos may be downloaded or only viewed online.

iMovie then puts your movie online.

NOTE ▶ Your .Mac Web Gallery can handle much larger video clips than YouTube does, so be aware that it may take some time for your movie to be published here.

Uploading to your .Mac Web Gallery

Uploading the medium movie...

[_____] (Cancel)

Time remaining: about 4 minutes

3   View your movie on your .Mac Web Gallery.

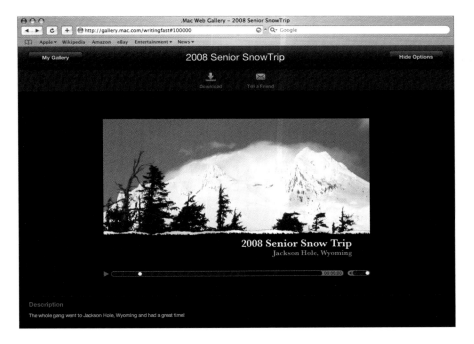

4   To remove a movie from your .Mac Web Gallery, choose Share > Remove from .Mac.

Publishing a Movie to the iLife Media Browser

So now you know how to share your movie with the world, but what if you're not quite finished with your movie yet? Maybe you need to polish the soundtrack in GarageBand, or prepare the movie for iDVD.

When you need to share your movies between programs, it's generally a good idea to publish them to the iLife Media Browser, rather than send them to iTunes. When you do so, the rendered movie files are associated with the project itself and embedded within the project file, instead of shared to a different place on your computer.

1   Choose Share > Media Browser.

2   Select the size(s) you want, and click Publish.

> **NOTE ▶** If you've already shared a particular size to iTunes, that option won't be available here. (And if you've shared all the file sizes to iTunes, the Share > Media Browser option won't even be available.) That's because everything in iTunes is accessible through the Media Browser. The opposite is not true, however—files published to the Media Browser are not accessible through iTunes.

Finding the Movies in the Media Browser

When you open GarageBand, iDVD, or iWeb, you'll find a small button near the bottom-right corner of the screen that opens the iLife Media Browser.

1   Open GarageBand, iDVD, or iWeb.

2   From within the program, open the iLife Media Browser.

In Garage Band

In iDVD

In iWeb

3 In the iLife Media Browser, select the Movies tab, and open the expansion triangle next to iMovie.

This will reveal your current iMovie projects.

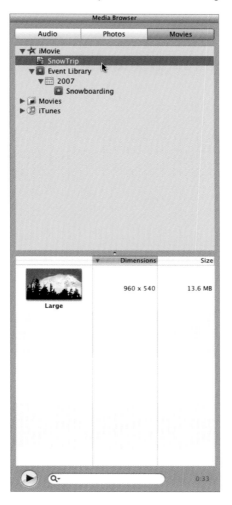

4 Select the Project name—in this case, SnowTrip—to reveal the movies that have been saved to the Media Browser for sharing with other programs.

You're now ready to use the rendered movie within the program.

Exporting a QuickTime Movie

When you need to share your movie with the other programs in the iLife suite, you'll use the Media Browser. But to share a high-quality copy of your movie with other people, the format of choice is QuickTime.

QuickTime has long been one of the most popular video formats on the Internet because of its impressive quality-to-compression ratio, and because of the enormous flexibility of your export options. You can choose precise picture quality, compression rates, screen dimensions, sound quality options, and more, to suit your exact needs and filesize requirements.

Suppose you're creating an iWeb video blog, and you need your movie to be exactly 320 pixels wide. You can easily export a QuickTime movie to fit.

1 Choose Share > Export using QuickTime.

2 Give your movie a file name and choose where to save it.

For our purposes, save it to the Desktop. That way it won't get lost.

3 Click Options.

From here, the Movie Settings dialog opens, enabling you to change Video and Sound settings (compression rates, size and scale, audio rates, and so on).

TIP Although most of the time you can accept the default settings, being able to customize your shared movie can help in a number of ways. For example, imagine that you're creating a video blog, and you need your QuickTime movie to be exactly 320 pixels wide. Simply open the Size dialog from this screen, and change the dimensions. iMovie will export a QuickTime file to the exact specifications you need.

4 Click Size, select Custom from the Dimensions menu, and enter 320 and 175 into the dimension boxes.

TIP If QuickTime saves your 16:9 widescreen video as a 4:3 full screen, you can easily find the custom dimensions by multiplying the width by 0.5454. For example, at 320 pixels wide, the standard 4:3 frame is 240 pixels high; to find the correct height for a 16:9 image, simply multiply 320 by .5454 and you get 174.5. Round up to 175 to make your pixel dimensions a whole number.

5 Click OK, and then OK again on the Movie Settings screen.

6 Click Save.

This will save a QuickTime copy of your file with the custom settings you selected to the destination you chose earlier.

Lesson Review

1. How many file sizes can you publish to iTunes?

2. When published to iTunes, where are your movies stored?

3. Are tags required when uploading to YouTube?

4. How do you share movie files between iMovie and GarageBand?

Answers

1. iMovie has four file size options: Tiny, Mobile, Medium, and Large.

2. They can be found in the Movies folder of the Library.

3. Tags are not required, but they are recommended to help visitors find your video when searching the YouTube website.

4. Publish to the iLife Media Browser, which embeds the rendered file within the iMovie project.

7

Lesson Files   No additional files

Time   This lesson takes approximately 45 minutes to complete.

Goals   Learn what kinds of events you can shoot for the best effect

               Get the best coverage in any shooting scenario

               Prepare for an efficient and productive editing session following
               your shoot

               Understand the many ways to import and capture video footage

Shooting and Importing: Movie-Making Basics

Once you've seen how shooting and editing are related, you'll under-stand why you'll want to add different kinds of shots to round out your videos. There are also some shooting tricks you'll learn in this lesson that will help you get particularly cool results in iMovie. Not special effects, mind you—just simple concepts for gathering footage that will give your videos a more sophisticated style.

As a hobbyist, you don't need to prepare for a video shoot in advance, and you don't need to bring a lot of equipment to an event. But you do need to keep certain ideas in mind—primarily, you must know what pieces of video you need for editing and remember to get this *coverage* during the event itself. Getting the right shots while you're shooting will make the time you spend editing much shorter and more enjoyable.

In many ways, shooting with a camcorder is the same as shooting with a still camera. All the rules of exposure and lighting apply (keep light behind you, not behind your subject), as do the rules of composition (don't always center your subject; remember the rule of thirds). It's important to hold the camcorder steady (two hands, always) and frame any shot before pressing the record button.

But a camcorder has the added feature of motion. It takes 24–60 pictures every second (depending on the camera), and consequently it can do lots of things that a still camera can't. You can move the camera or zoom the lens during a shot, and the camera records all of it. So in addition to basic photography skills, you need to learn some rules about moving pictures and good video.

Moving-Camera Techniques

Your camcorder is small. It's light. It fits in your hand. It seems natural to walk around with the thing recording, shooting up and down, left and right, following people around and so on. But effective camera technique involves keeping your camera work steady.

In Hollywood, the camera certainly moves a lot, but it's not a trivial matter. Professional filmmakers work in controlled environments using special equipment and rehearse their moves until they get them right.

This isn't you. You're trying to make a good-looking, enjoyable video, and you've got just yourself and your camcorder. If you break the habit of wandering around while recording, you'll see impressive results from this simple change. With some thought and planning, it's possible to add a little bit of movement to your projects to great effect.

The Lingo of Motion

Before you start moving your camcorder around, familiarize yourself with the relevant vocabulary.

Pan A move from side to side, along an imaginary horizon.

Tilt Similar to a pan but up and down, like scanning a tall building.

Tracking Moving the camera to keep a moving subject "steady" in the middle of the frame. If you pan on a car as it drives by, it's a tracking shot.

Zoom A change in frame size that moves toward or away from an object, using the lens, without physically moving the camera.

Shooting Pans and Tilts

The best way to move the camera, of course, is to use some equipment of your own: a tripod. A tripod is designed to hold a camera steady or still, and most tripods are outfitted with fluid heads that enable you to make smooth pans and tilts. But the camera motion must be very slow and deliberate. There is a natural tendency to pan for a long time—along a coastline, perhaps—but if you look closely at pans in movies, they're actually quite short. Not 180 degrees, but more like 10 degrees.

If you don't have a tripod (or a monopod, which is a single-legged camera-stabilizing device that you can carry as you shoot), it's almost impossible to make a pan or tilt look smooth and professional. If you feel compelled to pan or tilt, hold your body very stiff, hold the camera close with your elbows tight to your body, and then move the camera just a nudge between two relatively close points. If the move is short enough, sometimes the pan will be slick and usable.

Tracking

Pans and tilts are troublesome partly because the movement is often unmotivated— nothing on screen seems to naturally call for that movement. Tracking works a little better, however, because you typically follow an object and (generally speaking) keep it in the middle of the frame as it moves. The audience knows what it's watching in a tracking shot, and consequently the technique can be very interesting and effective. It takes some skill to follow a moving target, so practice as much as possible before you actually record the shot.

Think of moving the camera as a special effect—fun to do, cool-looking, but something you should do only once in a while when the moment is right.

Framing Your Shots

In addition to adhering to basic rules of composition, like the photographic principles described in Lesson 1, you'll need to pay attention to other important issues like how tightly you frame your subject. Wide shots help establish a scene; medium and close shots bring you closer to a subject or a person speaking once you've shown your audience where the action is taking place. You can also move from a wider to a tighter shot for dramatic effect, using your camera's zoom—but keep in mind that this needs to be done tastefully and in a way that doesn't distract the viewer from the content of your video.

When to Use—and Ignore—Zoom

Everything stated about moving-camera shots in the last section goes for zooming as well. When shooting, don't zoom. It's really, really tempting, and it feels slick while you're doing it, but the resulting video is less than ideal.

Of course, the zoom control is critical to your videos. It's front and center—under your index finger—and second only to the record button itself in importance. If you don't get to zoom, why is it there?

Instead of regarding this as a zoom, think of it as a bag of interchangeable lenses. What's great about the zoom lens on your camcorder is that it's the equivalent of a bunch of lenses in one. Zoom out, and you see the big picture with a wide-angle lens. Zoom in a little or all the way, and you've got a telephoto lens, up close and personal.

Use the zoom to help you frame your shot, using the rules of composition and thinking about the coverage you want for editing. Once you've set the zoom, you can then record— without touching the zoom control again until it's time to frame your next shot. After you stop recording, you can adjust the zoom and record again.

> **TIP** ▶ Once you're comfortable with the way shooting and editing are interrelated, you may find yourself leaving the camcorder on record while you zoom—from wide shot to close-up, for instance. The difference is that you're doing so only to get from one shot to another quickly, and you know you'll be cutting out the zoom part when you're editing.

A camcorder won't let you zoom carefully or slowly enough to produce good zoom shots. But you can create the same effect by shooting two or three static, non-zooming shots of an object with your camera set to wide, then closer, then as close as you can. Cut these shots together, and you get a professional-looking "push in."

Getting Wide, Medium, and Close-Up Shots

The three types of shots you'll use in most of your videos are wide, medium, and close (or close-up) shots. These naming conventions aren't rules so much as guidelines designed to help you distinguish the shots you're recording and help keep your shots distinct.

Why do you need three types of shots of the same subject? Because when you edit, you can't juxtapose two shots that are too similar. It ends up looking jarring, like a mistake. So although it's easy to cut from a wide shot to a close-up, cutting from a medium shot of a person to something only a tad different—say, to just their head and shoulders—likely wouldn't work. By recognizing the difference between shots and making sure they're appropriately distinct, you get material you know you can edit.

When you shoot scenes, you don't always need all three shots of each moment, but you should record at least two. That way, even if you get no other coverage, you have some way to edit the material into a video with impact.

Choose a subject to practice getting shots of various sizes.

1   With the camera zoomed out from your subject as wide as possible, record for about 15 seconds.

Wide shot (also written as WS or Wide)

This is a *wide shot*, which is defined as any shot in which the subject is fully inside the frame—a person seen from head to toe, for instance. A wide shot acclimates the audience to the setting of the scene. The wider a shot and the more details present in the frame, the longer the piece of video needs to be so that the audience can get oriented and see what's going on.

2   After you stop recording the wide shot, zoom in a little bit—about midway between the widest and the closest settings—and, once you've framed this shot, record again for about 10 seconds.

Medium shot (MS or Med)

This is a *medium shot,* in which you can see a person from head to waist. Medium shots should make up the bulk of your video material. They look good on TV and achieve a nice balance between being close enough to show what's going on and far enough to provide some perspective.

3   Finally, zoom in all the way to get a close-up shot.

Close-up shot (CU or Close)

Close-up shots are nice and often look more attractive than other shots because the subject is so clear. A close-up comprises just a person's head, and traditionally you crop off the top of the head to get a little closer. The eyes and face communicate expression, and the top of the head is considered superfluous.

An *extreme close-up* (ECU) is common too—just the eyes, or the eyes and nose.

TIP ▶ When working with a camcorder, it's easy to shoot everything too close. The LCD is often so small that it makes your subject look boring unless you get really close. Fight this urge, and trust that when you see the video on your TV set, the close-ups will freak you out with their intensity. The medium shot is the main kind of image you're looking for. Close-ups are powerful and a little scary, and they should be used more sparingly than it may seem.

> **TIP** ▶ A wide shot will often answer the question "Where are we?" A medium shot will answer the question "Who is here?" A close-up will answer the question "What is going on?"

> **NOTE** ▶ You can shoot a close-up with your camcorder even when the zoom setting is wide-angle (just stand really close to your subject) or telephoto (stand farther away). So there isn't a direct relationship between the zoom—in photo jargon, the focal length—and the size of your subject. In the end, when you work in iMovie, you won't care about wide angle or telephoto, but you will care about the distinct look of close-ups and medium shots.

Recording Sound

Unfortunately, sound can be really difficult to manage on your camcorder if you try to do it while you're shooting video. The built-in microphone is *omnidirectional,* which means it picks up sounds from everywhere around you while you record, resulting in a lot of unwanted noises. Also, because you shoot from a number of different positions—moving close to and far away from your subjects, starting and stopping the camera between shots—getting a consistent stream of audio is almost impossible.

> **NOTE** ▶ For some psychophysical reason, bad-quality video looks better with good sound, and, amazingly, good-quality video looks worse with bad sound.

Because it's so hard to get good-quality sound from the camera's microphone while you shoot video, the fastest way to get good sound in your finished projects is to mute most of the audio from your shoot when you're working with the footage in iMovie and replace it with music from a professionally created CD.

But if you want *production sound*—that is, the sound that's going on while you're shooting the video—it takes more effort. You need to use additional microphones and have someone carefully monitor how everything sounds while it's being recorded.

> **TIP** ▶ To get the best possible sound from your camcorder's built-in microphone, try to film in quiet locations and avoid loud or disruptive background noises. If your subject says something important while a car horn blares in the background, ask your subject to repeat what they've said. And try to keep the area nearest to the camcorder's microphone quiet whenever you're recording sound from further away.

Alternatively, you can use your camcorder not only as a digital video recorder but also as a digital audio recorder. And your Mac itself has a built-in microphone. With these handy audio tools and a little basic information, you can add professional-quality sound (and thus professional-quality production values) to your videos.

Getting Coverage in Your Scene

The bits of video you need for movie editing are called *coverage*. You need a certain minimum amount of coverage to have video elements you can edit.

Instead of shooting a series of interesting shots with your camcorder, think of every shot as having some kind of relationship to at least one other shot. If you shoot someone from far off, your next shot should be the same person from closer. If you shoot someone from the front, think about also shooting him from the back. If you show someone reading a book, show the audience what she's reading. Whatever you do, get a minimum of two shots of the same subject; you'll use these when you go to edit.

Using related shots highlights one of the most significant differences between video projects and still-image projects. With a still camera, you pick it up and shoot once in a while. You might shoot bits and pieces throughout an event. With video, you want to pick up the camcorder and shoot one scene, getting proper coverage from multiple angles, and then be done with it. You're not going to try to shoot many bits of lots of different scenes, but lots of shots of one scene.

Multiple Shots from Each Position

Don't move around too much with your camera. A common mistake is to shoot a little bit from here, wander around, shoot some more from over there, stop for a while, and then shoot from some new location. Video clips gathered in this manner will be more challenging to put together into a cohesive video.

From whatever position you make your first shot, you want to get two shots, as you did with the wide and medium shots earlier. For your first wide shot, record for about 15 seconds and then stop. Then try zooming in for a closer shot and record again, for 10 more seconds. If you're not in a hurry, you might shoot three shots from this location (a wide, a medium, and a close-up), but at least two are critical. Make two shots, then move to the next location.

Shots and Reverse Shots

When you record a couple of different shots from your first position, a question arises: Where do you go next? The answer is easy. Once you've shot everything you can see from the first vantage point, move to the other side of your subject and shoot back toward where you were standing. In very general terms, you're moving nearly 180 degrees from your original position. The name for this is the *reverse shot.*

> **NOTE ▸** Technically speaking, you're not going to move exactly 180 degrees opposite your original position. It's going to be closer to 120 degrees, but it's a detail that you can refine once you're in the habit of getting a reverse shot.

When you're done shooting from the reverse position, you'll have two sets of shots (called, of course, *shots* and *reverse shots*), and those have a very specific dynamic between them. As long as the action is similar from both positions, these shot/reverse combinations can be cut together to give a remarkable experience to the viewers—as if they were in two places at the same time.

This works wonderfully if a pair of people are talking or directly interacting. Focus on one of the two people for the first shot and on the second person for the reverse shot. Interaction between two people almost always gives a compelling core to your videos. Everything else is just setting and ambience. The back-and-forth of human interplay is, in many ways, the precise reason you're using video and not still photography. Consequently, the shot/reverse shot is often the main element of your projects.

If you want to try these basic shooting guidelines (and we encourage you to do so), set up a very basic scene. Two people sitting in chairs facing each other and playing a game—tic-tac-toe, perhaps, or chess, or cards. Let the two "actors" play a real game, ignoring you—and you shouldn't bother them. Shooting and getting this coverage will be straightforward, and although you won't use it for editing in the next lessons, once you've finished those exercises you could edit the material you just shot.

1   Find your subject, frame it as a medium shot, and start recording.

   This first shot should go on for a minimum of 10 seconds, probably more like 15. There are no rules; just hold still and let the person do whatever it is he's doing.

2 Before leaving the first position, get a second shot (zoomed either closer or wider).

Getting two shots will give you flexibility later when it's time to edit.

3 As soon as you stop recording, move to a position opposite where you were with the first shot.

The easiest way to do this is to imagine a line between the subject and the person your subject is interacting with. With luck (and for easier shooting), these two people should be facing each other, perhaps sitting on opposite sides of a table. Walk from position 1 to position 2 and, framing the subject in a medium shot similar to before, shoot for another 10 to 15 seconds.

4   Get a second shot (such as a close-up) from this same position.

When you've finished shooting from these two positions, you have the core of your video coverage. With a shot and a reverse shot, you can build a compelling moment easily in iMovie.

> **TIP** ▶ Another specific shot used often in Hollywood is the over-the-shoulder shot (usually shortened to OS shot). Instead of having a single shot of a person alone in the frame, keep the edge of the other person's back in the frame. This shows how close they are to each other and reminds the audience that two people are there, not just one. In conversations on film, particularly for medium shots, OS shots are the standard.

The Cutaway Shot

Shots and reverse shots may make up the core of your video, but it's almost impossible to watch these two shots all day. What you need is something else to look at, a break. Behold the *cutaway shot.* It's a close-up of something other than the people in your video. It doesn't include anyone's mouth moving. Its sole purpose is to show you details and texture of what is going on.

Any number of subjects can constitute a good cutaway shot. You'll probably find a half-dozen or more. You almost can't have too many, they're so useful. In some ways a good cutaway is almost a still photo: You frame some odd detail as a kind of still life. It doesn't have to be an image from the action—it could be anything that provides details within the environment.

Don't shoot your cutaway shots until you're satisfied with your shot/reverse coverage. You can cheat the cutaways a little bit; they don't have to fit precisely with the shot/reverse and can often be shot very late in the event. You don't know how (or even if) you'll use these shots while editing, but when you need one, you won't believe how important it is to have it. You'll end up picking one or two—whatever fits best with the video you're making. But those decisions will come later. For now, your job is to get all the coverage you might need.

Here are some cutaway shots that could be used with the shot/reverse combinations you saw previously.

Cutaways beg for creativity. From any position (wide from across the room, from the side getting the shot/reverse), you've always got the opportunity to point the camera in a slightly different direction, zoom in, and get a cutaway shot.

> **TIP** One of the great things about digital video edited with an application like iMovie is that it's a nonlinear medium. That is, you can cut together your shots in any sequence you want, regardless of when you shot them. For example, you might get your establishing shots last, but use them first, or get your cutaways last, but intersperse them with the main action, and have the main audio from the scene—such as your subjects talking—continuing as your cutaway shots appear.

The Establishing Shot

Finally, you'll always need at least one *establishing shot,* which shows where this event is taking place—a wide shot that depicts not only your main characters but also where they're situated. Sometimes this is the first shot you get; remember how you started wide and far away before getting close for the shot/reverse? But don't be limited to a wide shot or a shot that includes your subject. A shot of the building outside might be a better establishing shot.

Sometimes it's natural to get the establishing shot at the end, after the cutaways. Because the participation of your main actors isn't required, it's good to focus on them first and get the extra material afterward. It doesn't matter when you take the shot; just remember that establishing shots, particularly if they're wide, often need to play onscreen for a little longer than normal. Hold still (don't pan—it isn't necessary). If the venue or vista is too large for a single shot, stay in your position and point in a few different directions, changing from wide to closer as necessary. You can combine all these bits into a short establishing shot sequence.

> **TIP ▶** Like cutaways, establishing shots can be exceptionally creative. Don't just wander far away and shoot a big wide shot. Think about shooting from up high, over your head. Shoot through a window—reflections and all (just try to keep your own reflection out of the shot). Look for signage around that might help place your scene ("Welcome to Petroglyph Ceramic Lounge" or "Hot, Hot, Hot. Careful around kilns!") Signs are good for establishing your location, but they don't need to be full frame, dead center—just an edge of a sign or a snippet of a logo is often enough.

Looking for Story Structure

The final aspect of coverage is that of story structure—that is, finding shots that in some way represent what might be a "beginning" of your video as well as an "ending." Your video isn't just a random sequence of shots, but a short story. Although you can build a sequence that is visually dynamic using shot/reverse combinations with the occasional cutaway, your videos will be better if they have a natural beginning, some climax or punch line, and then a natural ending. Only the best videos nail these story elements—you can't script them. But when you're shooting, you should be looking for them so that you can record them when the moment arrives.

A few tricks can facilitate good beginnings and endings. Because you now know not to move the camera, you can achieve the excellent effect of letting your characters move into and out of the frame. If you know where something is going to happen—say, the girls just arrived at the studio and are about to start looking for ceramics at the shelf of bisque— you can point your camera there, start shooting, and hold still. In no time, the girls will wander into the frame. Presto: a beginning shot. Similarly, if you know they've found their pieces and are about to go sit down, frame them and hold still. They'll exit the frame, and you'll be left looking at a shelf of ceramics—a nice ending.

Many natural events make good endings. People walking off into the sunset is a classic (even clichéd) finale. Somebody pulling up in a car, opening a door to enter a house, or walking into a room are all natural introductions to a scene. Shooting these moments isn't required, of course. If you don't get this kind of coverage, you'll force the editor (again, you) to improvise. A simple fade-in or fade-out is the fallback position.

Getting Clips into iMovie

When you've finished shooting an event, such as a birthday or a wedding, you'll often have all the footage you need to begin working on a project. But video is a flexible medium— you can always go back and add extra shots, clips, or whole sequences later.

So it's helpful to think of importing as a step in the production workflow. You'll import from your camcorder, an iSight or compatible camera, a cell phone, or even your still camera that takes video footage.

Importing from a Digital Camcorder

Most of your footage is likely to come from your camcorder. Fortunately, importing video from your camcorder into iMovie is easy.

1   Plug your camcorder into your Mac with a FireWire cable.

NOTE ▶ FireWire is the standard type of computer connection for digital video (and other high-bandwidth computer connections). Its technical name is IEEE 1394, but it's also referred to as i.Link, Sony's brand name.

FireWire jacks: A 4-pin jack on a digital camcorder (left) and a 6-pin jack on the back of a Mac (right)

At each end of your FireWire cable is a different type of connector. The tiny one, which generally plugs into a camcorder, is a *4-pin connector*. The big one is shaped like a D and is called a *6-pin connector*. A 4-pin-to-6-pin FireWire cable, then, is the essential link between camcorder and Mac.

FireWire connectors: The smaller 4-pin side (left) and the D-shaped 6-pin side (right)

NOTE ▶ The common connector between a Mac and an external hard drive is a 6-pin-to-6-pin FireWire cable.

2   Make sure your camcorder is turned on and set to play back your tape.

That setting is probably labeled something like VCR or VTR; it's often a switch located near the red Record button on the back of the camera.

Once you've made the connection, iMovie opens the Import window.

> **NOTE** ▶ Occasionally, DVD software will automatically launch. If it does, just close it.

3   Select the footage you want to import.

Note that iMovie treats tape and non-tape devices differently:

▶   If you're importing from a DVD- or flash-based (tapeless) device, you'll see a list of all the clips you've shot. Use the playback controls at the bottom of the viewer to review clips, and then decide which ones you want to import.

▶   If you want everything, choose the Automatic option, or select the Manual option, and deselect the clips you don't want to import.

▶   If you're importing from DV or HDV tape, you'll see the viewer window. The simplest way is Automatic. Select Automatic and click Import. iMovie will rewind and capture the whole tape. Or switch to manual controls to queue up footage.

4   Click Import, Import Checked, or Import All, depending on your system and what you've selected for import.

5   Save to hard drive (or FireWire drive if you have one).

TIP ▶ Video files (particularly HD and HDV) consume large amounts of space. If you're going to be working with a lot of video, an external FireWire hard drive can be enormously useful. Any footage that has been imported into iMovie and stored on a FireWire drive will be instantly available through the Event Library as soon as you plug in your drive. This can free up resources on your computer tremendously, and offers a clean and simple way to maintain archives of your video projects.

6   Choose "Add to existing Event" if the Event for this video has already been created, or choose "Create new Event" to start one from scratch.

7   If you're working with 1080i, choose whether to save full or half size, and click OK.

It takes about 13 Gigabytes (GB) to store an hour of standard definition DV video and 40 GB to store an hour of high-definition HDV, so make sure you have enough space on the disk you choose. The amount of free space on each available disk is shown in parentheses next to the disk's name in the pop-up menu.

TIP ▶ Even if you're recording in high-definition format (which records a picture whose dimensions are either 1920 x 1080 pixels or 1280 x 720 pixels, depending on your camera), it's generally better to import to the Large size, which saves your video at 960 x 540 pixels. File sizes are considerably smaller, without any real loss in quality. For most everyday situations, including if you're publishing your work to the Internet, iPod, iPhone, or even high-definition television (HDTV), the Large file size is more than enough.

iMovie then imports your footage and creates thumbnails for the library.

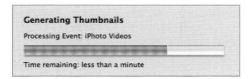

Importing Movies from iPhoto

When you're working with a still camera that shoots video, you won't import directly into iMovie. Instead, you'll import your footage into iPhoto, as we saw in Lesson 1.

The first time you open iMovie after importing video into iPhoto, iMovie asks if you want to generate thumbnails now or wait until later.

1   Click Now.

The filmstrips and thumbnails are automatically generated and placed into the Event Library.

2   Select iPhoto Videos in the Event Library.

If you named your events in iPhoto, the event names will be visible in the Event Browser.

Your iPhoto videos are now available to use alongside any other footage you've shot.

NOTE ▶ Any video that you capture with a cell phone that captures video, such as an iPhone, will be treated the same way as a still camera that captures video. In both cases, simply import the video into iPhoto, and access it through the Event Library in iMovie.

Capturing from an iSight

In addition to capturing movies using camcorders and other recording devices, you can also record straight to your computer using your Mac's built-in iSight camera, or any FireWire-enabled camera or camcorder.

1   Connect your camera if your computer doesn't have iSight built-in.

2 To open the Camera Import Window, click the camcorder icon above the Event Library or choose File > Import from Camera (Command-I).

3 If "Built-in iSight" is not selected from the Camera drop-down menu at the bottom left, select it now.

4 Click Capture.

5 Choose the disk where you want to store the video.

   TIP Make sure your disk has enough available storage space for the video you're recording. The amount of free space on each available disk is shown in parentheses next to the disk's name in the pop-up menu.

6 To create a new Event, type a name for it in the "Create new Event" field. To add the recorded video to an existing Event, choose its name from the pop-up menu.

7 When you're ready to begin recording, click OK.

   The camera begins recording immediately.

8 When you want to stop recording, click Stop.

   A new video clip is created and the thumbnail images are generated. You can start and stop as often as you like. Each time you start and stop the camera, you must click OK to add the next clip to the same Event, or select a different Event, or type the name for a new Event.

9 When you're finished recording, click Done.

Importing Movie Files

When you import footage you've shot using your camcorder, iSight, or other recording device, it's known as *capturing* your video. In those cases, importing into iMovie involves getting footage into your computer for the first time.

But you'll frequently want to work with video files that already exist as computer files. In that case, you'll be importing those movie files directly into iMovie. iMovie '08 can import MPEG-4, DV, or .mov files from most discs or hard disks. As you learned in Lesson 5, importing movie files is quick and easy.

1   Choose File > Import Movies (or right/Control-click within the Event Library and select Import Movies).

2   Select the file(s) you want to import.

3   Choose which disk to save to, and whether to create a new Event or add the footage to an existing Event.

iMovie will be copying the original files (or moving them, depending on your selection) to a new location, so be sure to select a location with sufficient disk space.

4   Decide if you want to import any 1080i files as Full-size or Half-size.

5   Click Import.

Importing from iMovie HD

Before you import your iMovie HD project, it's important to understand that iMovie '08 marks a significant departure from the old way of editing video. To migrate as smoothly as possible, a little planning goes a long way.

Because iMovie '08 imports only the RAW video from iMovie HD projects, any additions or changes you've made, such as transitions, effects, or music, are not imported.

> **TIP**▶ To retain transitions, effects, or music for use in iMovie '08, simply export the part of your iMovie HD project that you want to keep as an independent movie clip, and import it into iMovie '08 using the Import Movies dialog. But note that these transitions and effects will not be editable in iMovie '08.

The actual steps for importing your iMovie HD project are almost identical to those for importing a movie file.

1   Choose File > Import iMovie HD project.

Unless you've saved them elsewhere, you'll usually find iMovie projects in the Movies folder.

2   Choose the hard drive you want to save the project to, and click Import.

iMovie '08 automatically creates new Events and projects from the existing iMovie '06 project video clips. All clips from the clip viewer are added to a new Event. All clips from the timeline are added to a new project. All transitions are replaced by cross-dissolves.

NOTE ▶ Any clip that was dragged into the project from the Finder will not be added to the new project.

Now you're ready to begin working with your raw footage.

Lesson Review

1.   What do WS, MS, and CU stand for?

2.   From how many positions should you shoot to get sufficient coverage of an event?

3.   Which shots should you, at the least, record from each shooting position?

4.   Which kind of shot generally needs to be longer than the others and why?

5.   About how long should your shot types be?

6. List three examples of shot pairs that make editing a snap and give your projects a sophisticated look.

7. Name three ways to capture footage you can import into iMovie.

8. What part of an iMovie HD project can be imported to iMovie '08?

Answers

1. WS stands for wide shot, MS for medium shot, and CU for close-up.

2. Shoot from at least two positions—possibly three or four. Any more than that will likely produce too much coverage, with the majority of it not useful.

3. Record a wide shot and a medium shot from your position. If you have time, shoot a close-up too. Remember, the medium shot is your primary shot.

4. Wide shots usually need to be longer because there's more detail in the picture. It takes the audience a bit more time to "read" all the information wide shots contain.

5. Record your wide shots for around 15 seconds each. Medium shots and close-ups can be closer to 10 seconds.

6. Complementary shot pairs include a shot/reverse shot, a shot/cutaway shot, and a shot/establishing shot.

7. You can capture footage with a camcorder, a still camera that records video, or your Mac's built-in iSight camera.

8. iMovie '08 imports only the RAW video from iMovie HD projects, including clips from the clip viewer as well as video from the timeline.

8

Lesson Files iLife08_Book_Files > Lessons > Lesson08 > Start_project_8

iLife08_Book_Files > Lessons > Lesson08 > Finished_project_8

Time This lesson takes approximately 90 minutes to complete.

Goals Organize your workspace

Use Keywords and Keyword Filtering to streamline your editing

Find the natural structure within your video footage

Assemble a rough cut while building a documentary narrative

Learn to extract audio

Master the cutaway to create engaging video

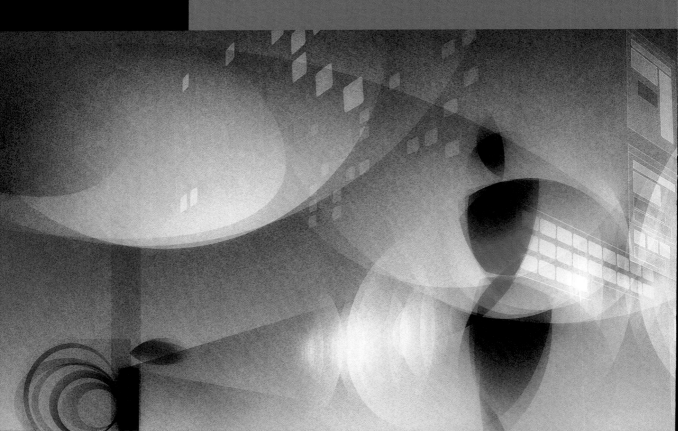

Editing Your Movie

As you learned in the previous lesson, when you approach a filming situation with a good shooting plan, you'll leave the shoot with a wide variety of shots and footage that can be used to craft a well-rounded and well-told story.

But regardless of what you planned, when you get to the computer to start editing, it's time to shift gears. Editing is the process of cutting, rearranging, and manipulating your source video to create a new work. It's a time to forget about what you *didn't* get, and focus on shaping what you *did* get into a movie that engages the viewer.

Over the next four lessons, you'll create a short documentary-style movie aimed at generating sponsorship for an amateur bicyclist riding for charity. You'll fine-tune and polish the picture and audio in the lessons that follow. But here, you'll focus on editing the raw video together to create a compelling story.

Make no mistake about it—good editing is good storytelling. In this lesson, you'll plan your edit to get the most out of iMovie, and then use a two-step approach to build your story. First, you'll identify the natural story within the footage, and then you'll weave a narrative through it.

Preparing Your Project

Rather than having you import clips again, this lesson's project has been partially prepared for you. But because iMovie doesn't give you the option to Save or Open a project (your work is saved automatically, and projects are always available to you in the project browser), bringing in the pre-prepared iMovie project means copying the Events and project files onto your hard disk from the included DVD in a way that makes them visible to iMovie.

So let's go behind the scenes, and discover how to move a full iMovie project, as you prepare the files for this lesson.

1   Close iMovie.

2   Open a new Finder window, and select the column-view layout.

3   Press Command-N to open a second Finder window, and position them one above the other on your screen, resizing the Finder windows if necessary.

4   In the top Finder window, navigate to the **Lessons > Lesson08 > Start_project_8 > iMovie Events** folder. You'll find it on the DVD or on the hard drive if you moved everything over earlier. Inside, you'll see two folders: **MB** and **Ride**. In the bottom Folder window, navigate to the **User > Movies > iMovie Events** folder. Holding down the Option key, drag *both* folders from the top Finder window into the folder in the bottom Finder window.

   NOTE ► If you're copying the files directly from the DVD, don't hold down the Option key.

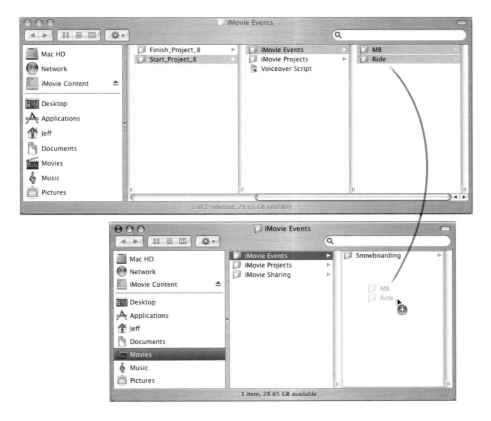

This will make copies of the prepared Events where iMovie can see them.

TIP ▶ iMovie recognizes the iMovie Events folder on any FireWire-enabled hard drive. To save space on your hard drive, you can create an iMovie Events folder on your FireWire drive, and copy the files there.

5   From the top Finder window, navigate to the **Lessons > Lesson08 > Start_project_8 > iMovie Projects** folder. Inside, find the **BikeRide** file, and Option-drag it to the **User > Movies > iMovie Projects** folder in the bottom Finder window.

6   Open iMovie.

7   When iMovie has opened, you'll see a new project called BikeRide in the Project browser, and two new Events in your Event Library—one called MB and the other called Ride.

You're now ready to get started on the project.

Organizing Your Workspace

When you're working with a lot of footage, taking the time to organize your material before you start editing is essential. It enables you to locate clips when you need them, and ensure that the perfect shot isn't forgotten.

Let's start by organizing the workspace. Because you'll only be using the footage from the Events you just imported (and not from the Snowboarding Event or any other Event you may have on your hard drive), you can hide the Event Library to give you more space for editing.

1   In the Event Library, select the MB Event and Shift-select the Ride Event.

With the two Events selected, all your footage is displayed in the Event Browser.

2   Click the Show or Hide Events button at the bottom left of the Event Library to hide the Event Library.

Because this project will be considerably larger than the SnowTrip movie you made in Lesson 5, you'll need to give yourself a bigger Project area, too. You'll do this by swapping the Project and Events areas of the interface to give more space to the Project area.

3 Click the Swap Events and Projects button on the center toolbar to move the Project area to the bottom and the Events area to the top.

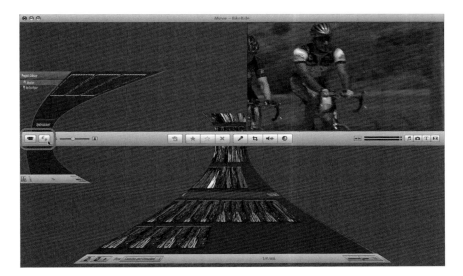

NOTE ▶ Although iMovie's default setting places the Project area on the top half of the screen, during the video editing exercises in this book we'll be keeping the Project area at the bottom of the screen because it gives us additional space to build a more complex project.

Finally, you'll need to maximize space for your Project area by closing the Project Library, the same way you closed the Event Library.

4 In the Project Library, select the BikeRide project, and click the Show or Hide Projects button.

5 To further avoid confusion, set the zoom sliders of both the Project Browser and the Event Browser to 10s, so you'll see the same thumbnails as presented on the screenshots in this lesson.

Skimming Your Video to Select Shots You Want

Once your footage is in iMovie, the first step is to watch it. You'll want to watch yours several times to familiarize yourself with the shots you have. As you look through the material, always be on the lookout for story—what's happening here, where is it happening, to whom is it happening, and why?

The basic structure of all stories is "Beginning, Middle, End." In the beginning, we meet the characters and set up the situation. In the middle, we watch the characters acting on their situation. And in the end, the situation is resolved.

As you watch the material, think about how you can shape the interview footage into a story. Look for a natural story within the Tour de Cure bike ride footage. Is there a natural beginning, middle and end? Is there an order that might help you convince a potential sponsor to give Michael a donation? Even though your editing will be directed in this exercise, think about the editing choices made in the exercise and how you might craft the story differently once you know how to use the iMovie tools.

Selecting Your Favorites

As you familiarize yourself with your footage, you can mark Favorites, reject footage you know you'll never use, and organize clips with Keywords. You'll start by marking Favorites.

1   Select the clip of the cyclist wearing a US Postal Service jersey.

2   Click the star button to mark your selection as a Favorite.

Whenever you mark a clip as a Favorite, a green line appears at the top of the clip.

Showing the Advanced Tools

There's an even easier way to select Favorites and reject clips, but it requires that you open the Advanced Tools. This is good, because there are some great advanced tools you'll use throughout the rest of the lesson.

1 Choose iMovie > Preferences.

2 Select the "Show Advanced Tools" checkbox at the very bottom of the Preferences window.

iMovie Preferences

- [ ] Display Timecodes
- [ ] Show date ranges in Event list
- [ ] Use large font for project and Event lists
- [x] Show "Play" reminder in viewer
- [ ] Clips in Event browser use project crop setting
- [x] Exit fullscreen mode after playback is finished
- [x] Check for iMovie updates automatically

Fullscreen playback size: [Entire Screen ▼]

- ( ) Clicking in Events browser deselects all
- ( ) Clicking in Events browser selects entire clips
- (•) Clicking in Events browser selects:

4.0s

- [x] Add automatic transition duration

Video Standard: [NTSC – 30 fps ▼]
Changes take effect the next time you start iMovie.

Import 1080i video as: [Large – 960x540 ▼]
This setting has no effect for DV, MPEG-2 or MPEG-4 video.
Selecting Large significantly reduces file size with little image quality loss.

- [x] Show Fine Tuning buttons
Note: Cmd-Option can be used at any time to access Fine Tuning.

- [x] Show Advanced Tools
Enables dual mode toolbar and keywording controls.

Two buttons appear on the toolbar (an Arrow and a Key), and the Favorite, Unmark, and Reject buttons get a little plus (+) sign next to them.

NOTE ▶ With the Advanced Tools preference on, the plus appears when a clip is selected to let you know that clicking the button will mark the clip accordingly.

Showing the Advanced Tools enables additional tools we'll discover later.

3   Close the Preferences window when you're finished.

Rejecting Footage

When you're viewing a lot of footage, such as what you've imported from a camcorder, you can eliminate a lot of waste by rejecting footage you know you'll never use. Obvious camera wobbles or unusable moments are both reasons to reject footage.

NOTE ▶ iMovie is a non-destructive editing tool. Which means that regardless of the edits, marks, and changes you make to your video in an iMovie project, the underlying video clips on your hard drive remain unchanged.

TIP ▶ Although working in iMovie doesn't affect the clip itself, it's always a good idea to back up your video files in case your hard drive fails.

1   Click the background of the Event Browser to deselect any selected clips.

You'll know that no clips are selected when the plus sign disappears from the Favorites tool.

2   Click the Reject Tool button on the toolbar.

3   Find the very first clip of the cyclists riding, in the Event Browser.

4   Drag your pointer over the entire 3.2-second clip.

Notice that the cursor changes to a red X, and the clip is red-highlighted as you drag your selection.

5   When you've selected the entire clip, release the mouse button.

Instantly, the selected portion of the clip disappears, and you never have to see the offending clip again.

TIP ▶ Don't reject everything you don't like. It's best to think of the Reject Tool as a way to help you streamline your editing work. If you begin rejecting every shot that isn't perfect, you may hide shots that can save your story when you need a shot later.

Retrieving Rejected Clips

If you accidentally reject a clip you want, don't panic. You can view all the clips you've rejected by telling the Event Browser to show them.

1   Select Rejected Only from the Show menu at the bottom of the Event Browser.

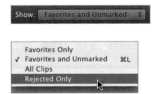

You'll notice that all rejected clips have a red line across the top of the rejected portion.

NOTE ▶ If you're certain you'll never use a clip, you can select Move Rejected to Trash, but be aware that this will delete the underlying video file, and you won't be able to retrieve it.

2   Select the Unmark Tool (the clear star between the Favorite and Reject buttons), and drag your pointer over the clip you want to restore (in this case, the entire 3.2-second clip).

As you drag the pointer, a clear white star appears beside the playhead.

When you release the mouse button, the clip disappears, because the Event Browser is set to show rejected clips only.

3   Select "Favorites and Unmarked" from the Show menu at the bottom of the Event Browser.

You should see the selected clip unmarked in its original position.

Using Keywords

You may have noticed a blue line across the tops of most of the clips. The blue line indicates that the clip has been tagged with a keyword.

Keywords can help you quickly and easily identify clips that share common attributes. For example, you can give all establishing shots, close-ups, or shots with audible dialogue their own keyword. Or mark all the shots with a particular person in them.

The project for this lesson comes prepared with several keywords assigned to a number of clips. In this exercise, you'll add one more keyword.

1   Click the Keyword Tool button on the iMovie toolbar, or press K on your keyboard.

The Keyword HUD (Heads-Up Display) appears.

2   If it isn't already selected, click Auto-Apply at the top of the Keywords HUD.

Auto-Apply lets you tag keywords by simply dragging your pointer across the clip.

3   In the New Keyword box at the bottom of the HUD, type *Riding* and click Add.

This adds the keyword to your list. You can add or remove any keywords you like at any time.

4   Select the checkbox next to your new Keyword, and make sure none of the other checkboxes are selected.

TIP ▶ You can apply multiple keywords to the same clip for more elaborate keyword-tagging.

5   Drag your pointer over the first clip of the cyclists riding.

A Key icon appears at the playhead, and the selected area is highlighted blue. When you release the mouse button, the keyword will fade into the clip and the blue line will appear.

To apply the same keyword to several clips, it can be much faster to use the Inspector.

6   Click Inspector at the top of the Keywords HUD.

7   In the Event Browser, select the second clip of the cyclists riding and then Shift-click the clip of the cyclists riding into the sunset, which should be near the middle of the Event.

This will multiple-select all of the 14 remaining unmarked riding clips.

8   Click the Riding checkbox in the Keywords HUD.

All of the selected clips get a blue line across the top, and are now tagged with the Riding keyword.

Keyword Filtering

When you want to view clips by keyword, open the Keyword Filtering pane.

1   Click the "Show or Hide Keyword Filtering pane" button at the bottom of the Event Browser.

Show or hide Keyword Filtering pane button

2   In the Keyword Filtering pane, select the Michael's Family checkbox.

In the Event Browser, only the clips that have been tagged with that keyword appear.

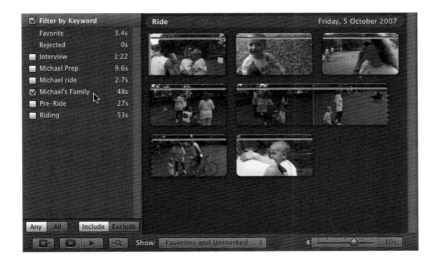

3   To close the Keywords HUD, click the X at the top of the window or press the
    Esc key on your keyboard.

If you take the time to label your clips, you'll save editing time later, as we'll discover in
the next exercise.

Assembling Your Edit

By now, you've had a chance to look through your footage several times, and you may
even have started to notice (or invent) a natural story or potential sequences you can
assemble.

Once you've identified the clips you want to work with, it's time to set up the basic
"beginning, middle, end" structure.

Fortunately, an event like a bike ride for charity has a built-in structure to it. The pre-ride
warm-up is the beginning, the ride itself is the middle, and the end is crossing the finish
line and whatever happens afterwards.

So let's start by assembling this structure into your project.

1   In the Keyword Filtering pane, select the "Pre-ride" checkbox and deselect every-thing else.

This will show only the warm-up footage.

2   Select all six clips, and press the E key to move them to your project.

3   When iMovie's Editing Tip comes up, click Continue.

NOTE ▶ After all or part of a clip has been added to the project, an orange line runs across the included portion of that clip in the Event Browser.

With your beginning in place, the next logical step is to add the middle—some shots of the ride itself.

For your own visual reference, add a cross dissolve to separate the beginning sequence from the middle. You learned how to add Transitions in Lesson 5.

4   Open the Transitions browser, and drag a Cross Dissolve transition so it's positioned just after the last clip in your project. Set the duration of the transition to 1.5 seconds.

5   In the Keyword Filtering pane, deselect the "Pre-ride" checkbox and select the check-box next to the Riding keyword.

Now the order of the riding shots has a natural flow. For now, add all of them to your project, and you'll adjust the edit later.

6 Select all 15 of the riding clips, and press E to add them to your project. Click continue when iMovie offers its Editing Tip.

7 Add a 5-second Fade Through Black transition to the end of the project to separate the middle and end sequences.

   NOTE ▶ iMovie will adjust this automatically to 3.7 seconds, because the sunset clip isn't long enough to sustain a 5-second fade.

   Now that a beginning and a middle are in place, we need an ending. The natural ending for the bike ride would be a shot of Michael crossing the finish line.

8 Using the methods you've already learned, filter the keywords so that only the Michael's Family shots are showing.

9 Making sure no clips are selected, click the Edit Tool on the center toolbar.

10 Drag your pointer across the clip of Michael crossing the finish line, and release the mouse button.

   Notice that the pointer has an Edit Tool icon, and the highlight color is gold. When you release the mouse button, your clip will automatically be added to your project.

An effective sponsorship video (and in fact, most of the movies you'll make) will highlight the human element. In Michael's interviews, he talks about how important his family's support is to him, and we can use that to shape our narrative, in the next exercise.

For now, let's add the family to the end sequence of the project, but rearrange the clips into a more natural order.

11 Add each of the other Michael's Family clips to your project using any method you've already learned, so they appear in this order:

If you play it back now, though, this ending sequence is out of its logical order, because he crosses the finish line, and then his wife says he's almost here.

12 Drag the clip of Michael crossing the finish to immediately follow the clip of the boy hitting the cowbell.

You're off to a great start. Play back the movie and you'll see that the footage itself has a beginning, a middle, and an end. The only thing it doesn't have is a compelling narrative.

Shaping the Narrative

Because you've only added the footage itself, when you play back your video, it looks like a video about the ride. But we're really trying to get Michael some sponsorship, and a video focused on the ride itself is not going to accomplish our goal.

So let's build the story of why Michael wants sponsorship. In his interview footage, he talks about how important his family's support is, how much he loves riding, how he's had diabetes all his life, how he's had a dream to raise a million dollars by riding cross country, and how he got involved with the Tour de Cure.

You can create an emotional connection with Michael by starting with his dreams and goals.

1 In the Keyword Filtering pane, show only the Interview footage.

2 Click the Arrow button on the toolbar.

This will give you greater precision when you insert clips into your project.

3   Select the 3.2-second clip where Michael says "I've had a dream since I was 14," and Shift-select the 7.4-second clip following it ("to raise a million dollars"), and drag them so that they become the first two clips in your project.

This is a great setup. It tells us exactly what this story is going to be about.

But after we've seen the pre-ride warm-up footage, it feels like we need to see Michael again, and find out what he's doing about realizing his dream.

4   Select the first 2.2 seconds of the last clip in the Event Browser—up to where Michael says "you have to start somewhere"—and place it in your project before the shot of the riders departing from the starting line.

TIP Where possible, draw parallels between interview quotes and onscreen action. In his interview, Michael says, "You have to start small." By placing that sound bite just before the start of the race, you tie the action together with the dialogue. The result feels natural and logical.

At the moment, there are long gaps between clips in which Michael speaks. Don't worry about that right now. We want to leave room for voiceovers, music, and audio extracted from Michael's video, which we'll do later in this lesson. For now, we just want to focus on giving the narrative some shape.

Let's break up the riding footage by having Michael tell us why this is so important to him.

5   Move the entire 14-second interview clip that starts with "I have diabetes" and the 5.5-second "it's out there" interview clip into your project between these two clips:

Doing so draws us into his world of cycling, so when he talks about his diabetes, it has greater impact.

6   Add the first 1.7-second "my family at the finish line" interview clip to your project immediately after the shot of Michael's wife on the cell phone.

This carries the continuity of the interview to the footage of his family.

Extracting and Shifting Audio from Your Footage

As you play back the final sequence with Michael's family, you'll find that we need to hear more of the words from his interview.

But rather than cut away from the action to the static shot of Michael being interviewed, you can extract the audio from the interview and place it on top of the action.

When you extract the audio from a clip, it will be placed in your project as an adjustable audio track.

1   Select the first 1.4 seconds of the 5.5-second interview clip to include only the words "that they stood behind me."

2   Holding down the Command and Shift keys, drag the selected part of the clip to the project, and release the mouse button when the pointer is over the middle of the clip of the boy with the cowbell.

A green audio track appears below the clip of the boy.

TIP ▶ If there's more audio on the clip you've extracted from, you can stretch the right or left edge of the green track to hear more or less of the audio.

3   Select the last two seconds of that same interview clip, and Shift-Command-drag the extracted audio to the middle of the next clip in your project.

4   Select the extracted audio, and drag it to the right until a yellow line appears, indicating that it's aligned with the end of the clip.

NOTE ▶ The left edge of an audio track has an angled upper-left corner that makes the audio track look like an inverted dialogue bubble from a cartoon. This is intentional—the upper-left corner points to the exact frame that is visible in the Viewer.

5   Select the full 16 seconds of the third interview clip and drag its extracted audio over the next clip, just before Michael's wife grabs her son's arm.

After the Tour de Cure starts, you have several clips of people riding. By adding audio clips that convey Michael's enthusiasm for riding, you'll give the audience more appreciation for the riding clips they see.

6   Repeating the steps above, place the extracted audio from the 10-second clip which starts with Michael saying "I don't know what it is" on top of the first riding clip after the Cross Dissolve, in the middle segment.

Extending Audio Over Cutaways

When you're watching an interview, it's common to cut away to action or a visual of what the person is talking about. Extracting audio gives you tremendous creative flexibility for achieving this, with a simple technique.

1   In the Project area, select the last 2 seconds of the second clip, in which Michael says "on my ride across country for diabetes," and choose Edit > Split Clip.

2   Right-click or Control-click the selected clip, and choose "Reveal in Event Browser."

3   In the Event Browser, Command-Shift-drag the clip to extract the audio and place it at the start of the next clip in the project, which is the overhead shot of the crowd.

4   Delete the part of the video clip you split in step 1.

Because you've extracted the audio from exactly the part of the clip you had split, the audio plays across the next shot seamlessly.

Using a Variety of Shots

Adding a variety of shots to your project keeps the viewer interested. But you don't want to add variety for its own sake. Add variety to create depth and meaning in your work.

At the moment, the very first shot of Michael talking is a little jarring, because we have no context for who he is or why we're about to watch him. We can smooth that introduction with an establishing shot.

As you look through the footage, you'll notice that we don't have an establishing shot of the area with Michael in it, but we can add a shot of Michael stretching to establish him.

1   Deselect all the checkboxes in the Keyword Filtering pane, and then click the Show or Hide Keyword Filtering pane to hide it.

You should now see all the clips in the MB and Ride Events.

2   Find the 1.5-second shot of Michael stretching, and drag it to the very start of the project.

> **NOTE** ▶ An effective establishing shot is wide enough to see the whole area and establish the context of the scene. In this video, the overhead shot of the crowd is the best example of an establishing shot.

Although it isn't necessary to *start* your video with an establishing shot, your audience is trying to make sense of your narrative from the very first frame. Anything you can do to establish "what's happening, where, and to whom" as early as possible in your movie will help viewers understand it and respond to it favorably.

Although this shot is not wide enough to be a true establishing shot, it gives us enough of a sense of place and context to establish our character. We can boost its effectiveness by adding a close-up.

3   Select all 2.1 seconds of the other stretching shot that ends on a close-up of Michael's face, and drag it to your project, immediately following the first shot.

A close-up is one of the most powerful shots available, because it is the human face we respond to most. By adding a close-up at the start of your video, you're effectively telling the viewer that this person is the central focus of your video.

By placing this close-up of Michael at the start of the video, as he's getting ready to do what he loves, you are immediately bringing the audience into his world.

Mastering Cutaway Shots

As you learned in Lesson 7, one of the most useful shots you can include in your movie is the cutaway. Let's add cutaways to where Michael is talking about his diabetes in the middle of the riding footage, and see just how valuable it can be.

1   Add the 2.7-second shot of Michael riding—it should be the last clip in the Ride Event—to your project immediately in front of the 14-second clip where Michael talks about having diabetes.

    We'll use this as the cutaway, and place some of the interview dialogue over it, so that Michael's comments play seamlessly from this clip into the interview, the same way you learned earlier.

2   Select the first 3.3 seconds of the 14-second interview clip, and right-click or Control-click and choose Split Clip.

3   Right-click or Control-click and choose Reveal in Event Browser.

4   Shift-Command-drag the extracted audio from the clip in the Event Browser to the shot of Michael riding.

5   Drag the right edge of the audio track to the left to make it 1.7 seconds long, and align it to the end of the video clip.

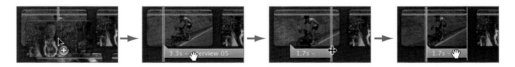

6   Delete the portion of the clip you split in step 2 to avoid repeating the dialogue.

7   Select the last 5.8 seconds of the remaining part of that interview clip, and choose Split Clip.

You should now have three interview clips in a row.

8   Find the shot in the Event Browser where Michael pricks his finger to test his blood on the machine on his bike, and drag it to the project, placing it between the second and third interview clips, as pictured below.

9   Select the first 4.5 seconds of the first interview clip in this sequence, up to where Michael says, "it's old." You will be omitting the "umm" from your selection. Choose Edit > Reveal in Event Browser.

10 In the Event Browser, extract the audio from this clip by Command-Shift-dragging the selection to your project, and place it over the cutaway shot of the finger. Align the audio track with the end of that clip.

    TIP ► By only revealing part of a clip in the Event Browser, you can quickly edit the audio before even extracting it.

11 Delete the entire first clip, from "It's just time" to "umm."

Play the sequence back.

Notice how effective cutaways bring dialogue to life and draw the audience into the world of the movie.

Recording a Voiceover

As you play it back now, the movie is starting to take shape. But the story is incomplete. If your Mac has a built-in microphone, or if you have an external microphone, you can use it to create a voiceover that can steer the narrative.

1 Open the text document called **Voiceover Script.rtf** located in your **Lesson08 > Start_project_8** folder.

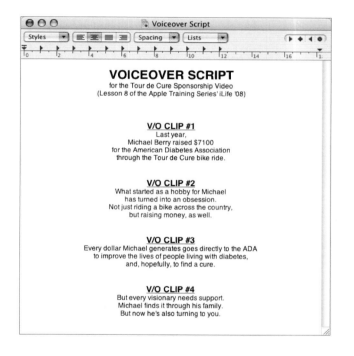

NOTE ▶ You can rearrange the document on your screen so you can see the script and the iMovie project simultaneously, or you can print out the Voiceover script. Either way, be sure you can read the script while you're working in iMovie.

2 In iMovie, click the Voiceover button, or press V.

3   In the Voiceover window, select your microphone.

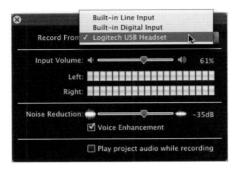

4   Speak into the microphone and notice the green lights expanding to the right of the meter.

The louder you speak, the further to the right the green lights go. If you speak too loud, your audio will be distorted, and you'll know this is happening when the meter goes red.

5   Practice reading the "V/O Clip #1" text. When you can say it in about 9 seconds, you're ready to record.

6   Move the pointer over the last third of the crowd establishing shot.

A microphone icon appears at the playhead.

7   Click the clip to start recording. iMovie gives you a three-second countdown timer, and then starts recording.

While you're recording your voiceover, you can see the progress in your project, as a red highlight expands until you stop recording.

8   To stop recording, press the spacebar.

iMovie turns your voiceover recording into a purple-colored audio track.

9   Practice and record the other three V/O clips.

V/O Clip #2 should be about 9 seconds, starting at the end of the fourth riding clip.

V/O Clip #3 should be about 10 seconds, and start on the clip after the V/O Clip #2 finishes.

V/O Clip #4 should be about 9 seconds, and finish on the sunset shot.

10   When you're finished recording, press the Esc key to close the Voiceover window.

When the Voiceover window has closed, you can shorten either side of the track or move it to a new position in the same way you can adjust any audio track.

With your voiceover in place, the story comes across effectively. And that's what editing your movie is all about.

When you're editing your own movie, you'll be adding these elements in varying order. Perhaps you'll want to start with the voiceover and add pictures—or start with pictures and drop audio over it.

As long as your story has a beginning, middle, and end, the rest is just fine-tuning.

Lesson Review

1. How can you move an iMovie project to another Mac?
2. What is the best way to prepare yourself for editing?
3. What is the basic structure of all stories?
4. Can you retrieve clips you have marked as rejected?
5. In the Keywords HUD, what is the difference between Auto-Apply and Inspector?
6. How do you extract only the audio from a clip?
7. Is it possible to cut away from a clip and continue its audio over the next clip?
8. How do you know when you've finished your rough cut?

Answers

1. Move the project file, found in the iMovie Projects folder, and any Events folders used by the project, found in the iMovie Events folder.
2. Watch your footage several times to familiarize yourself with the material. Search for possible storylines, and for a natural story within the footage.
3. Beginning, Middle, End. Effective stories introduce a character and a situation, follow the character dealing with the situation, and then bring the situation to a resolution.
4. Yes. Select Rejected Only from the Show menu at the botton of the Event Browser. Note that if you have selected Move Rejected to Trash, you will *not* be able to retrieve them.
5. With Auto-Apply selected, you choose keywords, and then apply them to your clips. With Inspector selected, you select the clips first and apply keywords from the list.

6. Select the clip in the Event Browser, and Command-Shift-drag the selection over any clip in your project. The extracted audio will be a green audio track running beneath the clip in your project.

7. Yes. Simply split the clip and reveal it in the Event Browser. Extract the audio and position it over the next clip. Delete the portion of the clip you split to avoid duplicate dialogue.

8. Editing is a subjective and creative process. There is no specific point at which you can say you're finished or not. However, a good rule of thumb is to ensure you have a beginning, middle, and end.

9

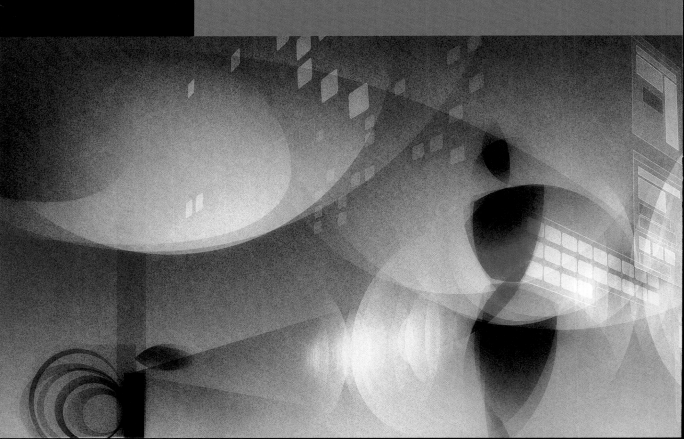

Finishing Your Movie

Once you've nailed your movie's story and presentation, there are a number of powerful tools available to you in iMovie to make your project look more professional.

In this lesson, you'll add some of the hallmarks of documentary-style editing to your project. You'll discover how to add photos to your movie and create still images from your video. You'll also learn how to use transitions more creatively, correct your color, and create cool advanced color effects. Then you'll add credits and titles that give your documentary impact.

Finishing your movie is primarily about making it look great. But as you begin to adjust the picture quality and add visual enhancements to your movie, you will also be fine-tuning the edit itself. Your objective, now as always, is not to create random pretty pictures, but to strengthen your story by enhancing the quality of the visuals.

Preparing Your Project

If you completed Lesson 8, your edited movie should be ready to start this lesson, and *you should skip this section.*

If you'd prefer to use the prepared file that came on the DVD, or if you skipped Lesson 8, follow these steps. If you skipped Lesson 8, you'll need to import the Events as well, so please refer to Lesson 8's "Preparing Your Project."

> **NOTE ▶** If you completed Lesson 8, continue with Lesson 9 using the BikeRide project in your Project Library. You do not need any other project files for this lesson.

1   If iMovie is open, close it.

2   Open and arrange two Finder windows as described in Lesson 8.

3   From the top Finder window, navigate to the **Lessons > Lesson09 > Start_project_9 > iMovie Projects** folder. Inside, find the **BikeRide_PICTURE.rcproject** file, and Option-drag it to the **User > Movies > iMovie Projects** folder in the bottom Finder window.

4   Open iMovie.

5   If the Project Library is not visible, click the Show or Hide Project Library button at the bottom of the Event Browser.

6   Select BikeRide_PICTURE from the list.

> **NOTE ▶** If you skipped Lesson 8, you won't have the BikeRide project in your Project Library.

7   Click the Show or Hide Project Library button to hide the Project Library.

> **NOTE ▶** The BikeRide_PICTURE project file references the same Events used in Lesson 8. If you didn't copy those Events into your iMovie Events folder, please do so before continuing.

NOTE ▶ If you skipped Lesson 8, be sure to Swap the vertical positions of your Events area and Project area to ensure that the screenshots here match what you're seeing.

You're now ready to get started on the project.

Trimming to Perfect Your Edit

When you assembled your rough cut, your focus was on the story and the narrative. To give your project a polished finish, you can trim your video at the edit points to achieve smoother cuts that feel more natural.

This process is called *trimming*, and it consists of removing unwanted frames from the start or end of a clip. iMovie provides two different ways to trim: the Fine-Tuning icons and the Trim tool.

Using the Fine-Tuning Icons

The Fine-Tuning icons appear on the clip itself, and let you extend or shorten either the start or end of a clip. Notice that in the last two clips in your project, Michael puts down the child, and in the next clip he's holding the child again. This is an awkward jump cut. Let's remove it to create the illusion of seamless action between the two camera angles.

1   Find the second-to-last clip in your project and click the Fine-Tuning icon.

This brings up a brown selection handle on the right half of the clip, which you can drag left or right to shorten or extend the clip.

NOTE ▶ When you've reached the end of the clip, you won't be able to drag the handle any further.

2 Drag the handle 27 frames to the left, shortening the clip to 2.0 seconds in length.

As you drag the handle, iMovie shows the number of frames on top, and the duration of the clip in seconds below it, as illustrated in this screenshot.

When you release the mouse button, iMovie trims the end of the clip, making the cut much more fluid.

TIP ▶ When an audience watches a cut that carries action forward from one frame to the next, it effectively masks the edit and gives continuity to the shot, which makes it flow naturally.

Next, let's trim a clip to remove some extraneous dialogue. Find the 5.5-second interview clip in your Project in which Michael says, "It's out there, the technology's there." The first part of that line—"it's out there"—is redundant and jumbles the meaning of what he's saying. You can make his point clearer by trimming it.

3 Click the left Fine-Tuning icon, and shorten the interview clip 30 frames by dragging the handle to the right.

Notice that the fine-tuning handles can be dragged a maximum of one second in either direction, depending on the length of the clip.

Getting Precise with Timecode

By default, iMovie shows clip durations in seconds or tenths of a second. But video runs at either 30 frames per second (for NTSC, the North American video standard) or 25 frames per second (for PAL, the European video standard). So a tenth of a second is not a precise measurement of the length of your clip.

You can edit more precisely by working with Timecode.

1 Find the 23-second clip where Michael's family greets him after he's finished his ride. Select 14 seconds of the middle of the clip.

When you drag the selection handle over more than 10 seconds of a clip, iMovie only shows you the length in whole seconds, making this selection imprecise.

2   Choose iMovie > Preferences to open the Preferences window, and select the check-box next to Display Timecode.

> **NOTE ▶** The Fine-Tuning and Trim tools will trim frame by frame regardless of whether you Display Timecode or not. Think of the Display Timecode feature as a way to see your clips with greater precision.

3   Choose View > Playhead Info.

As you move your playhead over the video, the time and keywords associated with that frame of video appear in a bubble above the playhead. Because you have chosen to display timecode, you will also see the exact frame the playhead is on.

> **NOTE ▶** The timecode on the Playhead Info bubble shows the duration of the project. In the screenshot above, the playhead is at 2 minutes, 21 seconds and 9 frames into this project, expressed as 2:21:09. Don't worry if your numbers are slightly different from what you see here. We haven't been working with frame accuracy before now, so your edits may have been at slightly different lengths, which will give you different timecode readings.

4   To reselect the clip with frame accuracy, select 14 seconds and 17 frames (14:17) from the middle of this clip.

TIP ▶ If you're having trouble selecting exactly 17 frames, you can set the zoom slider to a smaller number, which will show more detail in the thumbnails. Set the zoom slider to 2 seconds (2s), adjust your selection, and then return the zoom slider to 10 seconds (10s).

5   Press the Delete key to remove the selected portion of the clip.

This leaves two smaller clips on either side, totaling 9 seconds and 9 frames (09:09) in length.

NOTE ▶ Don't worry if your numbers aren't 5:00 and 4:09. As long as the numbers of your two frames add up to 9 seconds and 9 frames, you've trimmed 14 seconds and 17 frames correctly. Remember that there are 30 frames per second on this NTSC project, so the frame counter will roll over to the next second after it reaches 29.

6   Choose View > Playhead Info to turn off the info bubble.

Using the Trim Tool

The Fine-Tuning tool is great for smaller trims, but for greater control, you'll need the Trim tool.

1   Click the Trim Tool icon (it looks like a clock) on the bottom of the second clip you just made, or if the clip is selected, choose Edit > Trim.

2   In the Trim Clip area, slide the selection to the middle of the darkened clip.

This keeps the edited clip's duration, but plays a different part of the video.

3   Press the forward slash key on your keyboard ("/") or the Play Selection button to review the new selection.

You can preview your selections to determine the exact part of the clip you want to play. As you play back this selection, it's obvious that this isn't the right part of the clip.

4   Slide the selection back to the end of the clip.

5   Drag the left handle until the timecode reads 4:28.

6   Click Done.

All that's left is to trim the previous clip to exactly where you want it to be.

7   Trim the previous clip—where Michael's wife runs and gathers the kids to go greet Michael—keeping only the first 2 seconds and 18 frames, using any of the methods you've learned here.

> **NOTE** ▶ At the end of this shot, Michael's wife is picking up her son, but at the start of the next clip, she's already got her son in her arms. This jump in the action is called a *jump cut*. Although jump cuts can be used intentionally for effect, pros generally consider this bad technique, as this kind of jump is distracting to the viewer. We'll look at a way around this jump cut shortly.

Because we won't need timecode accuracy for the rest of the lesson, let's simplify things, and display time again.

8   Choose iMovie > Preferences and deselect the checkbox next to Display Timecode. Close the window when you're finished.

Adding Still Images to Your Movie

Adding images to a short documentary-style movie can have a tremendous effect on the final project. When you add a still image with a voiceover, you effectively detach from the immediacy of the video footage, and step back to present the whole story. This can help you shape the exact message you want to convey.

Importing Still Images

iMovie can see and quickly import any photo from your iPhoto Library, enabling you to add still photos to your movie project.

1   In the Finder window, navigate to the **Lesson09 > Start_project_9** folder and drag **GoneRiding.jpg** to the iPhoto program icon on your Dock.

    iPhoto will import the photo and create an Event for it.

2   Close iPhoto. Back in iMovie, click the Photos Browser button.

3   Find the GoneRiding.jpg picture, and drag it to the start of your project, in front of the first clip.

TIP ▶ Remember to hold down the mouse button until the vertical green line appears in front of the first clip.

4   Select the clip and right-click or Control-click, and choose Set Duration.

5   Set the duration to 6 seconds.

NOTE ▶ When you Set Duration while still in timecode format, you must tell iMovie the number of *frames* you want the duration to be. In this case that would be 180 frames.

Rotating a Photo

You'll notice two things about the photo you just added. First, iMovie has added an automatic zoom effect. Second, you'll notice that the picture is sideways, because the photo was taken vertically. Let's quickly rotate the photo.

1   Select the photo, and click the Crop tool.

2   Click the left Rotate button to rotate the clip to the left.

> **TIP** ▶ Because video is wider than it is tall, any time you use a still camera vertically—holding it so that the frame is taller than it is wide—you'll need to rotate your image in iMovie. The Rotate feature works for video as well as still photos. After you've imported it, you can choose to Fit to fit the whole image on the screen (which creates black bars on the left and right sides), or Crop to crop the tops and bottoms of the image to fit the screen.

If you've been following the lessons in this book in order, you'll see the Crop button highlighted. But that zoom effect is the Ken Burns effect, which you learned about in Lesson 4. Let's make the zoom perfect.

3   If it's not already selected, click Ken Burns.

Using the Ken Burns Effect

By default, iMovie adds an automatic Ken Burns effect to your imported photos. The automatic effect works well for wide shots, but you can customize the zoom to create a specific effect. Let's slowly zoom in to the Gone Riding sign in the photo.

1   Select the green crop rectangle and expand it as far as it can go.

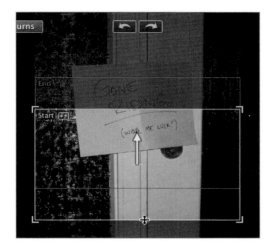

2   Drag the rectangle so that the entire sign and lock are within the frame.

3   Click the red rectangle to select the End frame, and resize and position it to surround only the words *Gone Riding*.

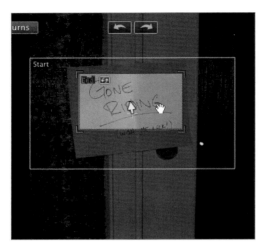

4   Preview the effect by clicking the Play Clip button.

5   Click Done when you're happy with it.

6   Click the Photos Browser button to close the Photos Browser and give yourself more space.

Next, you'll want to tweak the opening of this movie by extracting the audio from the first interview clip as you learned in Lesson 8.

7   Select the first video clip where Michael says "I've had a dream since I was about 14," and Reveal it in the Event Browser.

8   Extract the audio by Command-Shift-dragging the clip to the middle of the Gone Riding photo.

9   Delete the interview video clip from the project to avoid duplicate audio.

The addition of this photo to the start of your project sets the stage for who this character is, and how important riding is to him. And with the Ken Burns effect, you've created a polished, thoughtful intro.

Creating a Still Image from Your Video

One exciting feature of iMovie is the ability to take any frame of your video and use it to create a still image, or freeze frame.

1 Move your pointer to the very last frame of the final clip in your project.

2 Right-click (or Control-click) and choose "Add still frame to project."

iMovie creates a still image of the frame your playhead is showing, and adds it to the end of the project.

NOTE ▶ iMovie doesn't add an automatic Ken Burns effect to still frames generated from the video.

3 Select the new still frame, which is now at the very end of your project.

4 Open the Crop tool.

5 Click the Ken Burns button.

The Start frame is visible first.

6 Click the picture to select the End frame.

The red "End" comes to the foreground.

7   Resize and reposition the red crop rectangle to be a close-up of Michael.

8   Preview the clip, and click Done when you're finished.

9   Set the duration of the clip to 8 seconds.

> **TIP**▶ Because it's not always possible when skimming to rest your playhead over exactly the final frame of the clip, iMovie might make a still image of the second-to-last frame instead. If this happens, you'll notice a jerky motion just before the video freezes on the last frame. Using the Fine-Tuning tool, simply select the last video clip (just before the freeze frame), and make it one or two frames shorter. This will make the freeze frame much more precise, and create a polished result.

10   Play the end of your movie back to review the effect.

Getting Creative with Transitions

As you discovered in Lesson 5, transitions are a great way to bridge time and take us from one setting to another. Transitions can also be used creatively, such as to cover the jump cut we saw earlier.

1   Click the Transitions button to open the Transitions Browser.

2   Drag a Cross Dissolve transition between the two clips you cut earlier, where Michael's wife is gathering the kids to greet him, and where he gives her a hug.

Rather than simply masking a jump cut, this cross dissolve adds an emotional layer, because Michael's voiceover is talking about the time his family has spent without him.

Similarly, you can make the opening more dramatic by surrounding the still photo with transitions.

3   Add a 2.9-second Fade Through Black transition in front of the Gone Riding photo, and add a 1-second Fade Through Black transition *after* the photo.

4   Add a 1-second Cross Dissolve between the clip of the postal worker cyclist and the sunset shot.

By isolating the sunset shot, we can create a unique effect in a moment.

Avoiding the Cheese

Transitions—and, for that matter, most of the finishing techniques in this lesson—are easily misused and abused. As is often the case, when we're presented with cool creative tools, our first instinct is to use them anywhere and everywhere. They're *cool*, after all!

But we've all seen videos that are gaudy, cheesy, and otherwise over-the-top and amateur-ish because they overuse available effects. This can be easily avoided by following a simple mantra when adding transitions or other techniques:

►   Include only *motivated* transitions and effects. If it helps the story, keep it in; if it's window-dressing, get rid of it.

Identifying a cheesy effect or addition to your video is simple, really. The ones that are going to feel awkward or out-of-place or distract the viewer from the story are the ones that are there for no other reason than because they look cool.

Consider the transitions above. They heighten the emotion and add poignancy to the moment. Apply the same principle to your own videos to ensure professional-looking results.

Correcting Color

All light has a unique *color temperature*. If you shoot in a room with fluorescent lights, for example, skin tones can have a green hue. Shooting outdoors in bright sunlight will pro-duce different colors on video than shooting indoors under artificial light.

Most cameras have an automatic *white balance* feature, where the camera is programmed to understand "true white," and adjusts the rest of the colors accordingly. Unfortunately, cameras don't always recognize different color temperatures accurately.

Luckily, you can easily correct color problems in iMovie.

1   Select the first clip of the cyclists riding.

2   Click the Video Adjustments icon at the top left corner of the clip, or click the Video Adjustments button, or click V.

      The Video Adjustments window opens.

As you hover your pointer over the image in the viewer, you'll notice that the cursor has turned into an eyedropper icon.

3   Click the white line marking on the road.

By doing this, you're telling iMovie that this spot represents true white. iMovie adjusts the other colors accordingly, creating a simple color correction.

The difference in this example is subtle, but definitely perceptible to the human eye.

TIP ▶ To better understand the adjustments iMovie is making to the color, experiment by clicking the gray pavement with the eyedropper, and then click the green bushes, and then click the red of the second cyclist's sleeve. iMovie readjusts all the colors in the image to the selected point's color temperature.

4   Skim each of the clips in your project. When you find one whose colors seem muted, select the clip and use the eyedropper to click something white in the viewer.

Color is somewhat subjective, but taking the time to adjust your images can mean the difference between dull and vibrant images.

Adjusting Color to Create Effects

When you clicked the Video Adjustments icon, you opened the Video Adjustments window. As you can see, iMovie makes it easy to create powerful color effects in real time almost effortlessly. And the results can be striking.

Let's create a color effect for the sunset shot we isolated earlier.

1   Select the sunset clip at the end of the riding sequence, before the close-up of Michael's wife.

2   Move the playhead at least halfway through the clip, so that the sun is bright and flared in the viewer. This frame is representative of the image, and will help you determine what the effect will look like.

3   Move the Saturation slider to 0.

TIP ▶ When you completely desaturate an image, you are removing all color from it. This is an easy way to make your image black and white.

4   Create a sepia tone by sliding the Red Gain to 170%, the Green Gain to 140%, and the Blue Gain to 75%.

NOTE ▶ Sepia tones create an aged-film look, which we subconsciously link with old movie footage. The effect on an audience is to "age" the image being watched.

5   To take it one step further, drag the Contrast slider to 60%, the Brightness slider to -30%, and the Exposure slider to 145%.

With the Exposure level significantly increased, the bright areas of the frame will *blow out*—that is, appear over-exposed—giving the illusion of film that has aged.

6   Click Done.

Now you've created a unique and dazzling look that creates a wistful moment full of emotional impact.

> **TIP** ▶ If you want to apply the same video transition to multiple clips, close the Video Adjustments window, choose Edit > Copy to copy the clip, select the clips you want to apply the adjustments to, and choose Edit > Paste Adjustments > Video to apply the same adjustments to those clips.

If you're in the mood to experiment, try giving each of the interview clips a cool blue hue to give it a professional polish.

Adding Titles and Credits

No documentary project would be complete without title cards and credits, and the occasional information block that lets us know where we are and who we're looking at.

We had a quick look at adding titles in Lesson 5, but let's take it one step further. We want the audience to know who Michael is, and to establish the place of the bike race.

1 Open the Titles Browser by clicking the Titles button.

2 Drag the "Gradient – Black" title onto the first 5.4-second clip from Michael's interview.

Next, you'll make the title blend more effectively into the look and feel of your movie by changing the background color of the title, and adjusting the fonts to create a common (and less generic) style.

3 Click to the left of the words *Title Text Here* in the viewer.

A blue border will surround the background area, and the Colors window will pop up.

4 Click the magnifying glass icon on the Colors window, and move your cursor over the blue color on Michael's jersey. Click the blue to select it.

This makes the background of the title card the color you've selected. Note that if the title has a transparency or gradient, this is automatically applied.

TIP ▶ If you want to use a custom color again for another title card (such as for Michael's wife), you can save the color by dragging it to the bottom of the selection area.

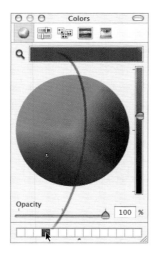

NOTE ▶ Not all titles have editable backgrounds. If you click the background of a title that does not have an editable background, nothing will happen.

Adjusting the Title Font

You can stylize the title with any font that's installed on your Mac.

1   Select the words *Title Text Here* and click "Show Fonts."

This brings up the Title Editing window and the standard Mac fonts dialog.

2   Scroll to the Arial Black font, and select it. Move the font size slider at the far right to 22.

3   Click the Right Alignment button.

Because Michael is positioned on the left third of the frame, it's more effective to have his title in the right position.

4   From the Colors window, take the magnifying glass and click the brightest yellow part of Michael's jersey, to turn the font the same color. Change the title text to read *Michael Berry*.

5   Change the subtitle text to read *Tour de Cure rider*.

6   Click Done in the Viewer to exit the Title Editing window.

7   To give a title to Michael's wife for continuity purposes, drag a "Gradient - Black" title over the clip of her on her cell phone.

8   Follow the steps above to create a title card for her in the same colors and fonts, with one key difference: because she's on the right side of the frame, align her title to the left.

9   Change the title text to *Michael's wife* and the subtitle text to *and #1 Supporter.*

Next, we need to establish the Tour de Cure bike ride. We'll do that by adding a title to the crowd shot, which is the clip immediately following Michael's title card.

10   Drag the "Echo" title card over the second half of the overhead establishing shot of the bike ride.

11   Change the title text to read *Tour de Cure* and the subtitle text to read *Bike Ride Against Diabetes.* Click Done.

12   Drag the title to 6.2 seconds and ensure that it's aligned with the end of the clip.

Creating Dramatic End Titles

Now we need something at the end that lets the audience know how to contact Michael. We could add scrolling credits, but for the style of this movie, it will have more impact with dramatic single title cards.

1   Drag three "Centered" titles to the very end of the project, following the last still image.

2   Select the first title, change the font to Helvetica, size 28, center aligned, and deselect the Outline style. If the Bold style is selected, deselect it also.

3   Change the title text to read:

   To date, Michael has raised
   over $80,000 for the
   American Diabetes Association

4   Select the text and Command-C to copy it.

5   In the second title, select the title text and Command-V to paste over the default text.

   Because you're pasting text, it retains the formatting you applied.

6   Change the text to read:

   Help him reach a million.
   Sponsor Michael today.

7   Select the last title, select the default title text and Command-V to paste the text. Change the text to *tour.diabetes.org*.

8   Place Fade through Black transitions before the first and second titles.

9   Set the duration of the first transition to 2 seconds, and the second transition to 1 second.

10   Set the duration of each of the title cards to 5 seconds.

TIP ▶ If you set the duration of the title card *before* you set the duration of the transition, your title's duration will change according to how it's affected by the transition. To avoid this, simply set your shortest durations first, and your longer durations next.

Effective video finishing creates a professional-looking result.

Lesson Review

1.   How does the Fine-Tuning tool differ from the Trim tool?

2.   What does the timecode number 6:09 mean?

3.   Can iMovie access photo images located anywhere on your hard drive?

4.   What is the Ken Burns effect?

5.   How can you avoid a stutter when creating a still image from the last frame of a video clip?

6.   Name the best method of avoiding cheesy or distracting transitions or effects.

7.   If not properly white balanced, fluorescent lights will make skin tones what color?

8.   Is it possible to take video adjustments made to one clip and apply them to another?

Answers

1. Fine-tuning allows you to adjust the start or end of your clip one frame at a time, to a maximum of 1 second. The Trim tool enables you to slide to a different part of the clip, and adjust the start or end to the maximum underlying clip length.

2. 6:09 means six seconds and nine frames of video.

3. No. iMovie can access any photos that have been imported into iPhoto.

4. The Ken Burns effect is a technique of moving a camera around a still image to create the illusion of motion. The effect was popularized by documentary filmmaker Ken Burns.

5. You can generally avoid a stutter by first creating the still image, and then fine-tuning the end of the video clip by one frame.

6. The best method is to ensure that all transitions and effects are motivated by the onscreen action, and not included simply because they're fun to look at.

7. Depending upon previous shooting conditions and the setting of the camera, fluorescent lights frequently apply a green hue to skin tones.

8. Yes. Select the clip you've adjusted, and choose Edit > Copy. Then select the clip you want to adjust in the same way, and choose Edit > Paste Adjustments > Video.

10

Working with Audio in iMovie

Up until now, you've focused on creating a movie that looks great, delivers a strong and clear narrative or message, and has tight, clean edits that go virtually unnoticed. To finish your movie as professionally as possible, you need to make sure your audio is as polished as your picture.

The audio tools in iMovie are surprisingly sophisticated. Although iMovie '08 simplifies audio editing and approaches it differently from its predecessor and traditional video editing systems, it's important not to underestimate what you can achieve.

In this lesson you will adjust the levels of your audio for consistent sound quality, learn how to fade, mix and duck your audio tracks quickly and easily, add and layer sound effects to create a full, dynamic sound, and look at two ways of working with music, to ensure the level of control that's right for you.

Working with audio is fun, and brings your movie to life.

Preparing Your Project

If you completed Lessons 8 and 9, your edited movie should be ready to start this lesson, and *you should skip this section.*

> **NOTE** ▶ If you completed Lessons 8 and 9, continue with Lesson 10 using the BikeRide project in your Project Library. You do not need any other project files for this lesson.

If you'd prefer to use the prepared file that came on the DVD, or if you skipped Lessons 8 and 9, follow these steps. If you skipped Lesson 8, you'll need to import the Events as well, so please refer to Lesson 8's "Preparing Your Project."

1   If iMovie is open, close it.

2   Open and arrange two Finder windows as described in Lesson 8.

3   From the top Finder window, navigate to the **Lessons > Lesson10 > Start_project_10** folder. Inside, find the **BikeRide_AUDIO.rcproject** file, and Option-drag it to the **User > Movies > iMovie Projects** folder in the bottom Finder window.

4   Open iMovie.

5   If the Project Library is not visible, click the Show or Hide Project Library button at the bottom of the Project Browser.

6   Select BikeRide_AUDIO from the list.

> **NOTE** ▶ If you skipped Lesson 8, you won't have the BikeRide project in your Project Library, and if you skipped Lesson 9, you won't have BikeRide_PICTURE.

7   Click the Show or Hide Project Library button to hide the Project Library.

NOTE ▶ The BikeRide_AUDIO project file references the same Events used in the previous lessons. If you didn't copy those Events into your iMovie Events folder in Lesson 8, please do so before continuing.

NOTE ▶ If you skipped Lesson 8, be sure to swap the vertical positions of your Events area and Project area to ensure that the screenshots here match what you're seeing.

You're now ready to get started on the project.

Adjusting Audio Tracks and Sound Levels

As you play your movie back, the first thing you'll notice is that you need to fix the audio levels. Some sounds are very loud whereas others are soft. Sounds compete for attention, making it difficult for the audience to follow the logic of the story. Background sounds like crowds and traffic start or end abruptly on the edit points.

Adjusting audio can be done at any stage of editing, and in practice, when you're familiar with all of iMovie's audio tools, you'll probably adjust audio levels while you're editing.

Normalizing Clip Volumes

We'll start with one of the easiest and handiest audio features of iMovie—its ability to *normalize* the audio level of a track. Normalizing audio means bringing its volume to the same level as all the other clips. For example, Michael's interview audio is much lower than the voiceover you recorded; normalizing brings them both to the same level.

With the click of a button, normalizing your audio ensures audio consistency throughout your project.

1 Select the first 5.4-second interview clip of Michael, where he says, "My dream as a kid was to ride cross-country."

2 Drag the playhead to the front of the clip and press the spacebar to hear the current level of the audio. Press the spacebar again to stop playback when the clip has finished.

3   Click the Adjust Audio button, or press the A key to open the Audio Adjustments window.

4   Click the Normalize Clip Volume button in the Audio Adjustments window.

iMovie displays a status bar as it processes the audio track to normalize the clip volume.

5   Play the clip again to hear the (much louder) normalized audio level.

Because all of Michael's interview footage was recorded at the same audio level, you'll need to normalize the volumes of every interview clip.

6   Keeping the Audio Adjustments window open, click to select the next interview clip where you see Michael talking, which comes just before the establishing shot of the start of the bike ride. When you've selected it, click Normalize Clip Volume in the Audio Adjustments window.

When you have multiple clips that need the same adjustment, you can paste the adjustments in the same way you can paste video adjustments.

7   Close the Audio Adjustments window, or click Done.

8   Select one of the two clips you've already normalized, and choose Edit > Copy.

9   Command-select the three remaining interview clips and the clip of Michael's wife on the cell phone, and choose Edit > Paste Adjustments > Audio.

> **NOTE** ▸ If the Edit > Paste Adjustments > Audio menu is dimmed, be sure that you actually selected the clip in step 8. If you attempt to Edit > Copy before you've selected the normalized clip, the Paste Adjustments properties won't be available to you.

The three clips are automatically normalized.

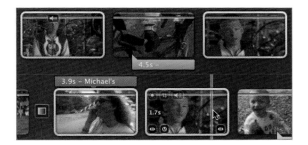

> **TIP** ▸ Before you edit, you can normalize the volume of all the clips in the Event Browser, and then when you edit them into your movie, the volumes will be normalized already. Because we've edited everything first and worked with audio last, you'll need to individually normalize each clip. Normalizing clips in the Event Browser will not affect any clips in the project.

> **NOTE** ▸ If you normalize the clip volume of clips in the Event Browser, any extracted audio will still need to be normalized again, because iMovie treats the extracted audio as its own reference file.

Mixing Your Sound with Audio Ducking

Even with sound normalized, audio tracks can compete with one another, and cause sounds or dialogue you want your audience to hear to be inaudible or unclear. iMovie enables you to choose a track as your primary sound source and *duck* all the others behind it, automatically changing their levels.

Here's how to normalize and set audio ducking for extracted clips and VOs.

1   Select the extracted audio track you placed at the start of the overhead crowd shot after Michael's first interview (it's the green one), and open the Audio Adjustments window.

The extracted audio from the interview is so soft it gets lost amidst the crowd walla (*walla* is industry lingo for that indiscernible background chatter). We need to normalize this audio, but we also need to drop, or duck, the crowd noise behind it.

2   Click Normalize Clip Volume.

3   Select the Ducking checkbox.

By default, iMovie ducks all audio on any other overlapping tracks to 15% of their original volume. This default setting has a pleasant effect in most situations and is generally preferable for longer tracks that extend over multiple edits, such as the voiceover tracks in your project.

But when you play this clip back to hear the results, you'll notice that the crowd volume is extremely low, and when the interview audio finishes, the crowd suddenly gets very loud. You can soften this by moving the ducking slider to keep it from dropping the other tracks too low.

4   Drag the Ducking slider to 35%.

This creates a more natural mix for these clips.

5   Normalize the volumes of each of the remaining extracted interview audio tracks and voiceover tracks in your project. Select the Ducking checkbox for each and accept the default value of 15%.

NOTE ▶ The Copy and Paste Audio Adjustments feature works only with video clips, and not with audio tracks. It's generally better to apply ducking manually anyway, to ensure the appropriate levels for the unique mix of individual tracks.

6   Click Done when you're finished.

Fading In and Fading Out

When you've finished normalizing and ducking, play back your entire project, listening carefully to the audio tracks.

One thing you might notice is that the interview clips fade in slightly at the start and fade out slightly at the end. That's because iMovie automatically adds a half-second fade to the audio in all your clips to smooth transitions between clips.

This automatic fade feature makes iMovie incredibly easy to use when you're quickly creating simple movie projects. But when you've made careful and specific edits as we have, you'll need to adjust fades manually.

1   Select the first clip of Michael's interview in your project (the first clip you normalized earlier) and open the Audio Adjustments window.

The automatic Fade In works nicely for this clip. But the Fade Out at the end drops the volume of his words, which stretch over the start of the next clip. To keep the volume through the cut, let's eliminate the fade.

2   Drag the Manual Fade Out slider all the way to the left, so that the number on the right reads "0.0s".

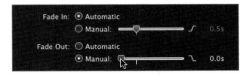

You can also fix the cutaway sequence of interviews in the middle of the project. In both of these cases, the clips follow from dialogue over the previous clip, so we'll remove the Fade Ins and leave the automatic Fade Outs.

3 Select the 5.8-second interview clip after the shot of Michael riding.

4 Slide the Manual Fade In slider to zero seconds.

5 Select the next 4.5-second interview clip, and adjust its Manual Fade In slider to zero.

6 Click Done when you're finished.

Adding Sound Effects

A powerful way to add texture to your video is the use of sound effects. iMovie comes with hundreds of professionally produced sound effects you can use to breathe new life into your video.

Ambient background sounds, such as traffic noise or the natural sounds of a forest, can stretch over many clips, creating an aural unity that makes the clips feel like they belong to part of a whole.

Let's start by adding some traffic sounds under the bike riding sequence.

1 Click the Music and Sound Effects button to open the Music and Sound Effects Browser.

2 In the Music and Sound Effects Browser, navigate to iLife Sound Effects > Ambience.

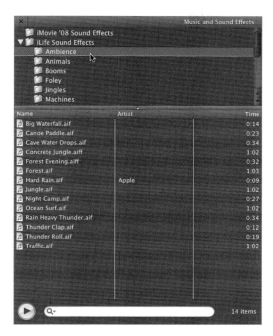

3   Drag the Traffic.aif sound effect file to your project, and place it on the first of the riding clips, just after the start of the ride, being careful to *avoid* releasing the mouse button when the entire project area's background turns green.

NOTE ▶ Don't worry if your clips aren't in the same position on your screen as shown in the image above—that will vary depending on your screen settings. As long as they're in the right order, you're fine.

The truth is, we don't want traffic noise to run through the background of this video. What we want is a subtle ambience that brings the picture to life. So let's drop the volume of the traffic sound to keep it soft in the background.

4   Select the Traffic track you just added, and open the Audio Adjustments window.

5   Drag the Volume slider to 18%.

The result is a consistent background sound that has the effect of smoothing out the cuts of your movie.

TIP ▶ You can adjust the overall volume of any track, adjust its fade in and out points, and choose whether to have other tracks automatically duck behind it, giving you exceptional control over the audio of your movie.

Stacking Multiple Audio Tracks in iMovie

Spot effects are those that match the onscreen action. If two cars are in a shot, you can add the sound of a car horn, and the audience will believe that the car onscreen honked at the other one.

You can create a richness to your movie by stacking multiple sound effects in the same place.

1   Locate the third riding clip, a 2.9-second clip of cyclists riding away from the camera.

2   In the Music and Sound Effects Browser, select the iLife Sound Effects folder.

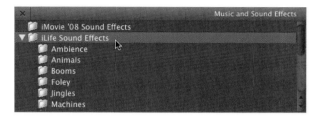

3   Type *coast* into the search bar at the bottom.

The search happens dynamically as you type, and the number of matching items in this folder or its subfolders appears at the right.

4   Select Bicycle Coasting.aif and drag it over the 2.9-second riding clip, being careful not to drop it on the green background.

TIP ▸ The search tool is handy if you know the exact name of the sound effect you're looking for. But it's worth navigating through the iLife Sound Effects folder to listen to all the sounds available to you. Bicycle Coasting is in the iLife Sound Effects > Transportation folder.

5   Select the track and align it with the front of the clip.

6   Drag a second copy of the sound effect to the same clip, but shift its start point to the right of the first sound, as shown here.

When you play it back, it's clear that the effect should be trimmed to the length of the clip.

7   Drag the right edge of the sound effect track to the left, until it's at the edge of the clip.

8   Adjust the other bicycle coasting sound effect track to the end of the clip.

NOTE ▸ As you shortened the lengths of the sound effects, their stacking order changed. iMovie displays sound tracks in such a way that tracks that extend to the next clip will appear higher in the stack than tracks that end on earlier clips. Note that the order in which the stacks are displayed does not affect volume or ducking levels.

The sound effect is great, but it ends rather abruptly now, and the volume is too loud.

9   Add a 1.7-second Manual Fade Out to one of the bicycle coasting sound effect tracks, and a 2-second Manual Fade Out to the other. Adjust the volume of one to 60%, and the other to 70%.

10   Click Done in the Audio Adjustments window when you're finished.

By giving them different volumes, start times and fade times, you create an authentic sound effect that feels like a natural part of the clip.

NOTE ▶ If two overlapping sound clips both have ducking applied, you might run into some issues with the audio levels of other tracks. In that case, you'll want to individually adjust each track's audio level.

11   Clear the word "coast" from the search box so that you'll be able to browse the Sound Effects library later.

Sharing Your Project to the Media Browser

Before we add music to the project, let's share this project to the Media Browser, so you'll have a clean copy of the movie available for Lesson 11.

1   Choose Share > Media Browser, and select only the Large option.

2   Click Publish when you're finished.

iMovie will prepare your project and publish it to the Media Browser, which will make your movie (without music) available to GarageBand.

Adding Music

As you saw in Lesson 5, adding professionally produced music to your video—such as an iLife Sound Effects jingle or a song you downloaded from the iTunes store—can instantly elevate your movie's quality by giving it professional production values.

You can add music to your movie in two ways: either as background music, or as a track.

> **NOTE ▶** If you use professionally produced music in your movies, you are not legally allowed to publish them to the Internet or record them to DVD without the written permission of the copyright owner, because professional music is subject to royalties. Be sure to use royalty-free music, or create your own in GarageBand. All the music and sound effects included with iLife '08 are royalty-free.

Adding Background Music

For quick-and-easy music in iMovie, you can drag a music track onto the background of your project, as you discovered in Lesson 5. But you can also get a lot more precise by pinning the background music to an exact moment of your video.

And if your music track isn't long enough, you can add another track to the background, and iMovie will automatically cross-fade into it when the first song finishes.

> **NOTE ▶** When you proceed with this exercise, iMovie will warn you that you've made changes to a published project. Simply click OK and continue with the exercise.

1 In the Music and Sound Effects Browser, navigate to the iLife Sound Effects > Jingles folder.

2 Scroll down to find the Two Seater Long.aif track, and drag it onto the background of your project, releasing your mouse button only when the background has turned green.

3 In the Music and Sound Effects Browser, scroll up to find Daydream.aif and drag it onto the background of your project. Don't release your mouse button until the gray area beneath the green area of the previous track turns green.

The second track begins at the end of the first one.

4 Drag Time Lapse.aif onto the background of your project.

5 In the background of your project, select the Time Lapse.aif track.

When you select a background music track, its border will turn yellow.

6 Hold the mouse button down on the name of the track—Time Lapse—and drag the whole background music selection to the end of the 4.5-second clip of cyclists in green and orange jerseys coming toward the camera (top, middle in the figure below).

If you timed your voiceovers correctly, the music selection will turn purple, and a pin icon will appear in the upper left corner of the track to denote that you have *pinned* the music to a specific frame of video.

TIP ▶ Dragging background clips may require a few attempts to get the hang of it. Be sure your pointer has turned into a hand before attempting to move the music track.

Arranging Your Background Music Tracks

As you play the music back to review what you've done, you might notice that the Two Seater Long music completely changes the tone of the intro to this video. In iMovie, you can easily swap the order of your background music.

1   Choose Edit > Arrange Music Tracks, or right-click/Control-click any background music in your project, and choose Arrange Music Tracks.

    This opens the Floating Music Tracks field.

2   In the green Floating Music Tracks area, select Two Seater Long and drag it beneath Daydream.

    As you drag the name of the song, a thin black line will appear to indicate where it will be placed when you release the mouse button.

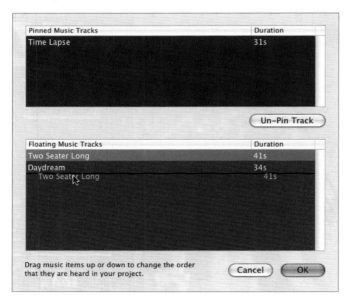

NOTE ▶ Think of your background music as the playlist at a radio station. The songs will play until they finish, and then the next song will begin. Any song pinned to a specific moment in your movie is not on the playlist, and must be un-pinned to join the playlist by clicking the Un-Pin Track button.

3   Click OK.

Trimming Audio for Precision

When you play it back, the Daydream.aif track is a much more effective way to start Michael's sponsorship movie. But it feels like the music should fade into the Two Seater track around the start of the ride.

You can achieve that with the Trim Music tool.

1   Click the Trim icon (it looks like a clock) on the Daydream track.

2   In the Trim Music area, drag the right handle to shorten the clip to 42 seconds.

As you drag the handle, the viewer displays the current frame in your project at that moment of the audio.

TIP ▶ You can edit any music or sound track with the Trim tool at any time by simply selecting the track and choosing Edit > Trim.

NOTE ▶ With the Trim tool, you can adjust the start or end of a track to clean up stray noises, and preview the track to make sure it's exactly what you imagine.

3 Click Done when you're finished.

Adding Music as a Track for Greater Control

Adding background music is easy, and offers you significant control over the way your music plays, and where it starts and stops. But you can also add music to your movie as a track, which has the added benefit of enabling sophisticated crossfades with other music tracks.

Let's add another copy of the Daydream track to the end of the project, creating an audio bookend to the movie. But let's do it by setting it as a music track.

1 In the Music and Sound Effects Browser, scroll to find the Daydream.aif track.

2 Drag it from the Music and Sound Effects Browser onto the sunset shot at the end of the riding sequence in your project, making sure to *avoid* the green background.

3 Move the new music track to align with the start of the sunset clip.

TIP ▶ Experiment with layering several music tracks in varying combinations over the end to see the different effects music can have on the finished movie.

Doing a Final Mix of Your Audio

When you play back your movie to listen to the music you've placed, you'll notice that the audio levels of your track have shifted. Some of the ducking has an unintended effect on the music.

So before you send your movie out into the world, take the time to go through your project and apply the skills you've learned in this lesson.

▶ Adjust the volume levels of each clip.

▶ Check the ducking levels, and change the ducking percentage if it sounds better.

▶ Manually Fade In or Out to smooth the start and end points of clips.

▶ Move or Trim any clips that need it.

When you've finished, press the Play Full Screen button to watch your completed movie.

Taking Audio One Step Further

As you discovered in this lesson, the audio tools of iMovie '08 give you the flexibility to create a rich and detailed audio score for your movie project.

But the iLife '08 suite has another application that will enable you to infuse the audio side of your movie with your own unique creativity, while adding an even greater degree of precision: GarageBand.

In the next lesson, you'll discover how to create a custom music score that fits your project exactly as you imagine.

Lesson Review

1. What does it mean to *normalize* a clip?

2. Does ducking change the volume of the selected audio track?

3. Are audio fades added automatically to video clips?

4. How can you add realistic sound effects to your movie?

5. Is it possible to pin background music to a specific clip in your project?

Answers

1. To normalize the Clip Volume means to bring the audio of a clip to the same level as the other audio tracks in your project or Event area.

2. No. Ducking reduces the volume of any audio that overlaps the track for which ducking has been selected.

3. Yes. iMovie adds an automatic half-second fade to the start and end of every video clip. To remove the fade, open the Audio Adjustments window and slide the Manual Fade slider to zero seconds.

4. Don't just place a sound effect and move on. When you add a sound effect to your movie, be sure to adjust the volume level and fade to fit appropriately within the aural context of your movie.

5. Yes. Simply drag the background music from the top, and move it where you want it to start.

Composing and Arranging Music

11

Lesson Files   iLife08_Book_Files > Lessons > Lesson11

Time   This lesson takes approximately 90 minutes to complete.

Goals   Find and preview video files in the Media Browser

Import a video file into a project

View a video as you work

Edit a video's audio track

Add and edit markers

Assign chapter titles to markers

Build a song using Apple Loops

Use Automation Curves to adjust levels

Modify a Software Instrument loop

Save a project with an iLife preview

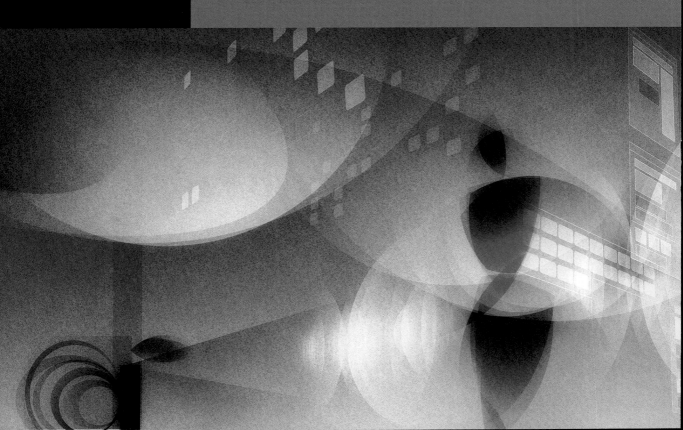

Scoring an iMovie or QuickTime Video

One of the best features of GarageBand is its ability to work with iMovie. This allows you to easily bring your movie into GarageBand and create a custom score. Your video will look and sound even better with a great musical identity.

Not only can you create your own music for your iMovies and QuickTime-compatible video files, but you can also choose from hundreds of finished musical pieces and sound effects to complete the soundtrack. By investing a little bit of time and creativity, you can really make your soundtrack shine.

In our previous lessons, you edited a video about the Tour de Cure bicycle ride. This video follows the story of a rider in his journey to raise money and awareness. By striking the right balance musically, we can reinforce the emotion of the video and enhance the audience's experience.

In this lesson, you'll import a finished video, and then create a soundtrack from scratch using some of the musical pieces that come with GarageBand '08. Along the way, you'll also add and label chapter markers that will be used in iDVD when you export the finished piece.

Creating a New Movie Score Project

A scored movie in GarageBand is similar to the default project setup. There are a few changes to make, though, to ensure that the tools you need are visible.

1 Open GarageBand. If GarageBand is already open, choose File > New.

2 In the GarageBand welcome screen, click the Create New Music Project button.

3 Save the project to your GarageBand projects folder as *Bike Ride Score*. The default options for tempo, signature, and key are okay.

4   Click Create.

If not already open, the GarageBand project opens, but needs to be customized to show the elements necessary to create a musical score.

5   Choose Control > Show Loop Browser.

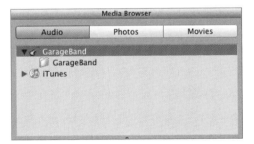

You'll use Apple Loops as the primary building block for your score. Apple Loops are prerecorded music files that can be used to add drum beats, rhythm elements, and other repeating patterns to a project. Loops contain musical patterns that can be repeated seamlessly as well as combined into new musical arrangements. You can extend a loop to fill any amount of time in a project.

6   You'll also want access to the iLife Media Browser. To open it, choose Control > Show Media Browser.

The Media Browser contains buttons for various types of media files (Audio, Photos, Movies). This is an easy way to navigate to the media files you want to use.

7   Choose Track > Show Movie Track to add a track to hold the movie that will be scored.

In the next section, you'll select a movie clip to place on this track for the project.

Working with Video Files in the Media Browser

For this lesson, you'll use the Bike Ride project you created in Lessons 8–10. If you haven't done those lessons yet, we'll give you a movie you can use instead.

Before you import the video file to your project, it's a good idea to preview it. Finding the right video file in this case is easy because the name is very obvious, and there is only one video clip to choose from. However, in your real-life workflow you may have dozens, or even hundreds, of video clips in your Media Browser, and the selection process may not be as easy.

Previewing a Video File

There are two simple ways to preview a video clip in the Media Browser: Select the file and click the Play button, or double-click the clip.

1   In the Media Browser, click the Movies button.

If the Movies folder on your computer includes movie files, they'll be displayed in the lower pane of the Media Browser whenever you select the Movies folder.

The Movies pane of the Media Browser may include iTunes if you've created your own mp4 files compressed for your video iPod or have downloaded video podcasts. Protected iTunes media will not appear in the Media Browser. You can also add other folders to the Media Browser by dragging them in, so you can access media files anywhere on your computer from within GarageBand.

2   If the projects on your computer aren't visible, click the disclosure triangle next to the iMovie icon to reveal them.

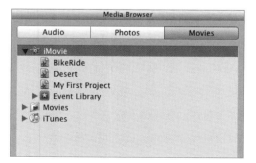

3   Select the project called BikeRide that you created in the previous lessons.

A large, shared movie is available with this project.

4   Double-click the **Large** shared movie file to preview it in the Media Browser.

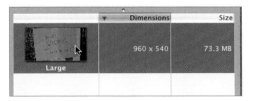

The movie icon becomes a small preview of the movie.

5   To stop the movie preview, press the spacebar.

Importing a Video File from the Media Browser

You can import any one iMovie project or QuickTime-compatible video file from the Media Browser. The movie you'll use in this lesson was created in iMovie. It was then added to the Media Browser by choosing Share > Media Browser. Let's add the movie to our GarageBand project.

1   Drag the **Large** movie into the Movie Track.

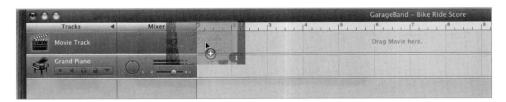

GarageBand generates thumbnails for the track to represent the video clips. It also adds a track called Movie Sound, and creates a new AIFF file that contains the soundtrack of the movie. The original movie file remains unchanged.

NOTE ▶ If you didn't create the Bike Ride Movie in Lessons 8–10, then you'll need to import a self-contained movie. You'll find a file named **BikeRide_to_Score.m4v** in the Lesson11 folder. Simply drag that file onto the Movie track in GarageBand instead of the iMovie project.

The Track Info pane also appears in place of the Media Browser, with the Movie Preview pane at the top where you can see the video as you play the project. The movie will update as you play the GarageBand project, which will make it much easier to synchronize the movie to the photo.

NOTE ▶ The video file always starts at the beginning of the project. Once added to a project, video files cannot be edited or repositioned in the Timeline. The Movie Sound track is a Real Instrument track, and it includes an orange (imported) Real Instrument region.

2   Select the Movie Track to see its info in the Track Info pane. Then select the Movie Sound track to see its information.

The Movie Preview pane will be visible as long as the Track Info pane is showing, no matter which track is selected in the Timeline.

NOTE ▶ A project can only contain one movie file. If you import a movie file into a project that already contains one, you'll see a dialog asking if you want to replace the existing movie with the new one.

3   Because we won't be using the Grand Piano instrument track, select it and choose Track > Delete Track.

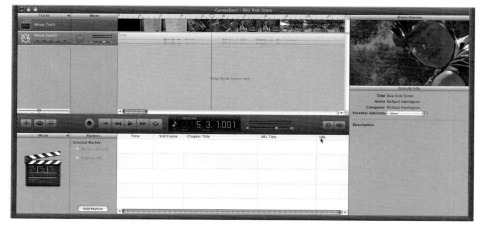

Your project is now ready to score.

4   Choose File > Save to capture your work so far.

Preparing the Project for Scoring

Once the video file has been added to the project, it's ready for you to begin scoring. However, there are a few things you should do first:

▶   Watch the video to get ideas about what type of sound you want to add.

▶   Clean up any problems in the video's audio track.

▶   Add markers that might be useful for planning the soundtrack or separating the project into chapters.

Viewing the Video

The Movie Preview pane is available for viewing your video as long as the Movie Track and Track Info pane are both showing. Because this project is based on video instead of music, you can change the time display to absolute time rather than musical time.

1   In the time display, click the Absolute Time button to view the project in absolute time (Hours:Minutes:Seconds.Fractions).

2   Press the End key to move the playhead to the end of the project.

The time display indicates that the project is about three minutes in length.

3   Press Return or the Home key to move the playhead to the beginning of the project.

4   Play the project once from the beginning to see the movie file in the Movie Preview pane.

The video has three major sections that we will score.

5   Press Return to move the playhead back to the beginning of the project.

This movie was edited in sections that can be divided into chapters for a DVD or played consecutively as a movie. To make the movie easier to navigate, you'll add chapter markers later in the lesson. First, let's clean up the audio track.

Working with the Video's Audio Track

You can make basic edits and change the mix for the Movie Sound track. This includes muting the track, and adjusting its volume and its *panning* (what portion of the audio is sent to each speaker in a stereo mix). Although you can edit the Movie Sound track anytime, it's always a good idea to clean up any obvious problems early, before you build the rest of the soundtrack.

> **NOTE ▸** If the movie has any major problems that you want to fix, you can always return to iMovie and update the project. Just be sure to share the project with the Media Browser when you close and save.

There are a handful of small things we can enhance. The sound of bike gears clicking is a bit loud in a few spots. We also have different volume levels for the interview soundbites that can be adjusted to match more closely.

You won't need the Movie Preview pane for this audio procedure, so let's close it temporarily to make more room in the Timeline for the task at hand.

1   Press Command-I to close the Track Info and Movie Preview panes.

2   Double-click the orange **Large** audio region in the Movie Sound track to open it in the editor.

3   Move the playhead to around 40 seconds in the Timeline (00:00:40.000).

TIP You can use the time display to navigate to a specific time by double-clicking the numbers in the display and typing the desired time. Press the right or left arrow keys to select a different field within the display. Press Return to send the playhead to the location in the display. You can also move the playhead in the Timeline by pressing the left and right arrow keys.

4 Press Control-right arrow several times to zoom into the waveform in the editor.

5 Listen to the track between 0:40 and 00:44.

You can hear several loud clicks as the bike riders begin to lock their cleats into their pedals and start the ride.

6 Move the pointer over the waveform in the editor until the pointer changes to crosshairs. Click near the center of the track and drag from left to right with the crosshair pointer from 00:41 to 00:43.

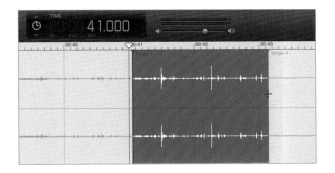

7 Once the selection is complete (blue), release the mouse button and click the selected area once to make it a separate selected region.

8   Press Delete to remove the unwanted section.

9   Move the playhead back to around 00:36 and play through the edited section.

The loud clicks are gone. You'll add music that will mask the silence in the Movie Sound track.

10   Choose File > Save to capture your work so far.

As you can see, the audio in the Movie Sound track can be edited just like any other Real Instrument region. The only difference is that it's orange, which indicates that it was imported.

Adding and Editing Markers

For this project, you'll add chapter markers between each of the movie's sections, which you can use in iDVD to create chapters for a DVD. The chapter markers can also be handy for navigating to different parts of the finished movie as you build the soundtrack.

In this exercise, you'll add four chapter markers that separate the different parts of the movie. You can add markers to the Movie Track in the editor. Because the editor is already showing, all you'll need to do is select the Movie Track.

1   Select the Movie Track to show marker information in the editor.

The editor changes to Marker view and contains the marker list with columns showing the start time, still video frame, and chapter title for each marker. The first chapter marker you'll add will be for the beginning of the video.

2   If the Track Info and Movie Preview panes aren't visible, press Command-I to open them.

3 Press Return to move the playhead to the beginning.

4 In the editor, click the Add Marker button to add a marker at the playhead position.

The first marker appears in the marker list. Also, the time position where you added the marker appears in the Time column, and the frame of the video at that position appears in the Still Frame column. The beginning of the video fades in from black, so the still frame for the first marker will also be black.

5 Click the Chapter Title text field and type *I've Had a Dream...*, then press Return.

Movie	Markers	Time	Still Frame	Chapter Title
	Selected Marker: ☑ Marks a Chapter	◆ 00:00:00.000	■	I've Had a Dream...
	☐ Displays URL			
	Add Marker			

Naming the chapter marker in the Chapter Title field automatically designates the marker as a chapter. If you want to name a marker without making it a chapter marker, you can deselect the "Marks a Chapter" option.

NOTE ▶ To delete a marker, select it in the marker list and press the Delete key.

Chapter markers you create in GarageBand will be recognized when you play the movie in iTunes, iDVD, or QuickTime Player.

Project Tasks

Now it's your turn to add the remaining three markers. First, you'll navigate to the right position in the Timeline, then click the Add Marker button. Once you've created the marker, you can name it accordingly. The last step is to press Command-S to save your progress.

▶   00:00:31 – Starting the Ride

▶   00:01:48 – The Finish Line

▶   00:02:37 – End Credits

> **TIP** ▶ Because you're working with whole timecode numbers and not fractions of a second, start with the playhead at the beginning of the Timeline so you'll have all zeros in the time display. Then you can simply type in the time where you'd like to move the playhead.

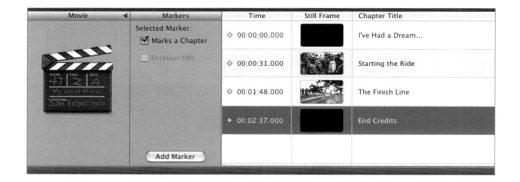

NOTE ▶ You can compare your project to **Bike Ride Score_Stage2.band** from the Lesson11 folder.

Building a Soundtrack in the Timeline

Now that you've viewed the project and added markers, it's time to add some music. In this exercise, you'll create and mix music in the Timeline, using some of the professional-quality prerecorded music selections and loops that come with GarageBand '08. As you add music, you'll adjust its levels to complete the project.

Locking the Playhead

This is a good time to mention the two different ways you can watch the playhead in action. When you play a long take or a full song, or simply navigate to a marker, your playhead may actually leave the screen. If you like to watch your playhead scrub across the tracks, click the Playhead Lock button. It's called that because it also lets you lock the playhead in the Timeline and the playhead in the editor so they remain onscreen.

The Playhead Lock button is located on the far-right side of the window, and it looks like two playheads, one on top of the other.

Playheads   Playheads
unlocked   locked

If the two playheads are lined up in the middle of the button, the playheads in the Timeline and the editor are moving in sync with one another (ganged). It also means that the playheads will stay locked in view in the Timeline, and the tracks will move behind the playhead. By default, the playheads in the Timeline and the editor stay centered in the middle of the GarageBand window once they reach the center.

If the button shows two playheads that are not aligned, the playheads in the Timeline and editor are not locked to the center of the screen. The playhead will continue moving left to right and can continue to move off screen as it plays the tracks in the Timeline. Sometimes you may want to see a different part of the song in the editor than the one shown in the Timeline. To do this, you can unlock the two playheads, so that the Timeline and editor can show different parts of the song.

Let's lock the playheads so that when you navigate to a marker, the playhead will be visible in the center of the screen even if you're zoomed in to the Timeline.

1   Click the Playhead Lock button once to set the playheads in the locked position, if they aren't already locked.

    The Ruler and playhead scroll until the playhead position is in the center of the Timeline.

2   Press Return to move the playhead to the start of the Timeline.

Browsing and Adding Loops to the Project

There are several strategies you can use when adding a soundtrack to your iMovie or video clip. One option is to import the video into GarageBand and add music and sound effects to the edited video. Or, you can create a song in GarageBand, then export it to iTunes, where you can then bring it into your video editing software such as iMovie and edit the picture to the music.

For this project, you'll use Apple Loops to create an original song. This process involves a fair amount of experimentation as you search for combinations to use. For the purpose of this lesson, the choices will be identified for you. Your goal in this exercise is to create a piece of music that works well with the video.

1   Press Command-E to hide the editor. Make sure the playhead is at the beginning of the project by pressing the Return key. Markers are shown as yellow diamonds at the top of the Timeline.

2   Play the project from the first marker to the second marker (around 30 seconds) and watch the video.

   What type of music do you think would work well with this piece? Let's try some upbeat music that builds in intensity as it progresses.

3   Press Command-L to open the Loop Browser.

   When the Loop Browser opens, the Track Info pane automatically closes.

4   Drag the gray bar above the Loop Browser upwards to make more room.

5   Click the Guitars keyword type to narrow your search.

6   Click some of the items in the results list in the right column.

NOTE ▶ There are two types of Apple Loops: Real Instrument loops and Software Instrument loops. The color of a loop's icon indicates which type each loop is. Real Instrument loops (which are recordings of real instruments) have a blue icon with an audio waveform. Software Instrument loops (which are generated by the computer using a synthesizer) have a green icon with a musical note.

7   Select the Loop Acoustic Picking 06 and drag it to an empty area of the Timeline. Be sure to drag it all the way to the left so the loop starts at the beginning of the video.

The loop is added to the Timeline and lasts for 8 seconds.

8   Choose Control > Snap to Grid and Control > Show Alignment guides to make it easier to drag your loop to the precise spot you desire. If these options are already enabled, leave them on.

Click play and listen to the guitar. It seems to work, but the loop can be longer.

9   Choose File > Save to capture your work so far.

Extending a Loop Region
You now need to extend the guitar loop so it lasts for the duration of the first section. The whole process is incredibly easy. Loop regions are designed to repeat (loop) over and over seamlessly. To extend a loop region, all you have to do is click the upper-right corner and pull.

1   Move your pointer over the upper-right corner of the Acoustic Picking 06 loop region.

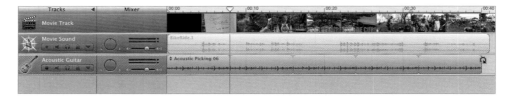

The pointer becomes a loop pointer, a curved arrow, which indicates the pointer is in the correct position to drag the loop to repeat.

2   Drag the upper-right corner of the guitar loop region and extend it so the loop repeats 5 times (to the 40-second mark).

You can identify a loop segment by the indented marks (like a capsule) at its ends. You don't have to extend a loop for the full length of the original region. If you make the looped section shorter than the original, you will hear only the notes included in the new loop segment.

Notice that as the loop repeats, you can see notches that show the beginning and end of the original loop within the new region.

3   Press Return to move the playhead to the beginning of the Timeline, then press Play.

The loop works well, but seems a little repetitive. We can modify the loop so it switches to a different, but compatible sound.

Splitting a Loop Region

By splitting a loop, you can make separate parts that can be modified individually. This makes it easier to use loops from the same family when building a song.

1   Move your playhead to the 00:16 mark (this is just after the loop has been played for the second time).

2   Select the Acoustic Picking 06 track so that it's active in the Timeline.

The track turns a brighter blue.

3   Choose Edit > Split or press Command-T.

The track splits into two parts. The first has two regions and the second has three regions.

NOTE ▶ If the track splits into multiple pieces, you didn't accurately position the loop at the start of your Timeline. To fix it, undo the split, then return to the start of your Timeline. Zoom in so you can easily see your location, then drag the loop so it starts at the exact beginning.

To make it easier to work with loops, they're often grouped into families. You'll see loops in the Loop Browser that have the same name, but with a different number at the end. For example, Acoustic Picking 06 and Acoustic Picking 07 belong to the same family. Loops in the same family often work well together.

4   Click an empty area of the Timeline to deselect any loops.

5   In the Timeline, select the second instance of the loop called Acoustic Picking 06.2.

6   In the Timeline, click the up and down arrows in the upper-left corner of the loop region to try different loops out.

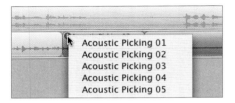

Be sure to listen to how the two loops fit together by playing your Timeline.

7   Set the second region to Acoustic Picking 16.

8   Choose File > Save to capture your work so far.

The loops are working well, but could use another instrument to complement them.

Using a Software Instrument Loop

Let's add a piano to the guitar. Earlier you learned about the two types of Apple Loops: Real Instrument Loops and Software Instrument Loops. For this part of the lesson, we'll use a Software Instrument loop.

1   In the Loop Browser, click the Reset button to remove the keyword filters.

2   Click the Piano, then select the Cheerful keyword type to narrow your search.

3   Click the Delicate Piano 08 loop to audition it.

This loop works well and can be added to the Timeline. When you add a Software Instrument loop, you can convert it to a Real Instrument loop. Real Instrument loops require less processing power for playback. This allows you to use more tracks and effects in a project without impacting your computer's performance.

4   Choose GarageBand > Preferences and make sure the Convert to Real Instrument checkbox is selected.

5   Drag the Delicate Piano 08 loop to an empty area of the Timeline.

The piano loop is added below the guitar loop.

6   Drag the upper-right corner of the piano loop region and extend it so the loop repeats 5 times (to the 00:40 mark).

The yellow alignment guides make it easy to tell when you've dragged the loop to the correct spot.

7   Press Return to move the playhead to the beginning of the Timeline, then press Play.

The loop works well, but again, could use some more variety.

8   Move the playhead to the 00:16 mark.

9   Select the piano track so that it's active in the Timeline.

10 Choose Edit > Split.

11 Move the playhead to the 00:24 mark and choose Edit > Split.

The piano track is now divided into three regions.

12 Change the middle piano region to Delicate Piano 10.

13 Press Return to move the playhead to the beginning of the Timeline, then press Play.

The music is working well for this section. It just needs to be mixed so that its volume swells at the appropriate time, then dips beneath when people are talking.

14 Choose File > Save to capture your work so far.

Using Track Automation Curves

To allow you to mix your music like a pro, GarageBand supports automation curves. These let you create changes in volume, pan, and other parameters over time. This means that you can take precise control over properties like volume change. After adding an automation curve to a track, you add control points where you want the change to occur. For example, if you add two or more control points to a track volume curve, you can then drag the control points to different values. The volume for the track will increase or decrease smoothly between the control points.

Showing a Track's Automation Curves

Every track has automation curves for volume, pan (except the master track), and other parameters. The track must be visible if you want to modify it.

1   Click the triangle next to the Lock button in a track's header. Do this for both the Acoustic Guitar and Piano tracks.

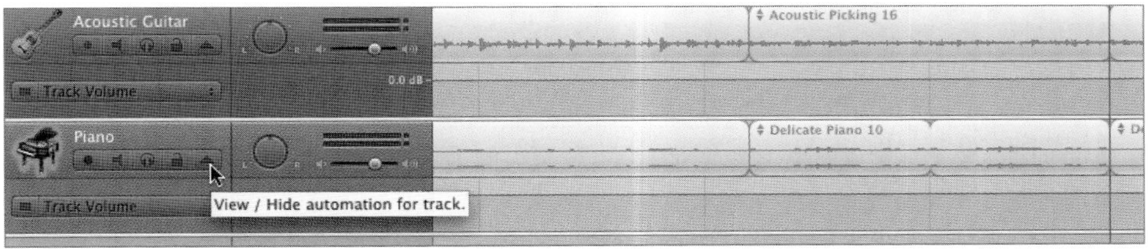

A new row for the volume and pan curves appears below the track in the Timeline.

2   By default, the Track Volume curve is selected.

   TIP ▶ You can choose the curve you want to work with from the pop-up menu at the left of the row.

3   Click the square next to the Track Volume label to turn on the curve for editing. Do this for both the Acoustic Guitar and Piano tracks.

Adding Control Points

Now you need to add control points to modify the automation curve. To add an automation control point, simply click the curve. To mix the track over time, we'll need several control points. These are chosen based on when there is narration in the movie.

TIP ▶ An easy way to see gaps in the narration is to look at the audio waveforms in the Movie Sound track.

1   Move the playhead to the 4.000 mark.

2   Click the automation curve for the Piano track and add a control point. Repeat for the Acoustic Guitar track.

You'll need several more control points for this mix.

3   Add control points for both tracks at the following times:

5.500, 16.000, 18.000, 20.000, 23.500, 30.000, and 35.000.

Now that you have control points, you can adjust the volume over time. The higher the control point is on the track, the louder it is. As you drag a control point, you'll see its volume displayed next to it in decibels (dB).

4   Shift-click to select the control points at the 5.500 and 16.000 marks for the piano track.

TIP ▶ If you have difficulty clicking, try zooming in on your Timeline by pressing Control-right arrow.

5 Drag the control point down to about -18.00 dB.

6 Repeat steps 4 and 5 for the guitar track.

The rest of the control points need to be mixed for both tracks.

7 Adjust the following control points to these approximate levels:

18.000	-6.0 dB
20.000	-6.0 dB
23.500	-18.00 dB
30.000	-18.00 dB
35.000	-144.00 dB

8 Press the Return key to move the playhead to the beginning of the Timeline, then press Play.

The music is working well for this first section. We can now go on and build the remaining two sections.

9 Choose File > Save to capture your work so far.

Monitoring Tracks

As you start to work with multiple tracks, you'll often need to limit what you hear. Otherwise, it can be overwhelming as you try to make decisions about the audio content and levels in your Timeline. Fortunately, GarageBand makes it easy to mute specific tracks. You can also solo individual or multiple tracks so only they can be heard. Using these two features together makes it easier to build and mix your musical score.

Muting a Track

You can silence, or *mute*, a track in your Timeline so that you hear only the other, unmuted tracks. This can be very useful when you want to hear how a track affects the overall project, compare tracks, or try different loops in a project.

1   Move the playhead to 26.000 in the Timeline.

2   In the Loop Browser click the Reset button. Then type *Electric Guitar Swell* into the search field at the bottom, and press Return.

FX	Bongo	Vibes	Experimental	Part	Fill
Harmonica	Harp	Harpsichord			
English Horn	French Horn	Celesta			

Scale: Any   Q- Guitar Swell   1 item

The results list shows Electric Guitar Swell 01, which we want to use.

3   Drag the loop so it starts at the playhead.

4   Press Play to hear the audio.

All four tracks playing at once is a little busy. You can mute the Movie Sound track so you can focus on just the music.

5   Click the Mute button (shaped like a speaker) for the Movie Sound track.

The track's contents are dimmed to indicate that they're muted.

6   Move the playhead to the start of the guitar swell and press Play.

Now it's easier to hear how the tracks interact.

7   Using the Automation Curve, adjust the track's volume so it fades in, rises gently, then fades out. You can use the following information and figure for guidance.

26.000	-144.0 dB
30.000	-10.9 dB
38.000	-3.1 dB
42.000	-144.0 dB

8   Click the Mute button for the Movie Sound track to toggle the mute status and restore the track.

Soloing a Track

Besides muting an individual track, GarageBand offers the ability to listen to individual tracks. This is called *soloing*. Soloing effectively silences the other tracks and is useful when you want to work on a track or region individually. In this case, we'll use the soloing feature to work on the music for the middle of the video.

So far, you've done a great job adding and sequencing loops. You've also effectively harnessed automation curves to control the volume of your tracks. To save you some time, you'll now open up a GarageBand project that has the rest of the Apple Loops added. This score, however, still needs some work before it's finished.

1   Open the file **Bike Ride Score_Stage3.band** from the Lesson11 folder.

This file is partially built, but you still need to mix the tracks and modify the ending.

2   Choose File > Save As and name the file **Bike Ride Score FINAL.band**. Save the file to your default GarageBand folder (located in your Music folder).

3   Move the playhead to about 24.000 and press Play. Listen to the music tracks.

Chances are, it's hard to hear because so many sounds are happening at once.

4   Click the Solo button (the one with the headphones icon) in the track header for the Kits track.

The other tracks in the Timeline are dimmed. They are now inaudible.

5   Click the Solo buttons for the Electric Guitar and Electric Bass tracks as well.

6   Move the playhead to about 24.000 and press Play. Listen to the music tracks.

It should be easier to hear the loops that need to be mixed.

7   Choose File > Save to capture your work so far.

Project Tasks

Now it's your turn to mix these three tracks. The goal is to have the music fade in quickly, swell when there is no narration, then quickly fade out. Make your own choices here about how to use automation curves. You can use the following figure for guidance when it comes to mixing your tracks.

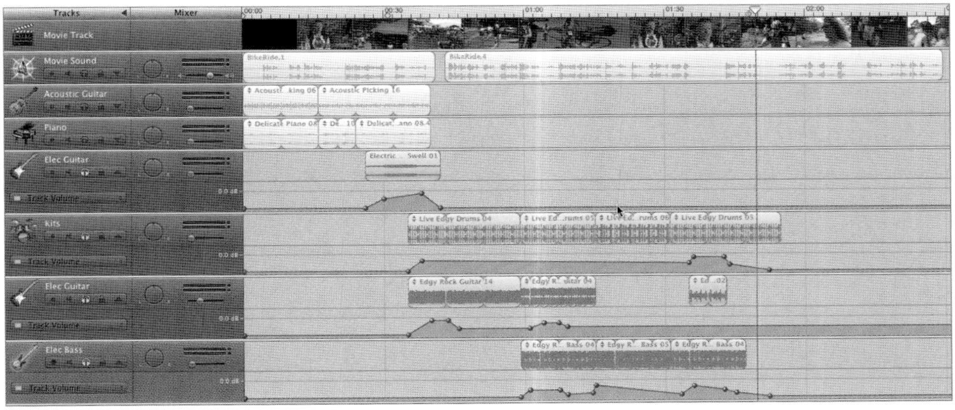

> **TIP** ▶ After you make an initial mix for your track, click the Solo button so you can hear the Movie Sound track as well. Adjust your Automation Curve until you're happy with the mix.

When finished with your mix, un-solo your tracks by clicking the illuminated (yellow) headphone icons. Then choose File > Save to capture your work so far.

> **NOTE** ▶ Mixing audio tracks like this takes practice. Remember your automation curve is very flexible and you can continue to move, adjust, add, or delete control points as needed. Hang in there . . . your reward is a great-sounding mix.

Working with a Software Instrument Loop

The last track in the Timeline contains a Software Instrument loop. You can tell the loop is different by both its color (green) and the appearance of notes within it. This type of loop works very similarly to the Real Instrument loops; the key difference is you can actually edit the notes within the loop.

1   Move your playhead to 1:46.000 in the Timeline.

2   Click to reveal the Automation Curve for the track.

3   Click the square next to Track Volume to turn the curve on.

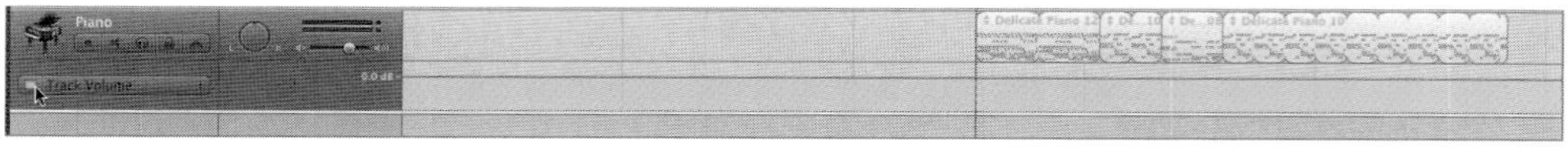

4   Add control points and adjust their volume using the following information for guidance:

1:46.000   -144.0 dB

1:53.000   -8.0 dB

1:57.000   -14.0 dB

2:27.000   -14.0 dB

2:31.000   0 dB

5   Move the playhead to about 1:44.000 and press Play. Listen to your music until the end of the video.

Everything sounds good except for a few stray notes at the very end. Because this is a Software Instrument Loop, we can edit its contents to change what music is played. The first step, though, is to isolate the region.

6   Move the playhead to 2:54.000.

7   Select the bottom-most Piano track and choose Edit > Split.

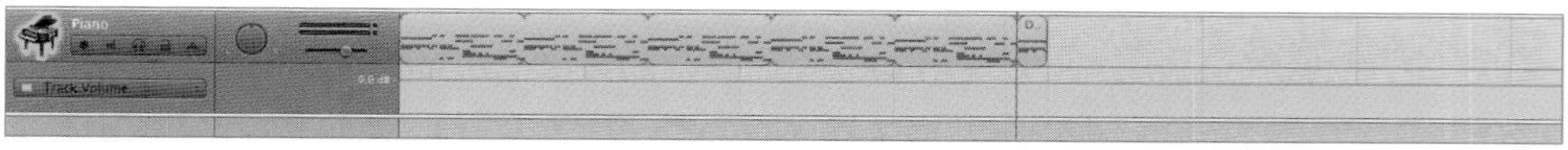

8   Double-click the last region to open it in the editor.

The gray bars indicate the notes that are being played. The default view is the Graphic view, but you can always switch to Notation view to see the notes. You'll find icons for both in the bottom-left corner.

9   Examine the notes that are being played. The small "twitter" you hear at the end is the bottom-most gray bars.

10   Shift-click the three bottom notes so they're selected. As you click each to add it to the selection, you'll hear the music play.

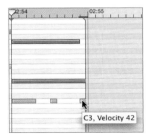

11   Press the Delete key to remove the notes from the region.

The notes are now gone and you've modified the Software Instrument loop.

12   Move the playhead back about 10 seconds and press Play. Listen to the modified ending of your score.

Sounds pretty good. You are now ready to save the project so it can be used by other iLife applications.

NOTE ▶ To compare your work to the final mix on the DVD, you can open the project **Bike Ride Score_Stage3.band** from the Lesson11 folder.

Sharing a GarageBand Project

When you finish a GarageBand project, you have some important choices to make. It's a good idea to save your project properly so it can be shared easily between applications.

1   Close your GarageBand project by choosing File > Close.

2   If you have made any changes, you'll be prompted to click the Save button to capture your changes.

3   When asked about saving your project with an iLife preview, click Yes.

This option generates an iLife preview that makes it easy to use or preview your project from within other iLife and iWork applications.

TIP ▶ You can also send the GarageBand project directly to other iLife applications with ease. With a project open, simply click the Send menu and click the Share menu. You can choose to send the project to iTunes, iWeb, or iDVD. The chapter markers that you've added will come through as chapters that work in iTunes, QuickTime, or a DVD player.

Lesson Review

1. What types of video files can be imported into a GarageBand project?

2. What is the maximum number of video files you can add to a GarageBand project?

3. If you import a movie file that includes audio, how does the imported audio appear in the Timeline?

4. Can you edit the audio region in the Movie Sound track?

5. How do you add markers to the Movie Track?

Answers

1. You can import any iMovie project or QuickTime-compatible video format.

2. A GarageBand project can include only one video file. It will always start at the beginning of the project.

3. A video clip's audio appears as an orange Real Instrument region in the Movie Sound track located directly below the Movie Track.

4. You can edit the audio in the Movie Sound track in the same way you edit any Real Instrument region.

5. Select the Movie Track, move the playhead to the desired marker position, then click the Add Marker button in the editor.

12

Lesson Files iLife08_Book_Files > Lessons > Lesson12 > Podcast_Open_Files

iLife08_Book_Files > Lessons > Lesson12 > Band_Photos

Time This lesson takes approximately 90 minutes to complete.

Goals Create a new podcast episode

Add and adjust the Speech Enhancer effects to voice tracks

Add artwork to the Media Browser and Podcast Track

Edit marker regions

Build a title sequence in the Podcast Track

Crop and resize artwork in the Artwork Editor

Add a URL and URL title to a marker region

Edit a project's episode information

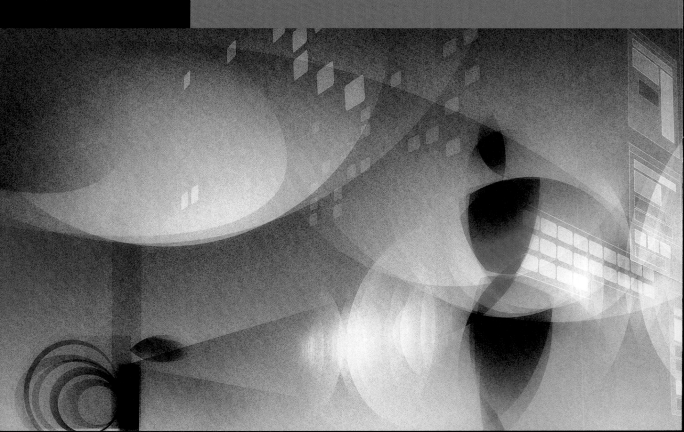

Recording a Podcast

Podcasts are one of the most popular sources of entertainment and information available on the Internet. Podcasts are similar to radio or television shows, in that they deliver audio and video to their audience. A key difference, though, is that a podcast is not broadcast using traditional means. Rather, a person subscribes to the show (usually for free) and then it is delivered to the subscriber's computer.

One of the reasons for podcasting's popularity is that shows can be viewed (or listened to) in a variety of ways. They can, of course, be watched on a computer, but they can also be sent to portable media players like iPods, as well as to television sets via an Apple TV or a Digital Video Recorder device.

With GarageBand '08, you can create your podcast episodes and then upload them to the Internet using iWeb or another application. There are four primary types of podcasts: audio podcasts; enhanced audio podcasts with markers, artwork, and URLs; video podcasts containing a movie; and enhanced video podcasts containing a movie, markers, artwork, and URLs.

In this lesson, you'll learn how to create a new podcast episode and set up voice tracks for recording. You'll then work on an enhanced audio podcast with multiple tracks, markers, artwork, and URLs. Along the way, you'll also build an opening title sequence, edit marker regions and artwork, and record sound effects directly to the Timeline.

Creating a New Podcast Project

Setting up a new podcast project is easy. GarageBand offers a useful New Podcast Episode template right in the GarageBand welcome screen. Let's build the opening sequence to our podcasting episode.

1   Open GarageBand. If GarageBand is already open, choose File > New.

2   In the GarageBand welcome screen, click the Create New Podcast Episode button.

3   Save the project as *Podcast Template* to your GarageBand projects folder (the default location).

4   Click Create.

The Podcast Template project opens, with the empty Podcast Track, editor with marker information, and Media Browser already showing. The Media Browser contains buttons for three different types of media files (Audio, Photos, Movies), a browser that lets you navigate to the media files you want to use, and a media list showing the media files in the current location.

You can use movie files to create a video podcast. Likewise, any files in the Photos pane of the Media Browser can be used as episode artwork for your podcast.

Besides the default items from your iLife media library, you can add other folders of still images and photos to the Photos pane so you can access artwork files anywhere on your computer.

NOTE ▶ To remove a folder from the Media Browser, hold down the Control key and click the folder. Choose Remove Folders from the pop-up menu that appears.

Showing and Hiding the Podcast Track, Browser, and Editor

By using the New Podcast Episode template from the GarageBand welcome screen, all of the basic tracks and panes needed for a podcast are already showing. However, as you work on your own podcast projects, chances are you'll need to show and hide some tracks and panes to maximize your Timeline workspace.

1 Choose Control > Hide Editor, or press Command-E, to hide the editor.

2 Choose Control > Hide Media Browser, or press Command-R, to hide the Media Browser.

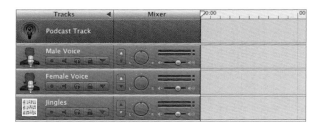

The podcast template includes a Podcast Track and three pre-built audio tracks, including Male Voice, Female Voice, and Jingles. You can always add more tracks or delete unneeded tracks from the Timeline.

To make your vocal tracks easier to hear, GarageBand has automatically enabled ducking. This means that some tracks take priority as lead tracks while others function as backing tracks. By default, the voice tracks are set as priority tracks, whereas the Jingles track is set as a backing track that will be ducked as needed to favor the voice tracks.

NOTE ▶ Whenever a sound is present on a lead track, the volume of the backing tracks is lowered. Ducking is indicated by the arrows pointing up and down next to each track's header. Click the up arrow to indicate a lead track. Click the down arrow to indicate a backing track.

3   Choose Track > Hide Podcast Track, or press Shift-Command-B.

Hiding the Podcast Track while you're working on a podcast is generally a bad idea. In fact, you're more likely to want to show the Podcast Track in a project you may not have originally designated as a podcast.

4   Choose Track > Show Podcast Track, or press Shift-Command-B. Click the Podcast Track to select it.

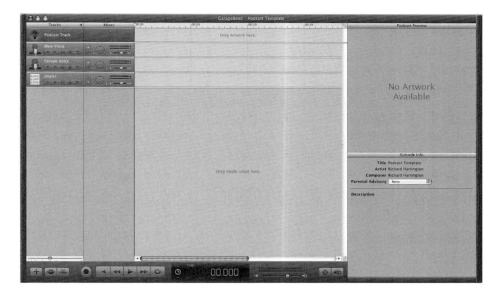

The Podcast Track reappears along with the Track Info pane for the selected track. You'll also see a Podcast Preview pane in the upper-right corner of the window. The Podcast Preview pane—which is similar to the Video Preview pane—allows you to see the podcast's artwork as you play the project.

5   Press Command-R to show the Media Browser and automatically hide the Track Info pane.

6   Press Command-R again to hide the Media Browser.

Hiding the Media Browser will not make the Track Info pane reappear. When a pane is hidden to make room to show another pane in its place, the previous pane remains hidden until you choose to show it again.

Now that you are comfortable with showing and hiding the various panes you'll be using during this lesson, let's move on to setting up a microphone to record your podcast. If you don't have a microphone, you can continue to read the lesson, and an audio file will be provided.

> **NOTE** ▶ A project can include either a Podcast Track or a Video Track, but not both. If you try to show the Video Track for a project that contains a Podcast Track, a dialog appears asking if you want to replace the Podcast Track with a Video Track and vice versa.

Choosing Podcast Recording Equipment

Recording audio for a podcast in GarageBand can be as easy or as complicated as needed for your project. For example, if your podcast needs only one voice track (which can contain more than one speaker), you can record the narration by connecting a microphone to your computer or by using the built-in microphone (if it has one). This could be the built-in iSight camera, which includes a fully functioning microphone. Additionally, you can record remote interviews directly to GarageBand with iChat users.

Voice tracks you record for a podcast are Real Instrument tracks, which means you can record a maximum of eight tracks simultaneously. To record more than one track at a time, you'll need to use an external audio interface, which is explained in more detail below.

> **NOTE** ▶ For this lesson, the audio tracks have already been recorded, so you'll just need to record the opening narration to the show. If your computer doesn't have a microphone, you can use an audio file in the Lessons folder.

Due to the popularity of GarageBand, a variety of third-party recording equipment is available. You don't have to invest in additional hardware, but most podcasters purchase a standalone microphone.

To record the introduction to the podcast, I used the Blue Snowball USB microphone, which plugs into any USB port. It doesn't require any additional software or drivers, and it works well for these types of projects. There are several different brands to choose from, however, so be sure to explore your options.

For the interviews with the band, we needed three microphones to be recorded discretely. For this, I used an FP10 24-bit/96K FireWire Recording System from PreSonus. The FireWire audio interfaces can allow for up to 8 audio sources to be recorded simultaneously.

MORE INFO ▶ You can find more information on GarageBand accessories on the Apple website.

Again, let me stress that additional equipment is not necessary to create a podcast. You can often get along with minimal equipment. A microphone, though, is a reasonable purchase and can greatly improve the sound of your podcast.

Before recording, make sure that your equipment is turned on and properly connected to the computer. For more specifics on the operation of your equipment, refer to the equipment manuals.

Exploring the Vocal Track Presets

In order to improve the sound of a recorded voice, GarageBand includes microphone settings and vocal enhancement effects. These can be applied to a vocal track before or after recording. Let's record a voice.

1   In the Timeline, double-click either the Male Voice track header or the Female Voice track header, depending on your gender.

The Track Info pane appears for the selected track. Notice that the Podcasting instrument category has been selected, and Male Radio (or Female Radio) is the specific preset.

There are five Male Voice presets: iSight Microphone Male, Male Narrator Noisy, Male Narrator, Male Radio Noisy, and Male Radio. The same presets are available for Female Voice.

The presets with *Noisy* in the title include an automatic noise reduction filter to help eliminate unwanted background noise in the track.

The iChat and iSight presets are made for tracks using those types of recordings.

2   In the Track Info pane, select the Male Narrator or Female Narrator preset.

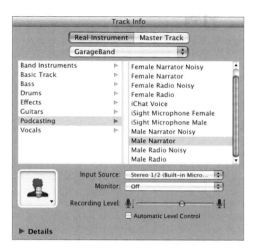

The preset effect changes, and the Track Header's name changes to reflect the new preset.

3   In the Track Info pane, click the Details disclosure triangle in order to reveal the effect's details.

This preset contains three effects to enhance a standard narrator voice recording. A Bass Reduction effect can pull out the low end (or rumble) in the recording. The slight Reverb effect can help fill in the sound by simulating reflections of sound. Finally, the Manual settings for the Speech Enhancer let you specify which type of microphone you're using. This is a helpful way to improve the recorded sound if you're using the built-in microphone on your computer.

4   Click the Edit button (which looks like a pencil) to open the Speech Enhancer controls for the Male (or Female) Narrator preset.

The Speech Enhancer controls include a preset pop-up menu, which will automatically change to Manual if you modify any of the current settings. There is also a Reduce Noise slider, which is currently at the lowest setting. In the Microphone Type menu, you can choose the type of microphone, and in the Voice Type menu, you can select the type of voice.

5   Select the Microphone Type box, then click the Microphone Type menu to see the different choices, ranging from MacBook to iMac Intel. Choose the microphone type that best fits your recording situation. Use Generic if you're using an external microphone.

6   Choose a preset from the Preset menu at the top of the Speech Enhancer dialog. Try a preset that best suits the type of recording you might use in a podcast. If you're unsure, try Male Narrator or Female Narrator.

    An alert appears, showing that you've made changes to the current instrument settings.

7   Click Save As, then name the preset My Podcast Voice, and click Save.

8   In the Speech Enhancer dialog, choose your new preset from the menu. Then close the Speech Enhancer dialog to add your custom settings to the selected track.

NOTE ▶ Once you've made changes to a track's preset vocal effect, you may want to change the name of the track to reflect the current effects.

Project Tasks

You now need to record the introductory voiceover for the podcast. Let's take a moment and try recording to the track you just set up. You can use the shortcuts R to start recording and the spacebar to pause. Be sure that the track you want to record is selected and the Record Enable button is turned on.

If you have a microphone attached to your computer, you can read the script below.

> Welcome to this week's edition of the Listening Room, bringing you the best in live music. Join us each week for interviews and music with bands coming to your neighborhood.
>
> This week's episode is brought to you by Raster Vector. For the latest in computer graphics news, visit Raster Vector Dot Com.
>
> This week's guest is the Brindley Brothers, a Washington, DC-based band led by singer/songwriter Luke Brindley. Luke is joined by his brother Daniel on bass, keys, and vocals, and brother-in-law Jared Bartlett on guitar.

If you aren't happy with your first try, you can stop the recording, erase it, and try again.

NOTE ▶ If you don't have a microphone attached to your computer, open the file **12_Podcast_Template_Stage_Two.band** to use in the next part of the lesson.

Working with Jingles and Sound Effects

Now that you know how to create a new podcast project and set up your vocal tracks, let's complete the show's opening by adding sound effects and a jingle.

1 Continue working with your current podcast project or open the file **12_Podcast_Template_Stage_Two.band** from the Lesson12 folder.

2   Click the View button (which looks like an eyeball) to show the Loop Browser.

You can now access a musical jingle to use in the show's opening..

3   Use the following path to access a musical jingle: Jingles > Rock/Blues > Glide Long.

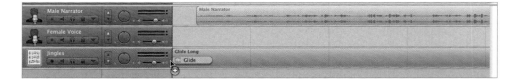

When you click the jingle, it begins to preview the audio. This is a useful way to audition clips. You can click other tracks to preview them.

4   Drag the Glide Long jingle into the Jingles track. Be sure to drag it all the way to the left to ensure that the music begins at the start of the Timeline.

Now that you've selected the music, let's add a sound effect to complete the background audio. Because GarageBand ships with several sound effects, you can quickly perform a search based on a keyword.

5   Click Sound Effects, then, in the search field, type the word *clap*, as shown in the bottom center of the image below. Because the Podcast Sounds View is selected, GarageBand will search the available podcast sounds.

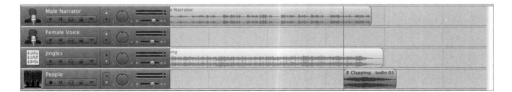

GarageBand should return four matches, three of a clapping crowd and one thunder clap.

6   Click each sound to audition it.

The sound Clapping Crowd Studio 03 should be the best match. It sounds like a small group and is the right intensity level for the audience size we're simulating.

7   In the Timeline, position the playhead around 33:00 (your narration should be finished by this point).

NOTE ▸ If your LCD display doesn't show the time in seconds, choose Control > Show Time in LCD.

8   Drag the sound effect Clapping Crowd Studio 03 to an empty area near the bottom of the Timeline and position it to start at 33:00.

A new track named People is created to hold the Clapping sound effect.

9   Click the "Go to Beginning" button in the transport controls to move the playhead to the beginning of the project.

10 Press the spacebar to play the project.

You'll notice that the music and sound effects automatically play lower under the vocal track. This is because ducking is enabled (as indicated by the up and down arrows next to the track names). The vocal track has been set to behave as the lead track. The jingle and sound effects tracks have their arrows pointing down, which indicates that they're backing tracks.

11 The overall volume of the Jingle track is a little high. To adjust its volume, use the track volume slider. Adjust until you find a value that balances with your voice. A negative value will work best.

12 If needed, adjust the volume of your narration track by moving your track volume slider.

13 Choose File > Save As.

Name the File *Podcast Open* and select the checkbox for Save as Archive to bundle the project. Save the project to the default GarageBand folder inside your User folder ([User] > Music > GarageBand). If you store the project in the GarageBand folder, it will appear in the Media Browser.

14 Close the project by choosing File > Close.

15 When prompted, click Yes to include an iLife preview.

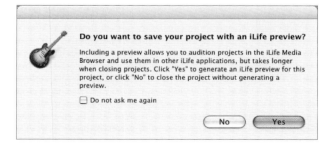

The preview file makes it easier to use the GarageBand project with the other iLife applications.

NOTE ▶ You can compare your work to the file **Lessons > Lesson12 > 12_Podcast_Open_END.band**, which is located in the Lessons folder.

Editing the Podcast

Now that you know how to set up and edit a basic podcast, we'll jump forward in time and work with a mostly completed show. You'll find a project called **12_Brindley_Brothers_ Interview_START.band**, which contains three recorded Real Instrument voice tracks, four music tracks containing orange (imported) Real Instrument regions, and one empty Podcast Track. Open this project so we are both working with the same project file.

You'll notice that the ducking controls are hidden. Due to the complex nature of this project, we'll use Automation Gain to manually mix the levels of the individual tracks. But before we mix our audio, there's a little cleanup to be done.

Adjusting a Recorded Track

The recording of the interviewer (Rich) contains a little background noise that can be removed. It'll be easier to make this fix by isolating the track temporarily.

1   Move the playhead to 01:00 (1 minute) in the time display. This is right before the Interviewer (Rich) speaks for the first time.

2   Press C to show the Cycle Region Ruler. A gold bar appears at the top of the Timeline.

3   Drag the cycle region so it begins just before the first waveform for Rich. Then drag its right edge and extend it slightly beyond the end of the first question (from 01:00 to around 01:10).

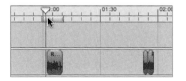

This will keep the audio playing in just this area as we make adjustments.

NOTE ▶ If you can't see the gold bar, drag the zoom slider (under the Master Volume checkbox) to the left until the bar is visible.

4   If you do not already have the Track Info pane open for the selected track, double-click the Rich track header to open it. Then click the Details disclosure triangle to see the track's details.

The track has the Speech Enhancer effect applied, with the Male Narrator preset.

5   Click the Edit button to open the Speech Enhancer controls.

6   Press the spacebar to begin playback of the cycle region.

7   Press S to solo the selected track (that is, to hear it independent of the other tracks).

You can hear a bit of room noise when Rich speaks. You may not be able to get rid of all the noise, but you can certainly remove some of it.

8   Continue playback and drag the Reduce Noise slider from the lowest setting (quiet noise) to the highest setting (loud noise). Feel free to choose a setting in between that you like better.

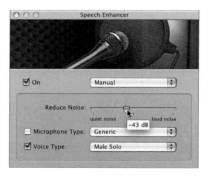

Can you hear the difference in the noise while he's talking? Let's also change the Voice Type effects preset on his track.

9   Continue playback and change the Voice Type pop-up menu from Male Solo to Male Voice Over.

10   Close the Speech Enhancer dialog and pause playback.

11   Press S to unsolo the Rich track, then press C to hide the Cycle Region Ruler.

As you can see, it's easy to apply the Speech Enhancer effects to a track before or after it's been recorded.

Importing a GarageBand Project

If you look at the entire Timeline, you'll notice a gap at the start of the project. This is where you'll place the show opening that you built at the start of the lesson. GarageBand makes it easy to import one project into another.

![GarageBand Timeline showing the project with multiple tracks and a gap at the start]

NOTE ▶ In order to easily add one project to another you should save it to the default GarageBand folder and include an iLife preview. You did both of these steps earlier in this lesson.

1   Click the Go to Beginning button to rewind your podcast to the start.

2   If it's not visible, press Command-R to show the Media Browser. Click the Audio button to show the Audio pane within the browser.

Your iTunes folder and default GarageBand folder are automatically showing in the Audio pane.

3   Click the GarageBand icon to show all of the contents of your GarageBand folder.

4   Scroll through the folder contents in the lower pane of the Media Browser.

Normal GarageBand project file icons look like a document (paper) with a guitar printed on it. GarageBand project files saved with an iLife preview show only a guitar icon.

5 Drag the **Podcast Open** project from the Media Browser to the beginning of the Timeline and drop it in an empty area below your music tracks.

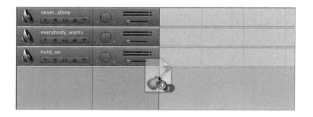

The project file appears in the Timeline as an orange Real Instrument region. The small guitar icon in the upper-left corner of the region shows that it's a GarageBand project instead of a normal audio file.

6 Play the first part of the project to hear the Podcast Open and the start of the interview.

The open works well, but the applause noise starts a little early. Because the audio track is a GarageBand project, we can easily modify it.

7 Double-click the Podcast Open track to open it in the track editor.

8 Click the Open Original button to modify the track.

GarageBand confirms that you want to close the current project and open the Podcast Open file.

9 Cick the Open Original Project button, then click the Save button to save the current project, then click No to skip the iLife preview.

The original Podcast Open file is now ready to edit.

10 Position the playhead at 35:00.

11 Drag the applause sound effect to start at 35:00.

NOTE ▸ For this exercise, don't worry if your narration isn't quite finished at the point where we add the applause. We have to use the same absolute time value to complete the exercise.

12 Choose File > Close and click Yes to save your changes. Click Yes as well for the iLife preview.

The Podcast Open project closes and you are returned to your full podcast project.

13 Because the duration of the audio file has changed, GarageBand prompts you to adjust the file in your Timeline. Click the Update Region button to make the fix.

> The length of "Podcast Open" has been modified and "12_Brindley_Brothers_Interview_MIDDLE" uses a region that links to an older version. Do you want to update the region with the most current version of "Podcast Open"?
>
> This could result in some regions being resized. If "Podcast Open" has gotten longer, this could even overwrite and delete other regions. Clicking cancel permanently breaks the Link between the two projects.
>
> [Cancel]   [Open Original Project]   [Update Region]

14 Choose File > Save to capture your work so far.

You've successfully added a GarageBand project to the Timeline of another project. Although you could have just exported a finished mix of the Podcast Open and added the mixed audio file to a project the same way, it would not preserve your flexibility. By placing one GarageBand project inside another, you can easily make modifications using the Open Original button. Best of all, when you save the changes, the project automatically updates in the Timeline.

Working with Automation Curves

Although GarageBand's ducking controls offer a quick way to mix between audio tracks, they do not offer precise control over audio levels. If you want a better mix you can harness automation curves to gradually adjust a track's volume (or other properties).

1 Click the arrows next to the Rich, Daniel, and Luke tracks to show the automation curves for the tracks.

This automation was previously added when the podcast project was built.

2   Click the automation arrow to disclose the automation for the music track called "hold_on."

3   Scroll the Timeline to the right to see the end of the podcast.

Notice that the "hold_on" music track has some automation applied at its start, but it must be mixed for the remaining part of the podcast. The goal is to have the music gently swell around the vocal interview tracks.

4   Drag the "hold_on" music track up in the Timeline so that it's directly below Luke's audio track.

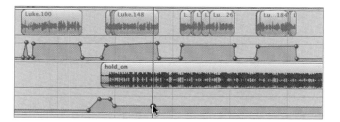

This will make it easier to control as we mix its volume in relation to the vocal interviews.

5   Scroll to approximately 5:50 (this is just before Luke finishes talking).

6   Click the automation curve to add a control point.

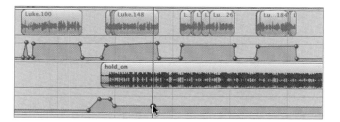

Control points allow you to adjust the automation over time.

7   Go forward to 5:55, then click to add another control point.

8 Drag the control point upward until it reads -6.0 dB.

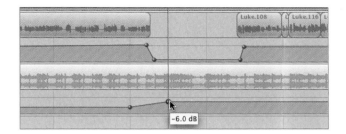

The music now swells to fill in the space between the interview segments.

9 Go forward to 6:02 and click to add another control point.

This will hold the music at this volume for 7 seconds.

10 Go forward to 6:06, click to add another control point, and drag it down to approximately -20.2 dB.

11 Drag the playhead to approximately 5:45 and then click Play to listen to the automation curve applied to the music.

12 On your own, add more control points to finish the automation curve. Adjust the levels so your audio track approximately matches the figure below. The goal is to swell the music in between the interview clips and then perform a gentle swell and fade at the very end.

13 Choose File > Save to capture your work so far.

Working with Artwork and Markers

The next step in building this podcast is to enhance it with artwork, photos, and markers. In this way, we can create a visual identity for the show and add photos of the band that will help the viewer better experience the music and interview.

When you add episode artwork to a podcast, the artwork appears when you play the podcast episode in iTunes (or on an iPod) and when you work with it in iWeb.

Artwork added to the Podcast Track creates a marker region the same length as the artwork in the Podcast Track. Marker regions are used in podcasts to literally *mark* a specific region in the Timeline to include artwork, a chapter title, or a URL. When you publish your podcast as an AAC file, iWeb or other software will use these marker regions to include the designated information for that region in the project.

You can edit, move, and resize marker regions at any time while creating your podcast project. You can also add and edit chapter title markers and URL markers in the Podcast Track. In addition to the artwork used as marker regions in the Podcast Track, you can designate the episode artwork in the editor. The episode artwork appears in the Podcast Preview pane whenever there is no artwork for the current marker region.

Adding Artwork to the Media Browser

The artwork you'll be using for this project is in two folders called **Podcast_Open_Files** and **Band_Photos** inside the Lesson12 folder. You can add artwork folders to the Media Browser by dragging the folders from the Finder into the Photos pane of the Media Browser.

1   In the Media Browser, click the Photos button to show the Photos pane.

2   In the Dock, click the Finder icon to open the Finder window. Locate the iLife Lessons folder on your computer's Desktop.

3   In the Finder, open the **Lesson12** folder and Shift-click to select the **Podcast_Open_Files** and **Band_Photos** folders. Drag them to the Photos pane of the Media Browser. Return to GarageBand.

The Photos for the GarageBand folder appear in the browser.

4   Click the disclosure triangle at the left of the Folders icon to view the folder's contents, if they're not already showing

You'll see that it contains two folders: Podcast_Open_Files and Band_Photos.

5   Press Return to move the playhead to the beginning of the project.

6   Select the Podcast Track to see it in the Track Info pane.

The Podcast Track is where you can view and edit marker regions for a podcast episode.

Adding Episode Artwork to the Project

Episode artwork represents the entire project—like a movie poster or CD cover. People will see it when they choose your podcast to download or preview. The project can have only one piece of episode artwork. Let's take a moment and assign a file as the episode artwork for this podcast.

1   If the editor is not visible, press Command-E to show it.

The editor appears for the Podcast Track. The Episode Artwork well on the side of the editor is currently empty.

The Podcast Preview pane shows that no artwork is available, because the playhead is at the beginning of the project where there is no artwork in the Podcast Track.

2   If the Media Browser is not visible, press Command-R to show it.

3   In the upper pane of the Media Browser, select the Podcast_Open_Files folder.

These titles are JPEG graphic files. You can create title graphics using programs like Keynote, Motion, and Adobe Photoshop.

4   Select the file **Open3.jpg** and drag it to the Episode Artwork well in the editor.

The episode artwork appears in the editor.

5   Press Command-I to show the Track Info pane.

The episode artwork appears in the Podcast Preview pane because there is no other artwork at the playhead position of the Podcast Track.

If you change your mind after you've added episode artwork, just drag the artwork from the well. Alternatively, you can add another piece of artwork to the well to replace the original.

Adding Artwork to the Podcast Track

Now it's time to add artwork to the show. First you'll add art to the opening introduction, then to the band interview. Let's zoom in to the Timeline for a larger view of the Podcast Track as you add the artwork.

1   Press Control-right arrow until the ruler shows 10-second increments instead of 30-second increments.

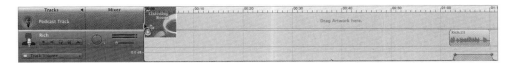

2   Press Command-R, or click the Media Browser button, to show the Media Browser.

If you add artwork to the beginning of an empty space in the Podcast Track, it will automatically fill the space.

3   Drag the file **Open1.jpg** from the Media Browser to the beginning of the Podcast Track in the Timeline and release the mouse button.

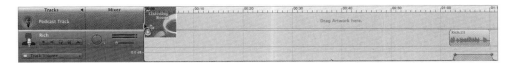

A marker region appears and fills the empty space at the beginning of the Podcast Track.

NOTE ▶   If you released the artwork too far to the left or right, it won't start at the very beginning of the track. Simply drag the beginning of the marker region toward the left until it extends to the beginning of the track.

4   Press the spacebar to play the podcast. When the announcer starts to discuss the show sponsor (around 13:00), press the spacebar to pause playback.

5   From the Media Browser, drag the file **Open2.jpg** into the Podcast Track.

6   Press the spacebar to play the podcast. When the announcer starts to discuss the show's guests (around 23:00), press the spacebar to pause playback.

7   From the Media Browser, drag the file **Open3.jpg** into the Podcast Track.

8   Press Command-I to see the artwork for the current playhead position in the Podcast Preview pane.

9   Press the Return key to jump to the beginning of your podcast, then play the project from the beginning to see the artwork in the Podcast Preview pane.

You're off to a great start, but you can further enhance the podcast by filling in some more photos. Keep in mind that although you don't have to use photos in a podcast, they can often improve the entertainment value of your show.

10   Press Command-R to show the Media Browser. Then select the Band_Photos folder.

This folder contains 23 images that you will use to fill in the rest of the podcast.

11   Drag the photos into the Podcast Track and attempt to synchronize them with the interview.

There is no "right" answer as to where these should be placed. You can use the list below for guidance, or make your own decisions.

```
00:00:00.000   Open1.jpg
00:00:13.000   Open2.jpg
00:00:23.000   Open3.jpg
00:00:39.000   01_Cover.jpg
00:00:50.000   02_Luke.jpg
00:01:10.000   03_Daniel.jpg
```

00:01:30.000	04_Club.jpg
00:01:52.000	05_Roof.jpg
00:02:05.000	06_Club.jpg
00:02:21.000	07_Luke.jpg
00:02:35.000	08_Club.jpg
00:02:58.000	09_Brindley.jpg
00:03:09.000	10_Luke.jpg
00:03:37.000	11_Luke.jpg
00:03:57.000	12_Daniel.jpg
00:04:10.000	13_Luke.jpg
00:04:35.000	14_Brindley.jpg
00:05:00.000	15_Daniel.jpg
00:05:10.000	16_Club.jpg
00:05:20.000	17_New_Cover.jpg
00:05:45.000	18_Luke.jpg
00:05:55.000	19_Club.jpg
00:06:23.000	20_Club.jpg
00:06:35.000	21_Club.jpg
00:06:45.000	22_Club.jpg
00:06:57.000	23_Roof.jpg

12 Press Command-I to show the Track Info pane and Podcast Preview pane.

13 Watch the beginning of the project and listen to the audio.

Any thoughts? A few of the pictures are cropped and can be adjusted to improve their appearance.

Resizing and Cropping Artwork

GarageBand includes a handy Artwork Editor you can use to resize and crop your artwork to show all or part of the original image. To access the Artwork Editor, double-click the artwork in the project.

1 In the Marker list, click the artwork at approximately 00:05:45.000 (it's a black-and-white shot of Luke).

2 Double-click the marker's thumbnail to open the Artwork Editor.

3 Drag the photo down so the head and shoulders are visible.

4 Click the Set button to apply the change.

5 In the Marker list, click the artwork at approximately 00:06:45.000 (it's a shot of Luke from the back of the stage).

6 Double-click the marker's thumbnail to open the Artwork Editor.

7 Drag the scale slider and reposition the photo so it's more tightly cropped. You want to make the photo look different because you used it earlier.

Click Set to apply the change.

8   Modify the last marker in your list so it's a tighter shot of Daniel and Luke.

9   Choose File > Save to capture your progress.

Good job. You've completed the podcast artwork. All that's left is to add URL markers and publishing information.

Viewing Marker Information
You can see more information about a project's markers, artwork, and marker regions in the editor. You can also select markers and change or update their information.

1   If the editor is not visible, press Command-E to open it.

The marker regions are listed in chronological order from the beginning of the project. The editor includes columns that show Time, Artwork, Chapter Title, URL Title, and URL for each marker.

2   Drag the vertical scroller to scroll down through all of the project's markers.

As you can see, there are several markers in this podcast.

The checkboxes in the Markers area of the editor show how the marker will be designated. Adding artwork to a marker region automatically selects the Displays Artwork checkbox for that marker.

Adding a URL to a Marker
You can add a URL (web address) to a marker region in a podcast or a marker in a movie and view the URL when you play the movie or podcast in iTunes. Not only will viewers

see the URL when they play the finished project, but they can also click the URL onscreen to open the webpage in their browsers.

If you add a URL title, the title appears in the Album Artwork window of iTunes (in a published podcast) and clicking it opens the webpage for the URL. An example of a URL title might be "For More Information," or "Check out our website."

Let's add a URL title and link to the end of the project. You'll add the URL to an existing marker region. To get there, you could navigate in the Timeline or simply double-click the marker in the editor.

1   In the editor, locate the last marker in your list. Then double-click any blank area on the marker's row in the marker list to jump to the marker's location in the Timeline.

The playhead jumps to the marker's location in the Timeline.

2   For the selected marker, click the URL Title field. Type *Visit the Brindley Brothers* and press Return.

3   For the selected marker, click the URL field. Type *www.brindleybrothers.com* and press Return.

GarageBand will automatically add *http://* to the address.

Notice the checkmark for the Displays URL option after you add a URL to the marker.

The URL also appears on the marker region in the Podcast Track to show that the marker includes a URL.

4   If the Track Info pane is not visible, press Command-I to open it. Play the marker to see the URL title appear in the Podcast Preview pane.

Feel free to click the URL title in the Podcast Preview pane to open the webpage. If your computer is not currently connected to the Internet, your browser will try to open the page and then tell you that you're not connected.

Project Tasks

The URL title and link you added work great. But the URL isn't onscreen very long. To give viewers enough time to see and click the URL, let's add the same information to the previous marker as well. Select the marker region that starts at 00:06:45.000 and add the same URL title and URL as you did in the previous marker. You can retype the information in each field, or copy and paste the information from a field in one marker to the same field in another. When you're finished, save your progress.

Adding Episode Info to a Podcast

The last step needed to complete your podcast episode is to add the episode information, which includes the title, artist information, a description of the episode, and a parental advisory. The episode information is available when you work on the podcast in iWeb and when you view the podcast in iTunes.

1   Select the Podcast Track in the Timeline.

2   Show the Track Info pane, if it's not already showing.

3   Click the Description area and type *An interview with Washington, D.C. band the Brindley Brothers.*

4   From the Parental Advisory menu, choose Clean.

5   Change the Artist name field to *the Brindley Brothers.*

6   Change the Title field to the Listening Room – Episode 45.

Episode Info	
Title	The Listening Room – Episode 45
Artist	The Brindley Brothers
Composer	Richard Harrington
Parental Advisory	Clean
Description	
An interview with Washington, D.C. band the Brindley Brothers.	

The description could be more in-depth if you'd like. You might include the names of the band members, list the songs included in the podcast, and provide other information.

7   Press Command-S to save the finished podcast.

8   Play the podcast from start to finish to see the completed project.

NOTE ▶ If you didn't complete all of the steps in this lesson and would like to see the finished version of the podcast, open the project **12_Brindley_Brothers_Interview_END.band** from the Lesson12 folder.

Congratulations! You've created an enhanced podcast and gained a good working knowledge of how to build your own podcasts. Once you've created a podcast episode, you can publish it using iWeb. You'll learn more specifics on how to export and share your finished podcast in Lesson 15.

Lesson Review

1. How do you create a new podcast using the Podcast Episode template?
2. Where can you add and adjust the Speech Enhancer effects for a voice track?
3. What must you do to a project so that it can be previewed or added to another project?
4. In what two locations can you add artwork to a podcast?
5. How do you crop or resize artwork in a podcast project?
6. Where do you add URL titles or URL information to a marker region?
7. Where do you edit the podcast episode information?

Answers

1. You can open a New Podcast Episode template from the GarageBand welcome screen.
2. In the Track Info details area, click the Edit button to open the Speech Enhancer dialog and modify the effects settings on the selected track.
3. You must save the project with an iLife preview in order to preview it in the Media Browser and use it in another project.
4. You can add artwork to a podcast as a marker region in the Podcast Track or as marker information in the editor.
5. You can crop or resize podcast artwork by double-clicking the artwork in the editor and modifying it in the Artwork Editor.
6. You add URL titles or URL information to a marker region in the editor.
7. You can edit a podcast episode's information in the Track Info pane for the Podcast Track.

13

Lesson Files iLife08_Book_Files > Lessons > Lesson13

Time This lesson takes approximately 90 minutes to complete.

Goals Create music with Magic GarageBand

Explore the GarageBand window

Add and change a software instrument

Record a software instrument

Explore real instrument tracks

Change the tempo of a track

Mix tracks

Share a song with other iLife applications

Creating Music with GarageBand

If you've completed the exercises in the previous two lessons, you already have a basic understanding of how GarageBand works. You've explored using tracks and adjusting those tracks, and have even recorded a new track using a microphone. Now it's time to dive in and start filling your tracks with custom music that you create using Software and Real Instruments.

In this lesson, you're going to learn editing and recording techniques for building music with Software Instrument regions. You'll also learn how to change the tempo, record your own beats, and split, join, and change instruments for Software Instrument tracks in the Timeline.

Once you know the basics of working with Software Instruments, we'll take a quick look at more advanced recording and arranging techniques. Along the way, you'll learn some new keyboard shortcuts and advanced techniques. But to get things started, we'll take a look at Magic Garage-Band, which can help you create a new song.

Exploring Magic GarageBand

Magic GarageBand is a great way to explore the music creation options of GarageBand. With it, you can use your Mac or a real instrument to play along with virtual musicians. When you create a Magic GarageBand song, you specify a genre (or style) of music as well as which instruments to use in the song. GarageBand then creates the song, which you can choose to play along with.

Creating a Song with Magic GarageBand

With nine musical genres to choose from, Magic GarageBand can serve as a catalyst for creativity. You can create a new song, then record your own part or practice playing along.

1   Launch GarageBand. If GarageBand is already open, choose File > New.

2   In the GarageBand welcome screen, click the Magic GarageBand button.

The Magic GarageBand stage appears and presents you with nine genres to choose from. For this lesson, I think a trip to a tropical island would be relaxing.

3   Click the Reggae genre button (located below the stage) to select it.

4   Click the Play button to audition the song.

TIP ▶ You can choose to preview the Entire Song if you'd like to hear it in its entirety. If you'd like to just hear a good sample, choose Snippet.

The music plays in its default arrangement. You can use the volume slider if you need to increase the song's volume temporarily.

5   Click the Audition button to customize the song and modify the instruments.

The curtain opens to reveal the Magic GarageBand stage. The instruments in your song are on the stage. To customize the song you can change which instruments are used.

Customizing a Song with Magic GarageBand

Once the stage is set, you can easily swap instruments and try out new musical combinations. Magic GarageBand offers more than 3,000 possible combinations of sounds for each genre.

1   Click the Play button to start the song playing again.

2   Click the Drums at the center of the stage.

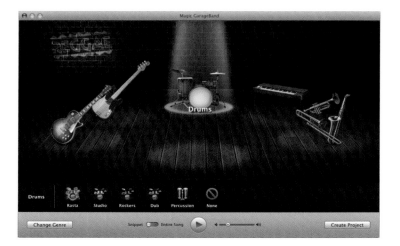

New instruments load below the stage.

3   Choose the Dub drums from the list below the stage.

The music preview updates to include the instrument change.

4   Click the Keyboard icon to select it, then choose the Electric Piano.

5   Click the Guitar at the front of the stage and change it to a Wah Wah guitar.

The stage is set and you can now create a song.

6   Click My Instrument at the center of the stage to specify which instrument you'd like to play.

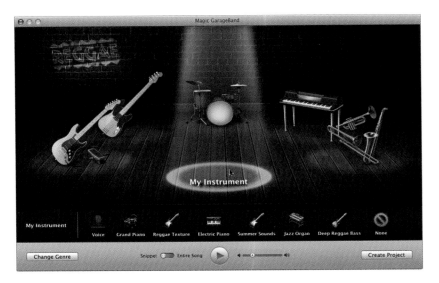

GarageBand offers you several choices. You can choose to record your voice with a built-in or attached microphone. You can record a piano or organ part using a MIDI or computer keyboard. If you own a guitar or other musical instrument, you can attach it to specialized hardware and record with GarageBand.

For this lesson, choose the Grand Piano.

7   Click the Create Project button to create a new song with the chosen instruments.

If it wasn't already open, the GarageBand window opens with tracks visible in the Timeline for each of the instruments in the song.

8   Choose File > Save As. Name the song Reggae Jam and save it to your GarageBand folder.

After you create a song with Magic GarageBand, you can edit, rearrange, and remix the song.

Exploring Tracks and Regions

Let's take a moment to examine what makes up the song in the Timeline. The song **Reggae Jam** contains six tracks. Each track, in turn, contains individual musical parts—regions—from a particular instrument. An instrument track may contain only one region, or it may contain many smaller regions—individual takes and retakes, often called overdubs—which, when arranged in a track, are the basic building blocks of an entire instrument's part for a song.

Regions come in a variety of colors (by type) and sizes. A track may have one region that lasts the entire duration of the song, or different regions representing different musical parts played by the same instrument at different times in the song.

Real Instruments

Purple, blue, and orange regions represent Real Instrument parts recorded from Real Instruments.

You can record Real Instrument parts into GarageBand through a microphone, guitar, or keyboard that is plugged into the microphone jack on your computer. You can also record Real Instrument parts through other input devices that you connect to your computer.

Real Instrument regions are placed in the Timeline as is. Once a Real Instrument region has been recorded into the Timeline, you can enhance the tuning, timing, and pitch. However, in contrast to Software Instruments, Real Instrument regions do not include individual notes, so you can't change the content of a Real Instrument region once it's recorded.

Software Instruments

Software Instruments are recorded performances that are more flexible than Real Instruments because they're recordings of MIDI note events, rather than sounds. Software Instruments utilize some of the same powerful music editing tools found in Apple's professional recording software, Logic.

> **NOTE** ▶ MIDI stands for Musical Instrument Digital Interface. It's an industry standard that allows all devices, such as synthesizers and computers, to communicate with each other.

Software Instrument regions are green and are recorded using a USB music keyboard, a MIDI synthesizer–type keyboard, the GarageBand onscreen keyboard, or Musical Typing, with the GarageBand software and your computer's keyboard serving as the MIDI instrument. Because Software Instrument regions don't contain sounds from actual musical instruments, they don't display the sounds, or notes, as waveforms, as do Real Instrument regions (purple or blue). Software Instrument regions represent individual notes as "note events" that look like a series of bars, lines, or dashes, which can be assigned to any Software Instrument, before or after it's recorded.

Later in the lesson you'll record a Software Instrument track that looks similar to this.

Once the notes for the Software Instrument region are recorded, you can change the sound of the instrument that plays the notes, fix the timing, notation, and velocity, or change the pitch of the region to a different key.

For this song, the Grand Piano track is a Software Instrument track, which is ready to be recorded.

Recording a New Software Instrument Part

Now that your project is set up, it's time to start recording an additional part. In this next exercise, you'll record a synth part for the song. Don't worry if you aren't a musician; you can just play along. There are several ways to play musical notes in GarageBand.

Using the Onscreen Music Keyboard

One option for playing music with GarageBand is the onscreen music keyboard. You can use the keyboard to both play and record Software Instruments.

1   To show the onscreen music keyboard, choose Window > Keyboard.

When you activate the onscreen music keyboard, it displays four octaves of keys by default. You can drag the lower-right corner of the keyboard to resize it, showing up to ten octaves.

TIP The onscreen keyboard includes an overview feature, which appears as a miniature keyboard above the main keyboard. This can help you quickly change the range of notes the keys play.

2   Play the onscreen keyboard by clicking the notes on the keyboard.

Although you can play music this way, it's not the easiest way to create complex music arrangements.

3   Let's change the range of the onscreen keyboard. You can use any of the following methods:

▶ Drag the blue rectangle in the overview area over the range you want to play using the onscreen keyboard. For this song, drag to the left to use a lower octave.

▶   You can also click an area of the overview outside the blue rectangle to move it to where you clicked.

▶   Finally, you can click one of the small triangles to the left and right of the keys. Clicking the left triangle lowers the range by one octave, and clicking the right triangle raises the range by one octave.

Working with Musical Typing

Musical Typing is a GarageBand alternative for recording Software Instrument tracks. Instead of using the onscreen keyboard or external MIDI musical instrument, you use your computer's keyboard. Let's try it.

For this test, you'll use the existing Grand Piano track.

1   Choose Window > Musical Typing or press Command-Shift-K.

TIP ▶ If the onscreen keyboard is visible, you can switch between it and the Musical Typing window by clicking the buttons in the upper-left area of the window.

The Musical Typing window opens and turns your computer keyboard into a fully functional MIDI keyboard.

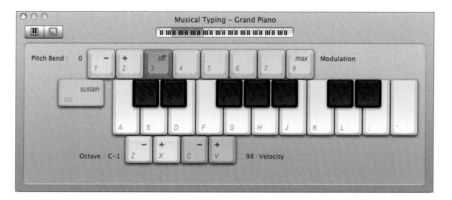

The Musical Typing window illustrates how different keys on your computer keyboard correspond to different musical notes.

2   Press various letter keys on your computer keyboard to hear the corresponding notes.

Whenever you press a key on the computer keyboard, the corresponding key is selected in the Musical Typing window. Because you currently have the Grand Piano track selected, you're playing that instrument.

The Musical Typing window includes keys for sustain (Tab) and changing octaves (Z, X), velocity or volume (C, V), pitch bend (1, 2), and modulation (3–8).

3   Press several keys and watch the time display carefully.

A small blue dot flashes in the bottom corner of the LCD. That flashing dot is the MIDI status light that indicates that GarageBand is receiving a MIDI signal. This reacts to any MIDI signal, whether it comes from an external MIDI device, your computer keyboard in Musical Typing mode, or the onscreen keyboard.

NOTE ▶ If you have another external MIDI device active when you open the Musical Typing window, you may see a steady blue dot rather than a flashing blue dot until you play notes on the device.

Connecting a MIDI Instrument to the Computer

If you prefer to use an external music keyboard, guitar, or other MIDI controller instead of Musical Typing for this exercise, you can connect a MIDI-compatible controller through a USB connection or MIDI interface.

A USB MIDI keyboard or other MIDI controller connects directly to the computer and to the keyboard with a USB cable.

To connect a standard MIDI controller such as a keyboard, you'll need a USB-to-MIDI interface. Connect the keyboard to the MIDI interface device using standard MIDI cables. Then connect the interface to your computer using the USB cable. Carefully read the instructions that come with the keyboard and MIDI interface, and be sure to install all of the necessary drivers.

> **MORE INFO** ▸ For more information about GarageBand accessories, including MIDI keyboards, USB keyboards, or MIDI interfaces, visit Apple's website.

Using the Arrange Track

If you listen to most songs, they're usually arranged into distinct sections such as introduction, verse, and chorus. GarageBand '08 allows you to use this kind of structure for your song. Besides making it easier to see the parts of your song, you can also rearrange your song at any time.

1   Click the Chorus arrange region located at the top of the GarageBand window.

> **NOTE** ▸ If the Arrange track isn't visible, choose Track > Show Arrange Track.

2   Hold down the Shift key and click Verse 1.

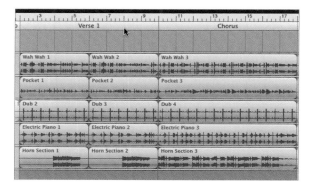

Now that you have the arrange regions selected, you can easily reuse them.

3   Hold down the Option key and drag a copy of the arrangement to the right of the Timeline.

A copy of the arrangements is now draggable.

4   Drag the cloned arrangements between the Chorus and Verse 2.

Two arrangements called Verse 1 Copy and Chorus Copy are added to the Timeline. The arrangements can be better named, though, to make it easier to navigate the song's Timeline.

5   Double-click the Verse 1 Copy arrangement region's title.

The title for the arrange region can now be edited.

6   Change the title for the region to Verse 2.

7   Rename the remaining two regions Chorus and Verse 3.

Mixer

TIP ▸ To add a new region, click the plus symbol in the Mixer area of the Arrange track.

Recording Multiple Takes

When recording your musical parts into GarageBand, it may take you a few tries to get it just right. Musicians often want to record multiple versions, or *takes*, in quick succession. This can be very useful when you're improvising and want to capture several versions, or if you'd like to record your practice takes to evaluate your performance. Later on, you can choose which take you want to use in the project as well as edit your selected takes.

> **NOTE ▶** You can record multiple takes for both Real Instrument and Software Instrument recordings. This is a great way to experiment with new options in your GarageBand project.

1   Near the bottom of the Timeline, click the Cycle button to turn on the cycle region.

A yellow cycle region appears at the top of the Timeline. You can move or resize the cycle region to identify where you want a recording to start and end.

2   Drag the edges of the yellow cycle region to resize it. Using the Arrange track as a guide, set the cycle region to the duration of the first chorus.

3   Click the track header for Grand Piano.

Now you're going to jam along with the song. Don't worry about your skill level as a musician; just jump up on the virtual stage and be a part of the band. You can use Musical Typing, the onscreen keyboard, or a MIDI keyboard to play along.

4   Click the Record button and start recording your Software Instrument.

As you record the take, the playhead moves from the start to the end of the cycle region. After the first pass, the playhead resets to the start of the region. A new take is recorded each time the playhead moves through the cycle region.

5 Continue recording for 5 or more attempts, until you're happy with your performance.

6 When you're finished recording, click the Play button.

A number appears at the end of the region name in parentheses, indicating how many takes you recorded. A circled number in the upper-left corner of the region also appears, showing the currently active take, which is initially the most recent take you recorded.

7 Click the circled number and select one of your earlier takes. Listen to a few of your takes and select the best one.

Besides switching takes, you can delete the current take, or delete all unused takes in the Takes menu.

TIP When working with Software Instruments, you can take multiple recordings with the cycle region and merge them into a single region. Simply open your Garage-Band preferences, choose the General pane, and select the Cycle Recording checkbox. Merging takes works well when recording drum parts and other layered recordings.

8 Click the Cycle button to turn off the cycle region option.

Changing a Track's Instrument

One of the major benefits of Software Instruments is the ability to preserve your recorded notes while retaining flexibility over the instrument. Essentially, once a Software Instrument track is recorded you can turn a piano into a guitar, or a trumpet, or whatever you like. All you have to do is open the Track Info pane and change the instrument for the track.

1   Double-click the top Grand Piano track header.

    The Track Info pane opens for the selected track.

2   Select Organs as the Software Instrument, and Classic Rock Organ for the specific organ.

3   Press Command + I to close the Track Info pane.

    The first track in the Timeline is now called Classic Rock Organ, and the track icon is an organ.

    NOTE ▶ Notice that the actual Software Instrument region is still called Grand Piano because that was its original name. You can always change the name of a region in the editor. At this time, it's fine to leave the original name as a reminder of how it was recorded.

4   Play the Grand Piano region in the Classic Rock Organ track to hear how it sounds with an organ as the lead instrument.

Fantastic! You'd never know it was originally recorded as a piano part.

Now you see how easy it is to change one Software Instrument to another. This is incredibly useful if you play keyboards but not guitar, for example, or the other way around.

You've done a great job so far. For now, you'll open an existing project file so your project will match the rest of this lesson.

5   Open the file **13_Reggae Jam_Takes.band** from the Lesson13 folder.

This file is nearly identical to the one you just built, but the software instrument track has been filled in more. This file will work well for the remaining steps in this lesson.

NOTE ▶ A special thanks to Megan Tytler for lending her keyboarding skills.

Working with Real Instruments

So far in this book you've utilized several of GarageBand's features including loops, Software Instruments, and microphone recordings. But GarageBand offers so much more. In fact, GarageBand is a full-featured multi-track recording studio. Whether you're a first-time musician or a seasoned pro, you can record, edit, and mix a song exactly as you want it. GarageBand allows you to hook real instruments up to your computer and run a virtual recording studio.

In the next few pages we'll give you a quick overview of using real instruments with GarageBand. Because we don't know which hardware and instruments you have, we'll review general terms and concepts.

TIP ▶ If you want to learn much more about the recording features of GarageBand, be sure to check out the official book by Mary Plummer. *Apple Training Series: GarageBand 3* explores more of GarageBand's capabilities. Even though the book covers the previous version of GarageBand, it still works very well for the current software.

What Are Real Instruments?

Real Instruments are exactly what they sound like: regions recorded from real instruments. With GarageBand, you can record a real instrument such as a guitar, bass, or keyboard directly into the Timeline. You can also use a microphone to record instruments that don't have an output jack, such as a trumpet, violin, grand piano, drum kit, acoustic guitar, or even vocals.

To record a Real Instrument into the Timeline, you have to physically perform or play the part using a real instrument in real time. In contrast to Software Instruments, Real Instrument recordings are "as is"—you can't edit the individual notes or change instruments. However, you can add effects and enhance the tuning and timing of Real Instrument regions once they're recorded.

Why would you record real instruments when you can use Software Instruments? Because they're *real* instruments! Certain instruments can't be simulated very well, so you want to record the real deal.

Suppose you're in a band and you want to record one of your new songs. How do you explain to your drummer that he has to play drums on a MIDI keyboard to get them into the computer? What about the lead vocal, guitar, and bass? Most musicians play best on their chosen instruments, not on a keyboard simulation.

Connecting Musical Instruments to Your Computer

There are basically two types of musical instruments: electric and acoustic. An electric instrument has a built-in interface for output of its sound, but an acoustic instrument needs a microphone to record its sound.

Electric instruments include electric guitars, keyboards, and electric bass. You can connect an electric instrument directly to the computer's audio-in port, if your computer has one. The computer audio-in port is a 1/8-inch mini input, so you'll need an adapter or cable to convert the 1/4-inch output from your instrument to the 1/8-inch audio-in port (mini input) on the computer.

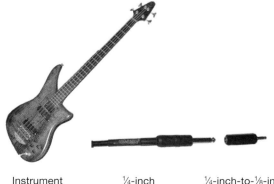

Instrument   ¼-inch   ¼-inch-to-⅛-inch   Computer's
                    instrument cable   mini adapter   audio-in port

To record an acoustic instrument or vocals, you can connect a microphone to your computer through the audio-in port. Mac Pro computers also include optical digital audio in/out ports for higher-end audio recording equipment.

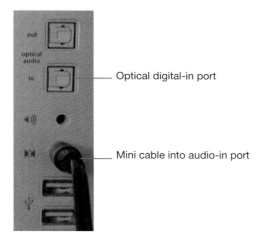

Optical digital-in port

Mini cable into audio-in port

You can also connect an audio interface to your computer and then connect your microphone or instruments to the audio interface. There is a wide range of audio interfaces and compatible formats, including USB, FireWire, PCI, and PC cards. With the addition of an audio interface, GarageBand allows you to record up to eight Real Instrument tracks and one Software Instrument track simultaneously. An audio mixer or console will also record more than one instrument or microphone at once, but it will mix all the inputs into only one stereo track. Our reggae song could have been recorded in a live session with multiple musicians using GarageBand-compatible hardware.

Make sure that whatever audio interface you use is compatible with Mac OS X 10.4 or later (for GarageBand '08) and that your computer supports the format used by the interface.

To set up recording using your Mac's built-in port:

1   Choose System Preferences > Sound > Input and select Line In Audio line-in port as your sound input device.

2   Play your instrument and adjust the Input Level slider until you achieve a good level without peaking/clipping.

Adding a Real Instrument Track

When you create a Real Instrument track for your own recording, you need to specify a few important options. First, choose whether you're recording mono or stereo, and whether you want to monitor (hear) the sound through your speakers or headphones.

At this time, you don't need to set up a musical instrument to record. The steps below are meant as an overview to illustrate the recording process. If you have an electric guitar attached to your computer, you're welcome to follow along.

1   Click the Add Track button (+) located in the bottom-left corner of the GarageBand window to add a new basic track.

2   Select Real Instrument from the New Track dialog, then click Create.

A Real Instrument track appears in the Timeline, and the Track Info pane shows on the right side of the window.

3   In the Track Info pane, select Guitars and No Effects.

4   From the Input Source pop-up menu, choose Mono 1 (Built-in Audio) if you are playing a mono instrument like a bass or guitar, or Stereo 1/2 (Built-in Audio) if you are playing a stereo instrument.

5   From the Monitor pop-up menu, choose On with Feedback Protection so you can hear your instrument through your computer speakers.

Setting Up Your Instrument

If you do have an instrument, play a riff on it now. Do you hear a delay between when you play and when you hear the sound? Depending on the audio hardware and computer you're using, there may be a slight delay when playing and recording Real Instruments. The short amount of time the Real Instrument input takes to reach the computer's input port and be processed is referred to as *latency*. You may not be able to eliminate latency completely, but you can reduce the amount of latency in the GarageBand Preferences.

1   Choose GarageBand > Preferences.

2   Click the Audio/MIDI button to open the Audio/MIDI pane.

3   Locate the "Optimize for" section. Select the "Minimum delay when playing instruments live" option if you're experiencing latency delays when you play your instrument.

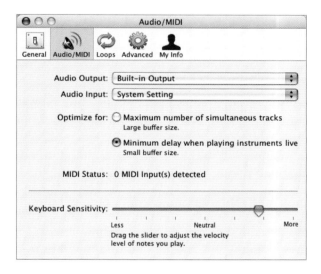

Selecting "Minimum delay when playing instruments live" will reduce latency by using more of the computer's processing power to process the audio input signal faster. However, this option can affect performance on slower computers. If you don't have latency issues and plan to record multiple tracks simultaneously, change the setting to "Maximum number of simultaneous tracks."

4   Click the General button to return to the General Preferences pane. Locate the metronome controls and select the "During playback and recording" option, if it's not already selected.

5   Press Command-W to close Preferences.

Recording a Short Take

Because the track you're about to record has no effects applied to it, the sound of whatever instrument you record will not be altered.

1   Select the empty No Effects track and make sure the Record Enable button for the track is on.

2   Press the spacebar to start the metronome and playback of the empty track in the Timeline. If you don't hear the metronome, press Command-U to turn it on.

3   Play a simple musical riff. Practice a few times until you're ready to record. Press Return to move the playhead to the beginning of the Timeline.

> **TIP** ▶ The keyboard shortcut to start recording is the R key. This is often easier than using the mouse to click the Record button—especially if you're holding a guitar or another instrument.

4   Choose Control > Count In to turn on the Count In feature.

    GarageBand will count in the first four beats before recording begins.

5   Press R, or click the Record button, to record your musical riff.

6   Press the spacebar to stop recording when you're finished.

Those are the essentials steps needed to record an instrument part into GarageBand.

Mixing and Effects

With GarageBand, you can record and create professional-quality music. However, to make your finished songs actually sound professional, you need to understand the fine art of mixing.

In previous lessons, you worked with automation curves to adjust volume over time. Those advanced controls work well for scoring and podcasting projects. For musical projects you'll often want to perform a more straightforward mix. Fortunately, the

GarageBand interface includes an easy-to-use Track Mixer with controls for volume level and pan position.

Your goal in this lesson is to take an arranged song to the next level to make it sound like a professional composition. To accomplish this, you'll need to apply professional mixing techniques, including balancing volume, panning, fixing timing, and adding effects.

Understanding Basic Mixing

Mixing a song is the art of carefully blending all of the different sounds and musical textures into one cohesive, balanced piece of music. Arranging regions in separate tracks is easy once you get the hang of it. Mixing takes a little more practice. It also takes some training. If you have a pair of stereo headphones (even those from an iPod) you should use them now.

Let's start by listening to the finished song.

1   Close and Save your current project as 13_Reggae Jam_Takes.band in your default GarageBand folder.

    Open **13_Reggae Jam_Finished** from the Lesson13 folder.

    This song is properly mixed to balance the different instruments.

2   Play the finished song.

    Now that you've heard the finished piece, let's compare it to the unmixed song.

3   Choose File > Open Recent > **13_Reggae Jam_Takes.band – GarageBand** to open your copy of the project file.

4   Play the first half of the unmixed song and listen for anything that stands out, in either a good or bad way.

    As you play the song, listen for the following:

    ▶   How is the overall pacing/tempo of the song?

    ▶   Are some parts difficult to hear? Do some parts seem too loud? Is the overall volume of the song even?

    ▶   Does the song sound and feel finished?

What was your impression of the unmixed song? My first impression is that the tempo seems a bit slow. Otherwise, all of the musical elements (instruments and parts) are there, but the levels are all over the place. The unmixed song doesn't sound or feel very professional.

Stepping up the tempo of the piece is so easy, let's go ahead and take care of it before moving on and saving the project. Tempo is pacing—the pulse or speed of the song—and it affects how the song sounds and feels. Software Instruments and Apple Loops automatically change tempo to match the project.

The current tempo is 75, which we've already established feels a bit slow. 78 ought to be fast enough to pick up the pace without feeling like it's no longer a reggae song.

5   In the time display, click the current tempo (75) and drag the Tempo slider up to 78.

NOTE ▶ If the tempo is not showing, click the left edge of the LCD and choose the Project display.

6   Play the song again at the new tempo.

Much better. Too bad you can't actually change the tempo of a live performance that easily.

TIP▶ If a part needs to be played faster than you can physically play it, record the part at a slower tempo, then speed up the project's tempo after you're done recording.

7   Press Command-S to save the final changes to the project.

Working with the Track Mixer

The first step to mixing a song in GarageBand is a basic understanding of the Track Mixer. The Track Mixer is located between the track header and the Timeline. You can hide or show the Track Mixer by clicking the disclosure triangle next to the word *Tracks* at the top of the window.

The Track Mixer contains three separate
tools: the Volume slider, the Pan wheel,
and the Level meters.

Adjusting Levels with the Volume Slider

You can adjust the volume levels for an individual track with the Volume slider. The over-all goal is to blend the different levels of all the tracks so that all the instruments can be heard, but the right tracks are emphasized.

By default, the Volume slider is set to 0 dB (decibels) for all tracks. 0 dB doesn't mean the volume of the track is 0 decibels. It actually means that there has been no change applied to the track's volume level. This applies whether the track contains recorded regions or loops. To change the track's volume level, you can drag the slider to the right to raise the volume level and to the left to lower the volume level. You can adjust the volume for an individual track while the playhead is static or while you're playing the song.

In our reggae song, there are 6 different tracks—which levels should you adjust first? Great question. Generally, you prioritize your tracks and start with the lead vocals or lead instruments. Because this song doesn't contain vocals, the guitar and piano tracks contain-ing the melody are the lead instruments, and therefore they take priority. Once the levels of the lead tracks are good, you then move on to the rhythm tracks.

Let's start by adjusting the volume level on the Wah Wah Guitar track. Before you adjust the volume, you'll need to solo the track so you can hear the level change without the other tracks.

1   Click the Wah Wah Guitar track header to select the track in the Timeline.

   The track turns brighter blue to indicate that it's been selected.

2   Press S, or click the Solo button, to solo the track.

   The soloed track becomes the only audible track in the Timeline.

3   Drag the Volume slider all the way to the left.

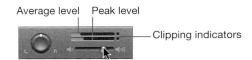

The slider turns blue when you click it to indicate that it's been selected. The lowest volume level is −144.0 dB (silence). That means the level has been lowered by 144.0 dB from the original volume level.

Next, you'll raise the volume while the track is playing.

4 Press Return, and then play the soloed track from the beginning of the song.

5 Drag the Volume slider to the right to raise the volume level while the track is playing.

6 Release the slider when you think you've reached a good volume level.

How do you know if your volume level is good? You can look at the Level meters.

Reading the Level Meters

The Level meters use colored bars to visually represent the volume level for the track.

Average level   Peak level

Clipping indicators

The lower the volume, the shorter the solid colored bars. If the color is green, the level is within a safe range and isn't too loud. If the color turns from green to yellow, that means caution—your sound is bordering on being too loud. If it turns red, you need to stop and turn the volume down immediately. The two circles at the end of the Level meters are the clipping indicators. Clipping means your music is not only too loud, but it could be distorted.

The Level meters in GarageBand are *sticky*, which means a single line of the colored bar will stick to the highest position on the meter while the average levels continue to change. The average volume level is marked by the solid colored bar, and the peaks are marked with the vertical line.

Let's create a cycle region and take a look at the Level meters in action.

1   Move your playhead back to the beginning of the Timeline.

2   Press C to open the cycle region.

3   Drag the ends of the yellow cycle region bar to resize the cycle region until it's approximately the length of the first region in the selected track.

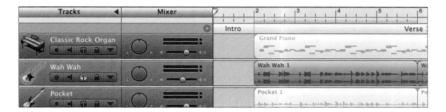

4   Press the spacebar to play the Acoustic Picking region in the soloed track.

5   As the region plays, watch the average levels and the peak levels in the meter.

    If any of the levels in the meter turn yellow or red, lower the volume for the track. You'll know your level is acceptable when the average stays within the green "safe" region of the meter, and the peaks remain within the green and yellow regions.

    Keep in mind that you can use the Level meters to see the levels, but the only way to make sure the levels are right for the song is to hear the track with the rest of the song.

6   Press C to hide the cycle region.

Project Tasks

Now that you've set the volume level of the Wah Wah Guitar track, let's take a moment to find a good level for the Electric Piano track. You'll start by unsoloing the Wah Wah Guitar track, soloing the the Electric Piano track, and finding a good level. Then solo the Wah Wah Guitar track again so you can hear both guitar and piano tracks and make sure the combined levels are good. Instead of using the cycle region, play the entire song with the guitar and piano tracks soloed, and watch their Level meters. I used a volume level of -4.8 dB for the guitar track and -6.7 dB for the piano track.

Using the Pan Wheel

The Pan wheel controls the left-to-right placement of a track within the stereo field. The *Pan* in Pan wheel stands for *panoramic*. A panoramic photograph is an image that includes everything you can see without turning your head. A stereo field is everything you can hear from the far left to the far right, without turning your head.

Imagine a panoramic photograph of the Rocky Mountains with a train cutting through the far-left side of the image. Visually, you place the train on the left side of your field of view. You would also place the sound of the train on the far-left side of the stereo field.

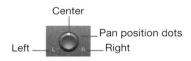

By default, all of the tracks in GarageBand start with the pan position set to the center. With center pan position, the sound is heard equally out of both speakers—it sounds like it's directly in front of you in the center of the audio space.

To adjust the pan position of a track, click the small white dots around the Pan wheel. Let's adjust the pan position of the selected track.

This exercise works best if you're listening through headphones, so take a minute and put on your headset before you start. Make sure your headphones have the right speaker (R) on the right ear and the left speaker (L) on the left ear.

1   Unsolo the Electric Piano track.

2   On the Wah Wah Guitar track, click the dot next to the L on the lower-left side of the Pan wheel to change the pan position to the far left of the stereo field.

3   Press C to show the cycle region. Press the spacebar to listen to the cycle region.

Notice that the guitar part sounds like it's coming from the far left.

NOTE ► If you hear the guitar coming from the far right, you probably have your headphones on backwards.

4   Click the dot next to the R on the lower-right side of the Pan wheel to change the pan position to the far right of the stereo field.

Notice that the sound of the guitar jumps to the far-right side.

5   Click the dot on the left side that's one dot away from the center position.

If the Pan wheel were a clock, the dot would be at 11:00.

Notice that the guitar still sounds like it's on the left, but closer to the middle of the stereo field. Now let's add the other guitar and make it sound like it's playing on the opposite position from the center of the stage (1:00 on the Pan wheel).

6   Solo the Electric Piano track so that both the guitar and piano tracks are soloed.

7   Press C to hide the cycle region.

8   On the Electric Piano track, click the dot on the right side that's one dot away from the center position (1:00).

9   Listen to the panned tracks.

Notice how it sounds like two different guitar players sitting on the right-center and left-center of the stage.

10 Press the spacebar to stop playback.

NOTE ► To quickly reset the volume and pan controls to the default settings, Option-click the controls. The default volume level is 0 dB, and the default pan position is Center.

Now that you have a better understanding of the Track Mixer and how to use it, let's start mixing the song.

Creating a Rough Mix

When mixing, you start with a rough mix, then fine-tune the mix, and finally polish the mix in the final master. There are five basic steps for creating the final mix:

1   Adjust the volume levels of the individual tracks to balance the sound of the different instruments.

2   Adjust the pan positions of the individual tracks to place them in the correct location in the stereo field.

3   Find and fix any musical imperfections in timing, tempo,or performance. (This may require editing in the editor, or rerecording a section of the song.)

4   Add and adjust effects to enhance the sound of individual tracks or the whole song.

5   Create dynamic volume and pan changes over time using the Volume and Pan curves on individual tracks and the Master track.

Let's start with step 1, adjusting the volume levels of the different tracks.

As you can imagine, there are hundreds of combinations of volume levels you could try on this song. Instead of experimenting, let's use logic and come up with a plan.

Planning Your Volume Mix

To mix volume levels, you need to know what type of sound you're going for in your song. What style of music is this song? A vocal ballad might favor the vocal tracks and the lead instruments and keep the drums low in the mix. A club song might favor the drums and synth bass tracks and bury the supporting tracks. Rock songs often favor the lead guitar and vocals and keep the drums about midlevel. Every song is different, every style is different, and every mix is different.

This song is a reggae song, so its guitar and organ tracks have taken a strong lead role. The drums also need to be very prominent in the final mix. The drum and bass rhythm parts as well as the supporting organ and horn parts are background parts that should be lower (quieter) in the overall mix.

Mixing Volume Levels for Individual Tracks

The first step is to adjust the volume levels to balance the song. Mixing music tracks is very much like mixing cooking ingredients. You start with the main ingredients, like water and tomatoes for a marinara sauce. Then you slowly add more ingredients, tasting along the way to make sure there isn't too much or too little of anything before moving on to the next. Following this analogy, the main ingredients (lead tracks) of the song have already been adjusted. Time to work on the next track, which in this case will be the Pocket Bass.

1   Select the Pocket Bass track.

2   Press S to solo the selected Pocket Bass track, then play the song from the beginning and listen to the bass along with the soloed guitar and piano tracks.

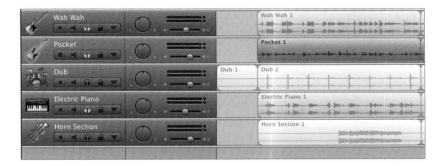

The default volume level (0 dB) is a good starting point for the Pocket Bass track. However, you may find it a little too heavy in the mix, which takes away from the lead guitars.

3   Lower the Pocket Bass track to -8.8 dB. Feel free to raise or lower it to your own liking.

Next, you'll add the Dub Drum Kit tracks.

4   Begin playback from the beginning of the song. Press the down arrow key until the Dub Drum Kit track is selected. Then press S to solo the track.

How do the drums sound and *feel* with the other tracks? They seem just a little dominant to me. In other words, they're a little too loud. Remember, your goal isn't to raise the volume of each track to match, it's to find balance between the tracks.

5   Start playback again from the beginning of the song and lower the volume level of the Dub Drum Kit track to -0.9 dB.

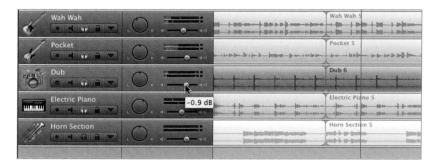

NOTE ▶   Adjusting track volume is like adjusting water temperature in a sink with separate cold and hot controls. If you're running both hot and cold water, and you want to make the overall temperature hotter, you can just turn down the cold instead of turning up the hot. The same goes for volume—instead of making a track louder to hear it better, you might need to turn down the other tracks a bit.

Before you mix the rest of the tracks, it's a good idea to mute the remaining tracks, then unsolo all the soloed tracks. That way you simply unmute the final tracks as you go. There's no sense in soloing all of a song's tracks; that kind of defeats the purpose of solo. You can click the Mute button on the remaining Classic Rock Organ and Horn Section tracks, or select the tracks and press M to mute.

6   Mute the two remaining tracks, then unsolo all of the soloed tracks.

Project Tasks

You should now add the remaining tracks one at a time to the Timeline. Simply unmute each track, then adjust its volume and pan. You can use your own judgment or try these settings:

Classic Rock Organ	Levels -5.6 dB	Pan -10
Horn Section	Levels -9.8 dB	Pan 0

Be sure to press Command-S to save your progress.

Sharing Your Finished Projects

Now that you know the basics of how to record, arrange, and mix your projects in GarageBand, it's time to learn how to share them with other iLife applications and export them to iTunes where they can be downloaded onto your iPod or burned to a CD.

All of the iLife '08 applications, including GarageBand, are designed to work together seamlessly. You can write music in GarageBand and export your songs to iTunes; score your iMovie video and export it as a QuickTime movie or send it to iDVD; send your finished podcast to iWeb to publish on the Internet; or create a whole playlist of original songs to be shared with any of your applications.

Sharing with iLife Applications

You have likely experienced the ease of working across multiple iLife applications as you've completed the lessons in this book. GarageBand is no exception. The key to this integration is the Media Browser that is accessible from both iLife and iWork (as well as many other applications).

1   Before sharing, always save your project by pressing Command-S to capture any changes.

2   When you're ready to share your project, click the Share menu and choose one of the following options:

▶   Send Song to iTunes—This option places a mixed copy of the track into your iTunes library. We'll explore it fully in the next section.

▶   Send Podcast to iWeb—You'll use this option in Lesson 15.

▶   Send Movie to iDVD—You'll use this option in Lesson 15. If you don't have a video track, this option is dimmed.

▶   Export Song to Disk—This option guides you through saving an MP3 or AAC file to a hard drive.

▶   Burn Song to CD—This allows you to place a song directly onto an audio CD.

Exporting Projects to iTunes

Exporting to iTunes is as simple as choosing Share > Send Song to iTunes. Before you begin exporting, however, there are a few things you'll need to do to prepare your songs.

In the next series of exercises, you'll set your GarageBand preferences to create a playlist in iTunes. Then you'll evaluate a song to make sure that you're exporting the whole song, and you'll check the output levels for clipping. Finally, you'll export your songs to a new playlist in iTunes.

Because you'll be working with a finished, mixed song, this is a great time to practice your "ear for music" so that you can hear beyond the basics.

Setting GarageBand Preferences for iTunes

To prepare a song to export to iTunes, the first step is to set your song and playlist information in the Export pane of the GarageBand preferences. You'll continue to use your reggae song for these exercises.

1   Choose GarageBand > Preferences to open the Preferences window.

2   Click the My Info button to open the My Info Preferences pane, if it's not already showing.

Next, you'll need to name your iTunes playlist, composer, and album. By default, GarageBand names the playlist and album after the registered user of the computer.

3   Type *iLife '08 Lessons* in the iTunes Playlist field.

4   Type your name in the Composer Name field.

5   Type *iLife '08 Book Album* in the Album Name field.

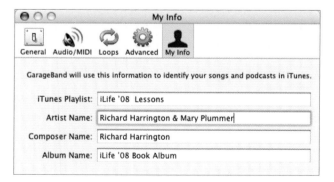

6   Close the Preferences window.

Now that you've set up the export information, iTunes will automatically create a playlist titled iLife '08 Lessons and include the composer's name as well as the album name information in the playlist.

Evaluating the Song's Output Level

Once you've set your information for iTunes, it's time to check the output levels for the song to make sure they aren't clipping. Remember, the Master Output Volume meters are located in the lower-right corner of the GarageBand window. You can use the Master Output Volume slider to raise or lower the output level as needed.

Also, because training your ears takes practice, remember to listen beyond the basic song: Check the left-to-right placement of the different instruments in the stereo field, as well as the balance between the volume levels of the different tracks.

Let's play the song and check the output levels. If the levels are too high, you'll need to lower the output. If the levels are too low, you'll need to raise the output.

1   Press Return, then the spacebar to begin playback. As the song plays, watch the Master Output Volume meters for signs of clipping.

> **NOTE** ▸ If you don't see the master level meters along the bottom of the GarageBand window, increase the size of the GarageBand window. You may need to change the resolution of your monitor to make more room. You can also hide the Track info if it's visible.

If you see any clipping (red) in the meters, stop playback.

You should discover red level meters and some clipping throughout the song.

2   Drag the Master Output Volume slider to -3.4 dB to lower the output volume and avoid clipping.

3   Play the song again from the beginning and check the new output level in the meters.

Be careful not to set your levels too low. Ideally, your levels should peak between the highest green and yellow portions of the meter.

The levels should be good, but the song ends a little abruptly.

4   Choose Track > Fade Out.

The master track appears and an Automation Curve is added to the track with a gentle fade. You can modify this curve as needed to control the fade out on your song.

5   Press Command-S and save the changes in your project.

> **TIP** ▶ Always save your project with the corrected levels before outputting to iTunes. That way, if you decide to output the song again or go back to work on the song later, the levels will be correct.

Sending a Song to iTunes

By default, GarageBand projects are sent to iTunes in AIFF (Audio Interchange File Format) at 44.1 kHz (kilohertz). Your songs can then be burned to an audio CD, downloaded to an iPod, or converted to another format, such as MP3, from within iTunes.

When you export a song to iTunes, the entire song or cycle region, if active—from the beginning of the first measure to the end of the last region—is exported. (If you mute or solo tracks, only those tracks set to play will be exported.) Let's export the song to iTunes.

1   Choose Share > Send Song to iTunes to export the song.

2   The Share dialog opens and offers several choices.

You can choose to modify the playlist information. You can also select the Compress checkbox, and then choose compression settings from the Compress Using and Audio

Settings pop-up menus. If you don't select Compress, a CD-quality AIFF file will be created.

3   Click Share.

GarageBand begins to mix down your song.

The mixdown process means that all of the different tracks are mixed (at the current levels) into one stereo pair (left and right) for iTunes.

A progress alert shows the progress of the mixdown. You can cancel the export process during mixdown by clicking Cancel.

When mixdown is complete, iTunes opens with your song in the new playlist, and the song automatically plays in iTunes.

You don't have to listen to the whole song.

4   Press the spacebar to stop playing the song, then press Command-Q to quit iTunes.

Once your song has been sent to iTunes, you can access it from any of the iLife applications through the Media Browser.

5   Select the GarageBand window to make it active, if it's not already active.

6   Press Command-R to show the Media Browser. Select the Audio pane, if it's not already showing.

The iLife '08 Lessons playlist appears in the iTunes library of the Media Browser.

Your song can now be used in any of the iLife applications, including GarageBand and iMovie.

7   Close and Save your project. When asked if you'd like to include an iLife preview, click Yes.

Lesson Review

1.   How do you create a Magic GarageBand project?

2.   How can you organize parts of a song like Chorus and Verses?

3.   Other than copy and paste, what is another method for duplicating selected regions in the Timeline?

4.   When using the Musical Typing window for recording, what keyboard shortcuts can you use to move the playhead to the beginning of the project?

5.   What should you do to a music project before exporting it to iTunes?

6.   What type of file does GarageBand export to iTunes?

Answers

1.   In the welcome screen, click the Magic GarageBand button.

2.   GarageBand '08 offers the Arrange track so you can quickly organize and rearrange sections of your song.

3.   The Option-drag method is an easy way to duplicate selected regions in the Timeline.

4.   The Return key can be used to move the playhead to the beginning of a song while the Musical Typing window is active. The Z and the Home key methods are disabled during Musical Typing.

5.   Check the master output volume levels to make sure the song is at a good level and not too low or too loud (clipping).

6.   By default, GarageBand exports songs to iTunes as 44.1 kHz AIFF files and places them in an iTunes playlist. You can also choose MP3 or AAC, which are compressed file formats.

Going Public

14

Lesson Files   iLife08_Book_Files > Lessons > Lesson14 > L14_Homepage Assets

iLife08_Book_Files > Lessons > Lesson14 > L14_Other Page Assets

Time   This lesson takes approximately 3 hours to complete.

Goals   Create a new website

Choose a theme for the site

Create a homepage

Add text to the homepage

Position text, shapes, and images on the page

Format and color text

Create links to external pages

Publish the site

Add additional pages to the site

Include a Google Map on a page

Incorporate an HTML snippet

Creating a Website

Once upon a time, if you wanted to publish something, you took it to the public square and read it out loud in front of the milling throngs. Later, inventions like the printing press, radio, and television made it possible to publish to a much vaster audience, but usually at a cost prohibitive to most people.

It sure would be great if there were an easy and low-cost way to publish and still reach millions of people—like, say, a worldwide web of interconnected computer networks capable of sending text and pictures and sound into hundreds of millions of homes and offices.

Wait a minute—there is! Today, if you want to publish something, you put it together on your Mac using iWeb and click a button to post it on your website. Then you wait for the milling throngs (or million web surfers) to come to you.

Deciding the Site's Purpose

If you're going to build a site and share it with a potential audience of hundreds of millions, it helps to have a plan. A good way to start is by answering these two questions:

▶ What are you trying to say?

▶ Whom are you trying to say it to?

The answers to these questions are connected. You may want to build your site in order to express your opinions, to share your experiences with others, or to sell something—or maybe even all three. In the following exercises, you'll build a site that combines those three motives: the website for a live-music concert venue, run by people who know the kinds of music they like, and want to share it with others. And the people they want to share it with are people who enjoy listening to the same kinds of music and are willing to pay to hear it performed live. The place is Jammin' Java, a popular cafe and music club based in Washington, D.C.

Choosing a Template

Now that you know what you're going to say, you want to look and sound good saying it—after all, millions may be watching.

iWeb, iLife's application for creating websites, has many good-looking professionally designed website themes from which you can choose. Each of these site themes provides templates for the various kinds of webpages you might use on your site: welcome pages, information pages, photo pages, podcast pages, blog pages, and blank pages that you can use for purposes that the other iWeb page templates don't address.

iWeb's icon

Let's pick a site theme for Jammin' Java and start jammin'.

1 Open the iWeb application.

The iWeb icon is placed in your Dock when you install iLife, but if you don't find it there, you can find the application in your Applications folder. Upon opening for the first time, iWeb displays a template chooser sheet (if you don't have a .Mac account, iWeb presents a .Mac sign-up dialog first before presenting the sheet). A list of themes appears in a scrolling list on the left of the sheet, and a pane of webpage template thumbnails for the currently selected theme appears on the right. The Black theme seems a suitable place to start for the site you're building, a popular coffeehouse that features nighttime entertainment.

NOTE ▶ If iWeb has been run previously, it may already have a site created, and you won't see the webpage template chooser. If that's the case, choose File > New Site to see the chooser.

2   In the theme list, click the Black theme. Next, click the Welcome page thumbnail on the right, and then click Choose.

iWeb displays the Black theme's Welcome page you chose in the *webpage canvas* on the right side of the iWeb window. The window's left side shows the *sidebar*, which lists the sites and pages you've created. Right now, there should be one site, named *Site*, and one page, named *Welcome*; you'll change these names later. Along the bottom of the canvas runs the iWeb toolbar. The page itself contains placeholder text and images that you can modify and supplement as you begin building your page.

NOTE ▶ You can change a page's theme any time you wish, and the site you build can comprise pages that use different themes. Use a set of pages that share a common style to help site visitors feel confident that they haven't accidentally wandered off into a different site as they move between the pages on yours.

Making the Homepage

The page you just added to the site is the *homepage*: the first page that visitors to your site see. Your homepage should help visitors find the information they came for as easily as possible. Most visitors to the Jammin' Java homepage probably want to find out which acts are scheduled to play at the cafe. You'll add a list of upcoming performances as well as prominent links that visitors can click to visit other pages on your site.

The Welcome page template you've selected contains a *navigation menu* at the top. It currently contains the name of the only page on your site right now: *Welcome*. As you add pages to your site, the names of those pages appear in this menu so your visitors can click a page name to go to that page. Below the menu is the page's header, which lets visitors know what page they're on. It currently reads *Welcome to My Site*.

First you're going to customize this page to add the Jammin' Java banner, and then you'll modify the header to be more informative and to match the banner design. After that, you'll add the performance calendar to the page along with some other information that visitors might find useful.

1 Drag the navigation menu down the page until it's 156 pixels from the top of the page.

As you drag, a yellow help tag follows your pointer, showing you where the item you're dragging is currently located on the page. The *x coordinate* shows how far it is from the left of the page and the *y coordinate* shows how far it is from the top. As an additional aid, a blue *alignment guide* appears when the navigation menu you're dragging is centered between the left and right sides of the page. You'll see these guides appear when you drag items around the page: They help you line items up with the sides and centers of nearby objects on the page, or with the page's top and sides.

Notice also that as you drag, all the other objects on the page move down. In iWeb, pages are divided into various regions: the navigation menu region, a header region where the *Welcome to My Site* header appears, the body region that contains the page's main contents, and a footer region at the bottom of the page. When you change the size of any of these regions, as you're doing when you drag the navigation menu down, the other regions move to accommodate the change.

2   In the Finder, open the **Lessons** folder that you dragged from the DVD that accompanied this book and find the **Lesson14** folder. Then open that folder and open the **L14_Homepage Assets** folder you find inside.

The items inside the **L14_Homepage Assets** folder contain the text and images you'll be adding to the Jammin' Java homepage.

3   Drag the **homePageHeader.gif** file from the folder to iWeb's webpage canvas, above the navigation menu you just dragged.

The Jammin' Java banner appears where you dragged it. There are a couple of problems, though: The banner is not big enough, and it isn't quite where you want it. The banner should be at the top of the page, and it should be as wide as the page's content area, which happens to be 700 pixels wide. You can fix the banner position and size using the Metrics Inspector window.

4   In the toolbar at the bottom of the iWeb window, click the Inspector button. In the Inspector window that appears, click the small ruler button that's third from the right in the Inspector window's toolbar.

You use the Metrics Inspector to see and change the size, position, and orientation of items on your webpage: Graphics, text boxes, and shapes can all be resized and repositioned precisely the way you want them. The name of the currently selected item, in this case the banner file, appears in the File Info area of the Inspector.

5   In the Size area of the Metrics Inspector, make sure that "Constrain proportions" is selected, and enter *700 px* for the banner's width. Next enter *0 px* in both the X and Y position fields in the Inspector's position area, and then press Return.

When you finish, the Jammin' Java banner appears at the right position above the navigation menu and at the right size. Notice that when "Constrain proportions" is selected in the Metrics Inspector, changing one of the dimensions of the selected item changes the other dimension automatically in order to keep the same proportions.

Adding a Shape

Now that you've repositioned the navigation menu and added the Jammin' Java banner to the page, you'll add a separator line above the navigation menu to match the one below the menu. This will help distinguish the navigation menu visually as a separate element from the others on the page.

1   In the webpage canvas's toolbar, click the Shapes button.

A pop-up menu appears, displaying various shape graphics that you can add to the page.

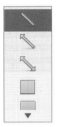

2   Choose the first item in the Shapes pop-up menu, a straight line.

A line appears selected in the center of the page. You'll use the Metrics Inspector to change its position and length, and the Graphic Inspector and Colors window to change its color to match the light gray color of the line below the navigation menu.

3   In the Metrics Inspector's toolbar, click the Graphics button immediately to the left of the Ruler button.

The Metrics Inspector window becomes a Graphic Inspector window. You use the Graphic Inspector to change various graphical characteristics of objects on a page.

> **TIP** ▶ Rest your pointer over each of the buttons in the Inspector window's toolbar to see a help tag that explains what Inspector the button represents. From left to right they are the Site Inspector, the Page Inspector, the Photos Inspector, the Blog & Podcast Inspector, the Text Inspector, the Graphic Inspector, the Metrics Inspector, the Link Inspector, and the QuickTime Inspector.

4   In the center of the Stroke area in the Graphic Inspector, above the Endpoint pop-up menus, click the white-colored button.

This button indicates the current color of the selected graphic item. The button remains highlighted after you click it and a Colors window appears. You use the Colors window to set the colors of things on the page: Text, shapes, borders, and backgrounds can all be set with the Colors window.

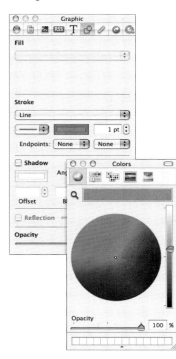

5   In the Colors window, drag the slider on the right down until just above the midway point.

The color chip at the top of the window shows a medium gray color; the line you added to the page becomes the same shade of gray.

6   In the Graphic Inspector's toolbar, click the ruler button again.

The window becomes the Metrics Inspector once more and displays controls suitable for controlling the length and position of a line shape.

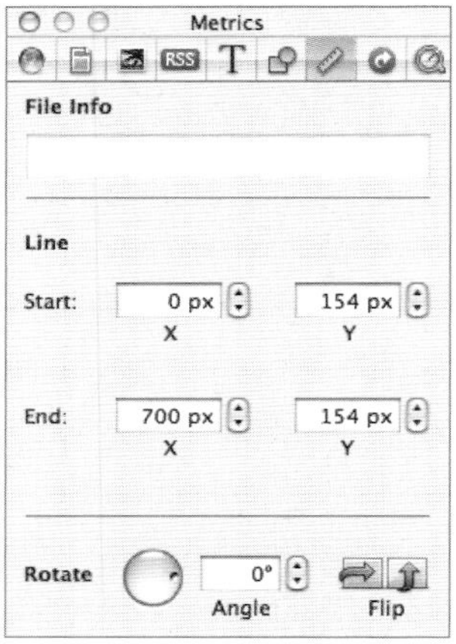

7   Set both the Start and End Y coordinates of the line to 154 pixels, then set the Start X position to 0 pixels and the End X position to 700 pixels, as shown above.

When you finish, the line moves to its new position directly above the navigation menu.

Now you need to adjust the length of the line below the navigation menu to match the one above.

8   Click the line below the navigation menu to select it, and then set its Start X position to 0 pixels, and its End X position to 700 pixels.

The bottom line now spans the page as well.

Modifying the Header

Now that you've added a banner and separator lines to the navigation menu region, your next step is to change the page's header to something more appropriate.

1   Double-click the *Welcome to My Site* placeholder text in the header, and type *Calendar*.

When you double-click a text box containing placeholder text, all the text is selected so you can immediately replace it by typing. *Calendar* now appears as the new header text for the page.

2   Select the new header text you just typed.

You need to have the text that's inside the text object selected for the next steps, which will change its color.

3 If the Colors window is not open, click Colors to open the window.

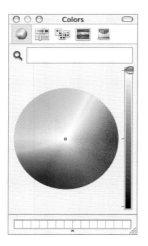

4 Click the magnifying glass near the top right of the Colors window.

Your pointer becomes a magnifying glass cursor. As you move it over the screen, the magnifying glass magnifies the area beneath it.

5 Position the magnifying glass over one of the colored letters in the Jammin' Java banner at the top of the page, and then click.

The header text becomes the same color as the text in the Jammin' Java banner graphic.

6   Choose File > Save, or press Command-S.

Whenever you finish a chunk of work on your page, as you've done here, it's good practice to save your work.

NOTE ▶ iWeb saves all your pages and sites in a single file in your user account's Library folder: ~/Library/Application Support/iWeb/Domain. You may want to copy this file to a backup location periodically so you don't lose all your work on all your sites should some disaster strike your Mac.

Adding Content to the Page

With the navigation area and header all squared away, it's time to turn your attention to the stuff that people actually come to this page to see: the main content. This content is a list of the acts scheduled to perform at the cafe.

NOTE ▶ The real Jammin' Java cafe has acts scheduled to perform almost every day of the month. For this exercise, however, we're only going to schedule four acts in order to save you time.

To do this, you'll create or duplicate a number of text boxes on the page, position them with the Metrics Inspector, and add the appropriate text to them from the files on the DVD that came with this book.

1   Click the big placeholder photograph on the page and press Delete.

This page will not feature a photograph, so you can reclaim the space the picture placeholder takes up and use it for the page's text.

2   Choose View > Show Layout.

This command outlines all the objects on your page with a thin line, so you can see them more clearly. Showing the layout can be very helpful when you work on a page that contains a lot of separate objects.

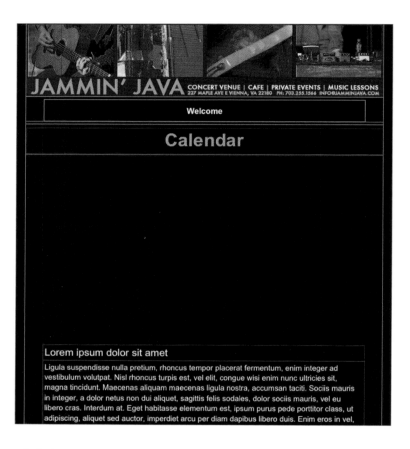

3   Click the page's title text box (the one that contains a single line of text reading *Lorem ipsum dolor sit amet*) to select the box, and then use the Metrics Inspector to position the box's top-left corner at these coordinates: X: 35, Y: 269.

The title text box now appears directly below the Calendar header text box.

4   Click the main text box to select it, use the Metrics Inspector to place the box at X: 147 and Y: 329, and then set its width to 345 pixels and its height to 285 pixels.

The main text box moves and changes shape to match your settings in the Inspector.

5   Choose Edit > Duplicate.

Another text box appears, slightly offset from the first one. The new text box is selected.

6   Set the text box's position to X: 147, Y: 622.

The text boxes no longer overlap and are now positioned in a column on the page.

7   In the Finder, drag the **ActOneText.rtfd** file from the **L14_Homepage Assets** folder onto the first text box in the iWeb window, then drag the **ActTwoText.rtfd** file from the same folder in the Finder onto the second text box in the iWeb window.

The placeholder text in the two text boxes is replaced by the text in the files you dragged. You now have two acts listed on the page.

TIP Although you can type and format text quite easily in iWeb, it's often easier to prepare the text in another program and then just drag the text file into a text box like you've done here. This allows you to reuse content you've written for other purposes. iWeb can incorporate text saved in RTF format, which can be exported from most word processing programs, including Pages and Microsoft Word. Depending on the program you use, the RTF file can even include images and links: Your Mac's TextEdit program, for example, can do this.

8   Set the height of the second text box to 193 pixels, then duplicate it and position the duplicate at X: 147, Y: 823.

9   Click in the duplicated box you just made so you have an insertion point in the box, choose Edit > Select All, and then press Delete.

The third text box is now empty.

10 Drag the file **ActThreeText.rtfd** into the third box, and then set its height to 351 pixels.

11 Duplicate the text box, position it at X: 147 and Y: 1182, and then delete the text it contains.

12 Drag the file **ActFourText.rtfd** into the fourth box, and then set its height to 409 pixels.

You now have four acts listed in text boxes on the Calendar page, all neatly arranged in a vertical column.

Adorning the Page

Next, you'll give the text boxes some style and illustrate them with thumbnail pictures of the performers.

First, you'll modify the appearance of the boxes containing information about upcoming performances at the cafe: Although white text on a black background looks stylish, it can be somewhat hard on the eyes. You're going to soften the look of these boxes, and, in the process, make them stand out more clearly on the page.

1   Click any one of the text boxes you just created, and then Shift-click to select the other three.

When you select multiple objects on a page, you can make changes to all of them at once.

2   Click the graphics button in the Inspector window's toolbar (it's the fourth one from the right) to show the Graphic Inspector.

Although the objects you've selected are text boxes, they still have some graphic attributes. The attribute you're going to change is the boxes' fill color.

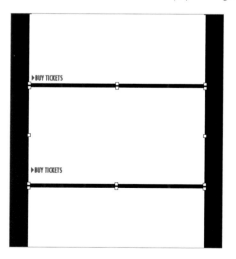

3   In the Fill area of the Graphic Inspector, choose Color Fill from the pop-up menu.

The text boxes immediately become filled with white, because that is the color currently displayed in the Fill area's color swatch. As a result, the text in the boxes seems to have vanished. Don't worry, you're going to fix that right now.

4   Click the white swatch in the Graphic Inspector's Fill area.

The Colors window appears. The Graphic Inspector will use the color you select in the Colors window as the fill color for the selected page objects.

5   Drag the slider on the right side of the Colors window about three-quarters of the way down so that the panel at the top of the window shows a medium-dark gray.

As you drag, the backgrounds of the selected text boxes change to match the color at the slider's position, and the text becomes visible again.

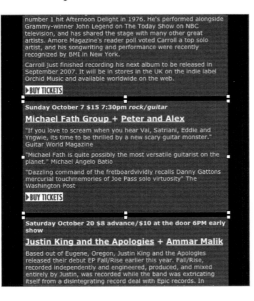

Your next task is to adorn the calendar entries for each act with small illustrations of the performers.

1   In the Finder, drag the `bencarroll.jpg` file from the `L14_Homepage Assets` folder to the left of the first text box in the iWeb window, then drag the `joncarroll.jpg` file from the same folder in the Finder to below the first picture in the iWeb window.

2   Click the first picture you dragged and use the arrow keys on the keyboard to move the picture up until it's just level with the top of the first text box. Then click the second picture and move it down so there's a small gap between the first and second picture.

3   Select both pictures and choose Arrange > Align Objects > Left.

The left sides of the pictures line up.

4   Drag the `king.jpg` file to the left of the third text box, then drag the `malik.jpg` file below the first picture, leaving some space between the two pictures.

5   Select both pictures and choose Arrange > Align Objects > Left.

6   Making sure both pictures are selected, drag the pictures slightly up and down until you see a horizontal alignment guide appear, then drag the pictures left and right slightly until you see a vertical guide appear.

iWeb shows the horizontal guide when two pictures are aligned with the center of the text box beside them. You'll see the vertical guide appear when the centers of the pictures line up with the pictures you placed above.

7   Drag and drop the **fath.jpg** file to the left of the second text box, then drag it so that
     it aligns with the pictures above and below and is also aligned with the center of the
     second text box.

8   Drag and drop the files **lgc.jpg**, **godgiven.jpg**, **tnyce.jpg**, and **samtim.jpg** so that they're
     arranged vertically beside the final calendar text box, and then select all four and drag
     them so that they align with the other pictures you've placed.

     When you finish, the bottom of the page should resemble the following picture.

By using the alignment guides and the Align commands on the Arrange menu, you can position objects on a page in relation to one another efficiently and accurately.

> **TIP** ▶ When you open iWeb's preferences, you can set whether alignment guides align with the centers of objects on the page, with the edges of objects, with both, or with neither.

Finishing the Homepage

With the homepage's main content in place, your final tasks are to replace the title placeholder text with something more meaningful and to add a small sidebar containing the week's current events.

1   Double-click the page title and type *Appearing in October* and then press Return.

The title lets visitors to the page know what all those text boxes and pictures that you've been placing are about.

2   On the iWeb window's toolbar, click the Text Box button.

A new, empty text box appears in the center of the page, ready for you to type something into it. You'll probably notice a problem: By default, new objects are always placed in the center of the webpage canvas, which means that your new text box is probably positioned directly over one of the calendar entries, making it very hard to see and manipulate. Fortunately, there's an easy solution: Use the Metrics Inspector to place it somewhere else.

3   Using the Metrics Inspector, set the box's position to X: 513, Y: 314, and set its width to 159 pixels.

The text box is now at the right side of the page, with the top of the box slightly higher than the top of the first calendar entry.

4   Type *THIS WEEK* in the text box.

The text appears in white. The text color of new text boxes on a page is controlled by the page template you chose.

5   Click the frame of the text box to select the box, and then, using the Metrics Inspector, set the text box's height to 38 pixels.

The box becomes shorter. This box is going to be a label for another box you'll place below it. But first, you'll format the text in the box.

6   In the Inspector window's toolbar, click the T button to show the Text Inspector and click the center text alignment button in the Inspector's Coloring and Alignment area. Then drag the Character slider in the Spacing area to the right until it reaches 30%.

![Text Inspector panel showing Color & Alignment, Background Fill, Spacing with Character 30%, Line 1.2 Multiple, Before Paragraph 0 pt, After Paragraph 0 pt, and Inset Margin 4 pt]

The text is now centered and widely spaced in the box. Now you'll add the text box for which this one is the label.

7 Click the Text Box button in the iWeb window's toolbar, then switch to the Metrics Inspector and use it to move the box to X: 513 and Y: 359, giving the box a width of 159 pixels.

A new empty text box appears beneath the label, with the same width as the label's text box. Don't worry about the box's height for now; iWeb will handle that for you.

8 Drag the **ThisWeekText.rtf** file from the **L14_Homepage Assets** folder into the new text box.

The box expands vertically to accommodate the text.

9   Click the edge of the text box to select it as an object, and then use the Graphic Inspector to give the box a white color fill.

Because the text is also white, it seems to vanish. This problem is easily fixed.

10   Using the Text Inspector, click the white swatch in the Color & Alignment area of the Inspector, and in the Colors window that appears, drag the slider on the right all the way down.

Voila! The text is now black and visible again. You can use background fills and text colors to create a variety of attractive text layouts.

NOTE ► Because the entire text box was selected, the text color adjustment affected all the text in the box. If you had selected just a portion of the text in the text box, the color change would have affected only the selected text.

The homepage is complete. If you haven't done so, now would be an excellent time to choose File > Save.

Publishing the Site

Although you still have some other pages to add to your site, publishing it once you've completed the homepage is not a bad idea. It gives you a chance to see how the site looks and works in a web browser, and allows you to tell a few friends about it and have them look and give you feedback for changes and improvements.

Before you publish your site, you have a few loose ends to clean up: the name of the site and of the homepage.

1   In the iWeb sidebar, double-click the top item, Site.

    The name of your site is selected for editing. It needs to be changed to something less generic than the word *Site*.

2   Type *JamminJava* and press Return.

    Your site is now renamed.

3   Double-click the next item, Welcome, then type *Calendar* and press Return.

    You've renamed the homepage. Notice that the navigation header on the page now shows *Calendar* instead of *Welcome*.

It may look odd to have *Calendar* in the navigation menu right above the page header, which also reads *Calendar*, but that's only because you haven't yet added any other pages to the site. Once you add pages, their names will appear in the navigation menu as well.

> **NOTE ►** You can move the navigation menu around, but you can't change its text or appearance. iWeb manages the menu: It uses the names of the site's pages for the menu's contents and the webpage template for its visual attributes.

With the loose ends all tied up, you are now ready to publish your site. You can publish either to .Mac or to a folder on your Mac.

> **NOTE ▶** Even if you own your own Internet domain, you can still publish your site to your .Mac account and have users visit your site by entering your domain's address. Choose File > Set Up Personal Domain to have iWeb walk you through the process of setting up .Mac hosting of a personal domain.

Publishing Your Website to .Mac

By far the easiest way to publish your site is to a .Mac account. If you have a .Mac account, iWeb can send the site there with a single click of a button. iWeb can detect whether you have your Mac configured to use a .Mac account, and displays the .Mac account it detects at the bottom of the iWeb window.

> **NOTE ▶** As mentioned elsewhere in this book, a .Mac account costs $99 a year, and in addition to giving you iWeb website publishing, it provides you with 10 gigabytes of online storage, email, software, and a bunch of other features. Most of the iLife programs can make use of a .Mac account. If you don't have a .Mac account and want to try it out, you can sign up for a free 60-day trial account.

iWeb also keeps track of which pages you've published, and which pages you haven't. It shows the pages and the sites you haven't published, or have changed since the last time you published, in red in iWeb's sidebar.

Ready? Let's publish the Jammin' Java site:

1   At the bottom left of the iWeb window, click Publish.

iWeb displays a Content Rights window with a reminder about using copyrighted material.

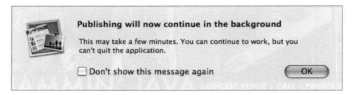

NOTE ▸ Clicking the Publish button is the same as choosing File > Publish. This command, like the Publish button, publishes any changed pages on your site to .Mac. In addition, you can choose File > Publish All, which publishes all the pages on your site, whether they have been changed or not.

2   Click Continue.

iWeb logs into your account, prepares your site for publishing, and then begins sending your site to .Mac. It presents a sheet telling you that the publishing is now taking place. You can continue working while iWeb sends your site to .Mac.

3   Click OK.

You can see how the publishing process is going by looking in your sidebar: iWeb displays a small round progress indicator as it transfers your site to .Mac.

That's it: three steps. If you select the two "Don't show this message again" checkboxes in the two sheets that iWeb displays, it's only one step the next time you publish.

As soon as your site is published, .Mac lets you know with one more sheet.

You can click OK to dismiss the sheet, click Visit Site Now to open your web browser and view the site, or click Announce to open your email program and send an email message with the site's address to anyone you want. iWeb even prepares the email for you—all you have to do is supply the addressees.

NOTE ▶ Once you've published your site to .Mac, the Visit button at the bottom of the iWeb window becomes active. You can click it at any time to visit your published site.

So let's take a look at the site you just published.

It looks almost exactly as it does in the iWeb window. If there are any discrepancies between how iWeb displays the site and how it looks in your browser (and often there will be), trust your browser because that's what people will be using to view your site. But keep in mind that what looks one way in your browser might look different in another browser on another computer.

> **NOTE ▶** In this example, a minor difference between the browser and iWeb has caused the top separator line on the page to appear a bit too high up. The solution is to lower the line a few pixels in iWeb and republish.

Publishing Your Website to a Folder

If you don't have a .Mac account, you can still use iWeb to design a site and then publish your site to a folder, which you can then upload to a web server operated by your Internet service provider or other web hosting service.

To publish to a folder, follow these steps:

1   Choose File > Publish to a Folder.

iWeb presents a sheet that lets you choose where to store the folder containing your site. The sheet also has an optional field where you can specify the address of your site, so that iWeb can set your site up for certain site functions. These functions include providing an RSS feed so that people can subscribe to any blogs on your site using an RSS reader (blogs are explained in a later lesson in this book).

2   Navigate to the place where you want to store your site folder, optionally provide the site's URL, and then click Choose.

iWeb presents the same Content Rights window that it shows when you publish to .Mac.

3   Click Continue.

iWeb saves your site folder and presents a sheet that tells you which features work differently (or not at all) between a site published on .Mac and one published to a folder. In particular, features that rely upon software running on the .Mac servers, such as hit counters and password protection, don't work for iWeb sites published to a folder.

NOTE ▶ Some of these features may be available from the Internet service provider that hosts your site, though making them work probably will require additional programming on your part.

Your site has been published to the folder you selected.

The following features are available only when publishing to .Mac:

- Hit counter
- Password protection
- Comments and attachments
- Personal Domains

For Subscribe buttons to work, you must type the site's URL in the dialog that appears when you choose File > Publish to a Folder.

Visit Site Now   OK

4   Click either button on the sheet to dismiss it.

Clicking the Visit Site Now button opens the site in your Mac's browser. This is an excellent way to check the appearance of your site in a browser before you actually publish it online, either on .Mac or on another web hosting service.

Adding and Linking New Pages

Your version of the Jammin' Java site now has one page on it: a calendar of upcoming performances. Now it's time to add a few more pages to round the site out.

You'll create the following pages: a Food and Drink page that offers the cafe's menu, an About page that tells visitors more about Jammin' Java, a Store page that gives visitors the opportunity to buy recordings, and a Contact page that gives site visitors a way to get in touch with Jammin' Java's staff for additional information or services.

The cafe's Food and Drink page is the first page you'll make. Although you can start this page by choosing File > New Page and then picking a page theme as you did when you created the homepage, doing so would require you to repeat all the preliminary layout work you did the first time. Because you want the Food and Drink page—and, in fact, most of the other pages on the site—to look similar to the homepage, it's easier to copy the homepage and then modify it.

NOTE ▶ Duplicating a well-designed page and modifying it is a very common method for giving a site visual consistency as well as reducing the amount of layout work you have to do as you add pages to the site.

1   In the sidebar, click the Calendar page, and then choose Edit > Duplicate.

A new page appears in the sidebar: Calendar 2. It's red, to indicate that the page has not yet been published. Also, the page's name appears in the navigation menu of the page displayed in iWeb's webpage canvas.

TIP▶ You can also duplicate a page by Control-clicking or right-clicking the page in the sidebar and choosing Duplicate.

2   In the sidebar, double-click the page's name and rename it *Food and Drink*.

The new name replaces the name in the navigation menu.

3   Double-click the page's header text and replace *Calendar* with *Food and Drink*.

Next, you need to get rid of everything on the page that you don't want to reuse.

4   Leaving the first calendar entry, the "THIS WEEK" label, and the white box below it alone, click to select each item on the page below the heading, and then press Delete to delete each in turn.

When you finish you have one calendar entry and the week's event list on the right.

5   Click the remaining calendar entry object to select it, click inside the entry to place an insertion point in the text, and then choose Edit > Select All and press Delete.

The calendar entry is now a single gray box. This box will become the home of the cafe's menu.

6   Using the Metrics Inspector, set the gray box's width to 498 pixels and its X position to 0.

The gray box becomes wider but retains its right and bottom margins.

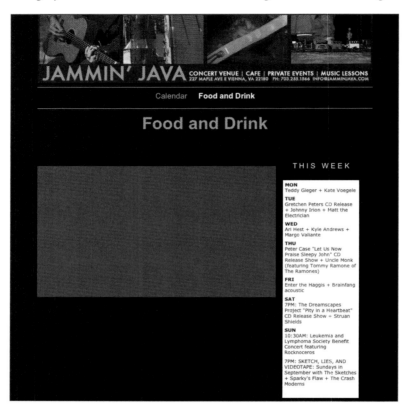

The page is now ready for you to add some new content. Before you do, duplicate this stripped-down page so you can use it as the basis for the other pages you're going to add:

1   Duplicate the Food and Drink page and rename the duplicate *About*.

2   Duplicate the About page and rename the duplicate *Store*.

3   Duplicate the Store page and rename the duplicate *Contact*.

4   Select the Food and Drink page again in the sidebar.

Filling Out the Food and Drink Page

Now let's add some content to the Food and Drink page: a graphic label to serve as the header for the cafe's menu, and the text of the menu itself. You can find these items inside the **L14_Other Page Assets** folder inside the **Lesson14** folder.

1   Drag the **cafe.gif** file from the **L14_Other Page Assets** folder above the empty gray text box on the page, making sure to align the left side of the image with the left side of the box.

2   Drag the **Cafe menu.rtf** file inside the gray text box.

The menu text appears inside the gray text box, expanding its length to accommodate the text. It's now ready for some additional formatting: For example, the entries on the menu are too close together, and the text is too small for older visitors to the site to see it clearly.

3   If the box is not selected, select it, then choose Format > Font > Bigger.

The text in the box becomes larger.

TIP ▶ You can press Command-plus to make text bigger and Command-minus to make text smaller instead of choosing those items from the Format menu.

4   Click to place an insertion point on the *Spinach Artichoke Dip* menu entry.

5   Using the Text Inspector, set the Before Paragraph spacing to 6 pt.

More space appears above that menu entry.

6   Repeat the spacing adjustment for the second and subsequent menu entries below each menu heading, but not for the prices.

Each menu entry is now separated more distinctly from the ones above and below it.

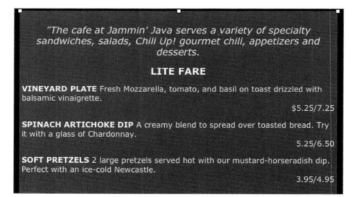

TIP ▶ Command-selecting in iWeb allows you to make text selections that aren't contiguous. For example, you can select a character or two in one paragraph and then hold down Command and drag to select a character or two in another paragraph so that you have simultaneous text selections in two places. You can use this technique to select portions of all the menu entries you want to change, and change them all at once with the Text Inspector.

7   Select the *Chili Up!* heading in the menu, click the color swatch in the Text Inspector to show the Colors window, and then choose a bright red color in the window's color wheel.

You can use the slider on the right of the Colors window to adjust how bright the color appears. When you finish, the *Chili Up!* heading indicates the spicy nature of the items below it.

Making the About Page

The next page you'll build is the About page. Most sites have such a page, which tells the story of the site or the business or owners who run the site. The Jammin' Java About page provides background about the owners of Jammin' Java and shares information about the cafe and its goals.

1   In the iWeb sidebar, choose the About page.

2   Add the About graphic by dragging **about.gif** from the **L14_Other Page Assets** folder and placing it above the empty text box, as you did with the Cafe graphic.

3   Drag the About.rtf file into the gray text box.

4   In the **L14_Other Page Assets** folder, open the file **wp-URL.txt** (it should open in the TextEdit program on your Mac), select all the text, and choose Edit > Copy.

This file contains the address of an article you want to link to. You're copying it so you don't have to type a long address. Copying and pasting web addresses to avoid making typing mistakes is a very common procedure when you build a webpage.

```
⊖ ⊖ ⊖                    wp-URL.txt
http://www.washingtonpost.com/ac2/wp-dyn?node=entertainment/
profile&id=1825912&typeId=5
```

5 In iWeb, find the section near the beginning of the About text where the reader is asked to check out an article in *The Washington Post*, and select the words *Washington Post*—they're on a separate line.

6 In the Inspector window, click the second button from the right in the toolbar to show the Link Inspector.

You use the Link Inspector to attach links to text and images on a page in iWeb.

7 Select the "Enable as a hyperlink" checkbox in the Link Inspector window, and then select the "Open link in new window" checkbox.

iWeb can detect a URL on your Mac's clipboard and will place it in the URL field of the Link Inspector when the "Enable as a hyperlink" checkbox is selected and some text or image is also selected on the page. If the link address you copied isn't already in the URL field in the Inspector window, select the text in the URL field, choose Edit > Paste to put the address you copied there, and then press Return.

8 In the Inspector window, click Format, then click the Rollover color button, and using the Color window's magnifying glass, choose the yellow-orange color from the page's About header text.

When you put your pointer over the link you've made, the text changes to the rollover color you selected.

9   Click Use for New Links on Page, and then click Hyperlink.

The same rollover color will be applied to any other text links you make on the page.

10 At the bottom of the About text, select the phrase *brindleybrothers.com*, check Enable as a hyperlink in the Inspector, and then type *www.brindleybrothers.com* into the Inspector's URL field and press Return.

The selected phrase is now a link.

11 Change the text of the page's header to say "About."

You've finished the About page. Save your site and get ready to build a store.

Making the Store Page

Many websites offer items for purchase, and Jammin' Java is no exception. In this exercise, you'll put some CDs up for sale and provide purchase links.

1   In the iWeb sidebar, choose the Store page.

2   Add the Store graphic by dragging **store.gif** from the **L14_Other Page Assets** folder and placing it above the empty text box, as you did with the Cafe and About graphics.

3   Drag **lb.gif** into the empty text box near the left side.

Rather than putting text into the empty gray text box as you've done previously, on this page you use the box as a container to hold a number of image and text boxes, such as the album cover you just placed on the page.

4   In the iWeb toolbar, click Text Box to place a new text box on the page.

5   Drag **lb.rtf** into the new text box, then drag the text box to the right of the album cover you just placed.

6   Drag the handles on the text box to adjust its size so that it spans the gray box from the album cover over to the right side.

You can use the alignment guides to help you position the text box more accurately after you resize it.

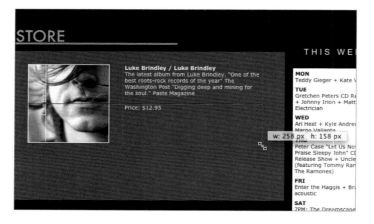

7   Use the Metrics Inspector, or select the gray box and drag its bottom center handle down to make the gray box longer.

You're going to be adding two more albums to the box, so you need to make room.

8   Repeat steps 3 through 6 twice to add two more albums below the first, using the files **pwtl.gif** and **pwtl.rtf** to supply the image and text for the second album, and **fwf.gif** and **fwf.rtf** for the third album.

When you finish, you should have three albums and their descriptions in the gray box. Next, you're going to provide the e-commerce buttons so that visitors can buy these albums.

1   In the iWeb toolbar, click Web Widgets, and choose HTML Snippet from the pop-up menu that appears.

A new HTML snippet appears on the page, with an editing panel where you can enter the code that goes into the snippet.

iWeb's HTML snippet feature allows you to place programming code directly on your page. In this case, you need to add something called a *form* to the page—when clicked, this link will produce a new page with items to be filled out. You won't need to write this code, though: It's already written and stored in text files in your **L14_Other Page Assets** folder. All you'll have to do is copy and paste it, as you did with the link URLs earlier.

2   Open the **lb-buy.txt** file and copy the text, then paste it into the HTML snippet editing panel.

3   Click Apply in the snippet panel.

The panel closes and the snippet becomes a red Buy button.

4   Drag the Buy button below the text description of the first album in the store.

5   Repeat steps 1 through 3 using the text in the **lb-itunes.txt** file.

This creates a link button that connects the user to the iTunes Store to buy the album.

6   Position the Buy button and the iTunes button so that they line up beneath the album description text.

7   Repeat steps 1-6 to create buttons for the remaining two albums, using **pwtl-buy.txt** and **pwtl-itunes.txt** for the second album's Buy and iTunes buttons, and **fwf-buy.txt** and **fwf-itunes.txt** for the third album's Buy and iTunes buttons.

8   Change the text of the page's header to say "Store."

When you finish, you'll have a completely operational online storefront.

Save your file, and get ready to make yet another page.

Making the Contact Page

Another page common to many websites is a contact page. This page provides a way for site visitors to contact the site creator. If it's a business site, the contact page often provides instructions for how to get to that location, sometimes even including a map.

The Jammin' Java contact page you're about to build provides all of these niceties.

1   In the iWeb sidebar, choose the Contact page.

2   Add the Contact graphic by dragging **contact.gif** from the **L14_Other Page Assets** folder and placing it above the empty text box, as you did with the Cafe, About, and Store graphics.

3   Drag the file **contact.rtf** into the gray text box.

4   Scroll to the bottom of the page, and drag the bottom center handle on the text box down to provide room for the map, which you'll add next.

5   In the iWeb toolbar, click Web Widgets, and choose Google Map from the pop-up menu that appears.

A Google map appears on the page, with a Google Map panel into which you can enter an address for the map to display.

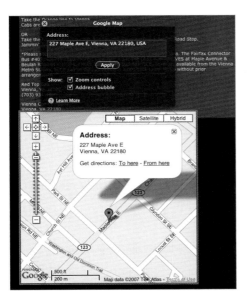

6 Enter *227 Maple Ave E, Vienna, VA, 22180, USA* into the Google Map panel's address field, and then click Apply.

The map displays the location of Jammin' Java.

7 Drag the map into position below the contact text, adjusting the map's height and width if necessary.

8 Change the text of the page's header to say "Contact."

Keep in mind that the map has to be large enough to show the controls: 400 pixels wide by 300 pixels tall is a reasonable size.

You now have a complete contact page. Again, save your work and, if you like, publish the site.

Jammin' Java is open for business!

Lesson Review

1. What are the regions into which iWeb divides a page?

2. What are two very good questions to ask yourself before designing a website?

3. If a site looks different in a web browser from the way it does in iWeb, which one should you trust?

4. Which Inspector do you use to set the background color of a text object?

5. How can you arrange objects precisely on the page?

6. How can you arrange objects precisely relative to one another on the page?

7. How can you copy a color from one object to another object?

8. What is an HTML Snippet?

9. What is a quick way to create several pages that have similar layouts?

10. What is the difference between the Publish button on the iWeb window and the File > Publish All command?

Answers

1. iWeb divides a page into a navigation menu on top, followed by a header region, a body region to hold the main content of the page, and a footer region.

2. Ask yourself what you're trying to say, and who you're saying it to.

3. You should always trust how the browser displays the page, because that's how people will be viewing it. A webpage will seldom look the same on all computers and in all browsers; webpages consist of instructions that tell the browser how to display the page, and different browsers may interpret those instructions in different ways.

4. You use the Graphic Inspector to set a text object's background color. You use the Text Inspector to change the color of the text itself.

5. To position objects precisely on the page, you use the Metrics Inspector, which allows you to set an object's size and page coordinates.

6. You can use iWeb's alignment guides or the options in the Arrange > Align Objects submenu to position items relative to one another.

7. Select the object you want to color, open the Colors window, drag the magnifying glass from the Colors window over the object that has the color you want to copy, and click.

8. An HTML Snippet is an object that allows you to place HTML programming code directly in a page. It is used to implement forms and other complex features that are not provided otherwise by iWeb.

9. Select the page in the iWeb sidebar and choose Edit > Duplicate to make a copy of the page and then modify the copy.

10. The Publish button, like the File > Publish command, publishes to .Mac only those pages that have changed since the last time you published. Publish All publishes all the pages to .Mac, whether they've changed or not.

15

Lesson Files iLife08_Book_Files > Lessons > Lesson15 > L15_Photo Page Assets

iLife08_Book_Files > Lessons > Lesson15 > L15_Blog Assets

Time This lesson takes approximately 90 minutes to complete.

Goals Build a photo page

Create a blog

Add blog entries

Incorporate additional photos in a blog

Make a video blog entry

Create a podcast entry

Creating Blogs, Photo Pages, and Podcasts

Blog. n. A website on which one or more people produce an ongoing narrative or discussion. (From *web log.*)

That's a fine definition as far as it goes, which is really not very far at all. It leaves out the most important point about blogs, which is that blogs—and their offshoots like podcasts and web photo albums—are among the most powerful, flexible, convenient, and enjoyable ways for you to get personal in public that civilization has yet seen. From the privacy of your own home, or from anywhere else you can get on the web for that matter, you can express yourself with words, pictures, and video, sharing your thoughts and experiences with a few million of your closest friends in a matter of moments—and those friends can tell you how *they* feel about it mere seconds after your fingers have left the keyboard.

Think we're exaggerating? Tell us about it on your blog.

Building a Photo Page

You've already seen how iPhoto makes it simple to post anything from your picture library online in a matter of moments. But if you already have a website, and want to post your pictures on a webpage that matches your site's other pages in style, you need something else. That something else is an iWeb photo page.

An iWeb photo page can slip seamlessly in among your site's other pages, and you don't have to abandon iPhoto's convenience either: iWeb uses iLife's Media Browser to let you reach right into your iPhoto library and get the pictures you want.

iWeb photo pages share some of the characteristics of a blog: People can subscribe to them, and they can (at your discretion) add comments to them. That's why we're covering them in this lesson.

In this exercise, you'll make a photo page on the Jammin' Java site to show photo highlights of acts that have performed at the cafe over the past year.

1   In the **Lesson15** folder, open the **L15_Photo Page Assets** folder, and drag the two folders, **JJ recent events** and **On the road**, into iPhoto.

You'll need the pictures in these folders for this exercise and the next. If you have iPhoto in your Dock, you can simply drag the folders onto it there. iPhoto will open and import the pictures, creating two Events, just as you saw in an earlier lesson. Once the pictures are imported, you can close iPhoto if you like. It doesn't need to be open for iWeb to use the pictures in the iPhoto library.

2 If you closed iWeb at the end of the last lesson, open it.

When iWeb opens it always displays the last page you worked on.

3 Click the + button at the bottom left of the iWeb window.

The New Page sheet appears, showing the available page templates from the theme you last used.

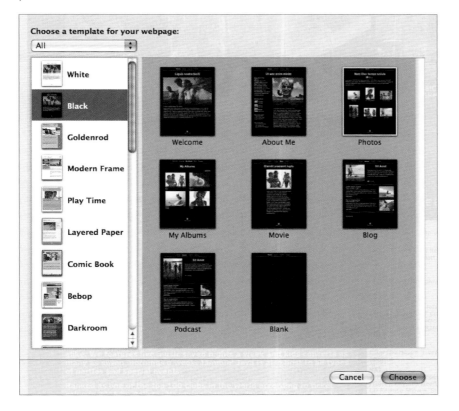

4 Click the Photos template and then click Choose.

A new photo page opens in the webpage canvas, and a Photos page appears in the sidebar. Notice also that the Photos page appears in the navigation menu along with the site's other pages.

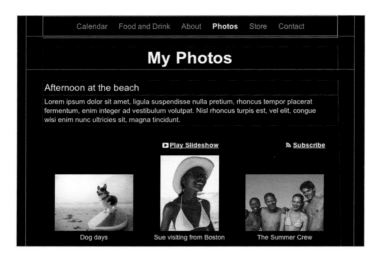

NOTE ▶ Although earlier you created other pages for the site by copying an existing page and modifying it, that shortcut won't work here—you need to use the Photos template in order to take advantage of the special photo layout and display capabilities built into that template. Fortunately, you'll soon learn some shortcuts to make it easier to customize a pristine page template so it blends into your site.

5   In the sidebar, double-click the name of the new page and rename it *Recent Events*.

   The new name appears in the navigation menu. However, it might be better if the Recent Events page came after the Store page and before the Contact page in the menu. That's an easy fix.

6   In the sidebar, drag the Recent Events page between the Store page and the Contact page.

   As you drag, a black line appears, showing where the page will be placed when you drop it. After you drag the page, the navigation menu changes to reflect the new top-to-bottom order of the pages in the sidebar.

7 Double-click the page header and type the new name for the page.

This page is not a personal photo page, as the placeholder text in the header suggests, but a collection of photos from recent events at Jammin' Java.

Recent Events

8 Choose View > Show Layout if the layout is not currently visible.

Having the layout visible will help you with the next part of this exercise.

Customizing the Photos Page Template

Now that the page is in place and appropriately named and labeled, your next task is to make it resemble the other pages on the site.

1 In the sidebar, click one of the other pages to display it in the webpage canvas, then click the banner graphic on that page and choose Edit > Copy (or press Command-C).

You're stashing the banner on your clipboard so you can quickly place it on the photo page. While you're on the other page, you can pick up a couple more useful items to use in the photo page makeover.

2 In the iWeb toolbar, click Colors to bring up the Colors window, then click the Color window's magnifying glass and click the magnifying glass pointer on one of the letters in the page's yellow-orange header.

The color you clicked with the magnifying pointer appears in the long rectangular swatch at the top of the Colors window.

3 Drag the color from the swatch at the top of the Colors window into one of the small squares in the palette at the Colors window's bottom.

The square you dragged the color onto now contains the yellow-orange color. The Colors window provides this palette so that you can store a set of colors in order to get to them quickly when you need to use them.

4 Use the Colors window's magnifying pointer to pick up the gray background color of a text box on the page and stash that color in the Colors window's palette.

5 Using the Metrics Inspector, click the navigation menu and note its Y position on the page as displayed in the Inspector window, then do the same for the separator lines above and below the navigation menu.

TIP ▶ When designing a webpage, it is often useful to have a pad of paper handy on which you can jot down things like object coordinates that you might need to refer to later.

6 Using the sidebar, click the Recent Events page, then click the Recent Events page's navigation menu and position it at the same Y position (154 pixels from the top of the page).

This provides room at the top of the page for the next step.

7 Choose Edit > Paste (Command-V).

The banner you copied from the other page now appears on the Recent Events page in the same location. When you copy objects on a page in iWeb, the copy includes the object's position information.

8 Select the *Recent Events* text in the header, then click the yellow-orange color you placed in the Colors window's palette.

The header color now matches the header color on the other pages.

9 Click the separator line below the navigation menu, and use the Metrics Inspector to set the line's Start X position to 0, set its End X position to 700, set both its Start Y and End Y positions to 204, and then choose Edit > Duplicate.

The first separator line now spans the page, and a new line appears selected just below and to the right of it.

10 Use the Metrics Inspector to set the duplicate line's X and Y positions to the ones you noted (for example, 0 and 158).

The line moves to the new position, which matches the layout on the site's other pages.

11 Double-click the page title text box and replace the placeholder text with the title *Highlights from the last 12 months*.

With the header and navigation menu areas set, and the title in place, it's time to address the main content of the page.

Adding Pictures and Other Content to the Page

An iWeb photo page's content region contains a title text box and a small main content text box. The rest of the page's content region is occupied by the photo grid, which can expand as you add pictures to the page or when you double-click a picture to show it in the detail view that the page provides.

For this part of the exercise, you'll add the pictures that depict recent performances at Jammin' Java, give those pictures captions, and provide a detailed description of the performers shown in the pictures.

The first thing you need to do, however, is to position the objects on the page so they're ready to receive the content you want to add.

1   Click the main content text box beneath the title and press Delete.

The main content text box goes away. Although you'll add a detailed description of the performers to the page later, the main content text box is not the best place for it: The description you'll be adding is long enough to push the photo grid too far down the page to look right. Moving the main text box below the photo grid is also not a good idea: When the grid expands, it will cover anything immediately below it. Later, you'll see how to work around these problems. Now, though, you need to take care of the blank space you left by deleting the main content text box.

2   Click once inside the photo grid area, making sure not to click a photo placeholder.

Clicking a blank area inside the photo grid selects its enclosing box so you can reposition the grid on the page.

3   Use the Metrics Inspector to set the grid's Y position to 342.

The blank space above the grid is eliminated.

TIP ▶ When you drag an object by hand, a help tag appears showing you the current coordinates of that object. If you don't want to bother with the Metrics Inspector, you can use the coordinates shown in the help tag to help you position the object accurately.

Now it's time to place the performer descriptions you want to add.

As has been discussed, the content region on a photos page changes size dynamically, so you can't add text content below the grid in that region. However, there is another region left on the page that you can exploit: the footer region. When the content region expands, the footer region—along with everything in it—moves down to accommodate the expansion. You can put your description text box there.

1   In the Inspector window's toolbar, click the second button from the left to show the Page Inspector, and then click Layout.

The layout pane of the Page Inspector allows you to adjust the height of the content region. Although its height changes dynamically depending on the content it contains, the size you set here still controls how far down from the bottom of the content region the footer region appears. You want to bring the footer region up closer to the bottom of the photo grid.

2   Set the Content Height in the Page Inspector to 400.

The footer moves up.

3   In the footer, click the Made on a Mac logo and press Delete.

4   In the iWeb toolbar, click Text Box.

A new text box appears on the page, right over the photo grid.

5   Click the frame of the text box to select it.

TIP The text box may be hard to locate. If so, you can type a few words to help you find it: iWeb puts the insertion point inside a newly created text box. You can also use the Graphic Inspector to set the text box's fill color temporarily to something that stands out on the page.

6   Hold down the Command key as you drag the box into the footer region of the page, and then release the mouse button once the box is in the region.

Ordinarily, dragging an object down below the bottom of the content region expands the size of the region. Holding down the Command key allows the object to cross a region's boundary.

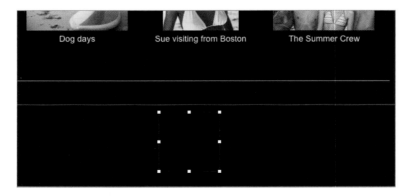

7   Show the Graphic Inspector, choose Color Fill from the Inspector's Fill pop-up menu, click the Fill color button in the Inspector, and then click the gray swatch that you placed in the Colors Window's palette.

The Inspector shows the gray color in its Fill color button, and the text object in the footer takes on the same hue.

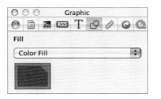

8   Show the Metrics Inspector, and set the text object's width to 623 pixels, its X position to 38, and its Y position to 690.

The text box spans most of the width of the footer region. You don't need to set its height: When you add text to it, it will expand as needed.

With all page's objects in place, you're finally ready to add content to the page.

1   In iWeb's toolbar, click Media. Then, in the window that appears, click Photos, click the disclosure triangle beside iPhoto in the window's top section, and click Events in the iPhoto source list that appears.

The Media Browser opens, and the bottom part of the window shows you the contents of the item you selected in the iPhoto source list. You're going to choose pictures from the JJ Recent Events folder you imported earlier. This iPhoto Event is the last Event in the window's bottom section.

NOTE ▶ Unfortunately, the Media Browser window doesn't show Event titles. If, for some reason, the JJ Recent Events Event is located elsewhere in the list of Events, don't worry. You can still find the pictures you need by using the Media Browser's search field as you'll see next.

2   Double-click the last Event in the window's bottom section to show the Event's contents.

The three pictures in the JJ Recent Events Event appear in the window. If you can't find this Event, however, you can find the pictures you need by their titles. To find the first picture, do the following: In the top section of the window, click iPhoto, and then type *chelsea* in the window's search field. The window displays the first picture you're going to add to your page, a picture of Chelsea Lee.

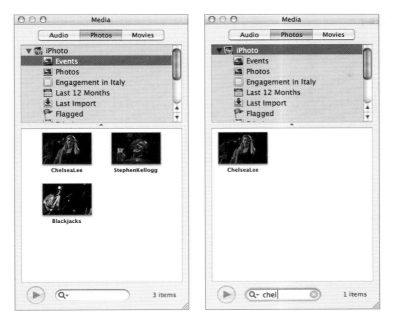

If you can't see the Event you need, you can find pictures by title, keyword, or rating.

TIP ▸ To make it easier to find and use pictures from iPhoto on your site, give them distinct titles, or use keywords, to take advantage of the Media Browser window's search capabilities. You can also open iPhoto and flag the pictures you want to use on your page and pick them up from the Flagged collection in the Media Browser window.

3 Drag the picture of Chelsea Lee from the Media Browser window and drop it on the first placeholder image in the webpage's photo grid.

The picture of Chelsea Lee replaces the placeholder and the other picture placeholders vanish. Even though the placeholders are gone, you can still add additional pictures to the grid just by dragging them.

4   Add the pictures of Stephen Kellogg and the Blackjacks to the grid.

If you need to search for these pictures, type *kell* in the Media Browser window's search field to find the first picture, and *blackj* to find the second one.

5   Drag the **Recent Events.rtf** file from the **L15_Photo Page Assets** folder and drop it on the gray text box you placed in the webpage's footer region.

The descriptions of the three performances appear in the text box. You're going to use the titles of the events from this text to provide captions for the pictures, replacing the picture titles.

6   In the text box, select *Chelsea Lee CD Release Show - Saturday 9/22/07* and choose Edit > Copy (Command-C).

This is the header of the first item in the box, and is in bold type, so it should be easy to spot.

7   Click the caption under the picture of Chelsea Lee and then choose Edit > Paste and Match Style.

You want the caption to retain its format and this command does exactly that: The caption is pasted without bold formatting and remains centered under the image. If you have nimble fingers, you can use the keyboard shortcut for this command: Command-Option-Shift-V.

8   Repeat steps 6 and 7 twice for the remaining two pictures, copying and pasting *Stephen Kellogg and the Sixers - December '06* for the Stephen Kellogg picture's caption, and *The Blackjacks - Saturday 5/19/07* for the Blackjacks picture's caption.

You may notice that some captions are too long to fit beneath the pictures.

9   Click any picture in the grid.

A Photo Grid panel appears with controls for adjusting the layout and appearance of the page's photo grid.

10 Choose 3 from the Caption Lines pop-up menu in the Photo Grid panel.

The captions now appear in their entirety. You can show as many as seven lines of caption below each picture. If you wish, you can edit the captions to make them lay out more neatly, such as inserting a Return between "Chelsea Lee" and "CD Release Show."

Fine-Tuning the Photo Page

The page is ready to publish, but before you do that, you may want to make some final adjustments and set a few more options.

1 In the photo grid, drag the Stephen Kellogg picture to the right of the Blackjacks picture.

As you drag, the Blackjacks picture moves to the left to make room for the picture you're dragging. Although not strictly necessary, this step puts the pictures in the same order as they appear in the descriptive text on the page.

2   Double-click one of the pictures in the grid.

You see a larger version of the picture in a detail view, and the footer moves down to make room.

3   In the Inspector window's toolbar, click the third button from the left to show the Photos Inspector.

On a picture's detail page, visitors are offered the option of downloading the picture. You use the Photos pane of the Photos Inspector to specify the size of the pictures visitors can download, or choose not to allow downloads at all, by making a choice from the Photo Download Size pop-up menu. The Inspector also provides an option you can set to allow visitors to the page to subscribe to the page with iPhoto, much like they can with an iPhoto Web Album. You can also choose to allow visitors to add their own comments to the page, much like they can do on a blog.

NOTE ▶ If you allow visitors to make comments, you need to keep an eye on them; iWeb keeps in contact with your site and tells you when new comments have appeared, and it gives you the ability to delete individual comments if someone posts an inappropriate or rude one. Monitor the page frequently after you publish it if you allow comments; otherwise, you may find inappropriate or offensive comments piling up on the page. The web is a big place, and not everyone who uses it is mature, responsible, and polite.

4   In the Photos Inspector, click Slideshow.

You use this pane to control whether your photo page allows visitors to view the pictures in a slideshow, and to set slideshow display options.

5   At the bottom of the iWeb window, click Publish.

The Jammin' Java Recent Events page is published. Go ahead and check it out.

Building a Blog

On the web, sites that don't add new content frequently don't get visited. One of the best ways to keep a site fresh is to add new content to it with a blog: an online diary, or log, of observations, announcements, and insights.

iWeb blogs provide the features and components that every blog needs:

▶   **A main page** that lists the most recent entries, and which gets updated automatically when a new entry is added

▶   **The blog entries** themselves, including links that allow the reader to move from one entry to the next

▶   **An archive of entries**, so that even when older entries have dropped off the main page, readers can still find them

For the Jammin' Java site, the blog is called From the Green Room. It comprises entries made by the site's owners, the Brindley Brothers, written and posted on those occasions when they leave their cafe and hit the road to perform.

In this exercise, you'll create the blog, customize its pages to match the rest of the site as you did with the Recent Events photo page, and add a few entries, including photos and a video, from the Brindley Brothers' road shows.

1   Click the + button at the bottom left of the iWeb window and in the sheet that appears choose Blog, then click Choose.

iWeb creates a new blog for you consisting of a main page, an entry page, and an archive page. The entry page appears in the webpage canvas. Before you start adding entries, you need to customize the three pages iWeb has created to have the same look as the rest of the site.

2 In the sidebar, click Blog to see the main blog page.

This page is the one visitors see when they click Blog in the site's navigation menu. You'll begin customizing this page first.

NOTE ▶ As you work, you'll find it useful to have the layout showing on the page (View > Show Layout).

3   Move the navigation menu down, adjust the bottom separator line, and add a top separator line as you did for the photos page. Then visit another page, copy the banner, return to the main blog page, and paste it.

If you don't remember how to do this, refer to the Customizing the Photos Page exercise earlier in this lesson.

4   In the sidebar, click Archive.

The archive page appears in the canvas. Even though you still have work to do on the main page, you should take advantage of the banner graphic that you still have on your clipboard.

5   Move the navigation menu, add and adjust the separator lines, and paste the banner, as you did with the main blog page.

6   Change the header text to *From the Green Room - Archive* and change its color to the yellow-orange color stored in the Colors window's palette.

7   Select the text *Green Room* in the header and change its color to a deep green. Then save that green color in the Colors window's palette so that you can use it again.

8   In the sidebar, click Entries, and customize the first entry's navigation menu, then change the header's text to *From the Green Room*, insert a return after "the," and then apply the colors as you did for the Archive page.

9   Go back to the main blog page and change its header to read *From the Green Room* and apply the same colors to it.

10 Delete the first placeholder image on the main blog page and resize the header text object so that it stretches across the page, then resize the placeholder text object below the header so that it spans the page as well.

11 Select and move the objects in the page's content region up to eliminate the empty space created by removing the placeholder image and resizing the two text objects.

You're now ready to tackle the first blog entry.

Adding the First Blog Entry

Once you have a blog set up in iWeb you seldom need to bother with the archive page or the main page—iWeb updates them itself, every time you add a new entry. You spend most of your time creating entries.

You'll finish formatting the first entry, which will become a model for subsequent entries, and then put some content in it.

1   Click Entries in the sidebar to see the first blog entry.

2   Click the text object that holds the entry's placeholder text and use the Graphic Inspector to change its color fill to match the same gray color used for text objects elsewhere in the site.

The gray color is still in the Colors window's palette ready for you to use.

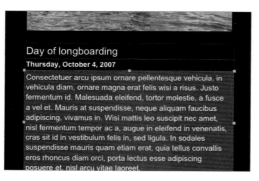

3   In the blog entry list at the top of the canvas, double-click the entry's date.

A calendar panel appears, allowing you to set the date and choose a date format.

4   Set the date to 12/23/2006 and then double-click the entry's title. Change it to read *JAMMIN' JAVA CD RELEASE SHOW.*

The entry's title changes on the page as well.

5   Open the **L15_Blog Assets** folder inside the **Lesson15** folder and drag the file **Blog 12-23-06.rtf** into the gray entry text object.

The placeholder text in the object is replaced with the contents of the file you dragged.

6   Drag the file **lb.gif** from the **L15_Blog Assets** folder and drop it on the entry's place-holder image, then click the image.

A picture resizing and repositioning panel appears.

7   Drag the panel's magnifying slider to the left to reduce the image's size so that it no longer fills the placeholder image object.

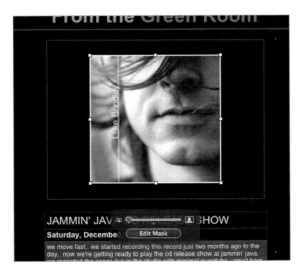

The first blog entry is now complete. Next, you'll make a few minor changes to the main blog page.

1   In the sidebar, click Blog.

The main blog page appears, with the first entry listed on it. The entry listing includes the picture you placed in the entry.

2   Replace the placeholder text in the blog description text object below the header with the following:

The green room is the room where performers wait before they go on stage. As long as we're waiting, we can fill you in on what's going on . . .

3   Move the objects on the page below the blog description up to eliminate some of the blank space below the description.

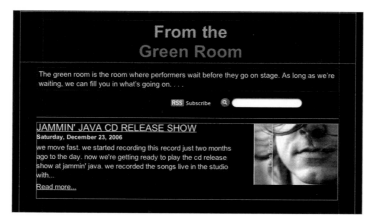

Adding Another Blog Entry

The main page is now ready to list additional blog entries, so let's create another one.

1 In the sidebar, click Entries.

2 In the entry list above the entry page, click the first (and only) entry listing and then choose Edit > Duplicate.

A new entry appears in the list. When you create a blog using a customized page template, it's usually easier to duplicate an entry than it is to use the Add Entry button and then customize the new entry that it creates.

3 Double-click the name of the duplicate entry and replace the selected title with *9:30 CLUB*, then set the entry's date to *3/10/2007*.

The title and date appear above the entry's main content text object.

4 Select the text in the entry's main content and delete it, then drag the file **Blog 3-10-07.rtf** from the **L15_Blog Assets** folder and drop it on the entry's main content text object.

The new blog entry text appears in the main text object.

5 Using the Photos pane of the Media Browser, click iPhoto in the source list and type *brindley* in the search field.

Three concert photos of the Brindley Brothers appear in the Media Browser's viewing area.

6 Drag the first picture shown in the Media Browser's viewing area and drop it on the picture above the entry's title.

The picture you dragged replaces the other picture.

This entry is ready to post as it is, but what about the other two pictures from the same performance? You can give this blog entry added flair by putting those pictures inside the entry's text object.

1 Drag the second picture of the Brindley Brothers' performance from the Media Browser to an unoccupied space on the page.

To embed a picture in a text object, you paste it directly into the text, but first you have to get the picture onto the page.

2   Click the picture you just dragged and choose Edit > Cut (Command-X).

3   Double-click the blog entry to make it editable, place the insertion point at the beginning of the entry's text, and choose Edit > Paste (Command-V).

The picture appears before the first words in the text, but it leaves a lot of empty space. You can change that with the Wrap pane of the Text Inspector.

4   Click the picture you just pasted to select it, show the Text Inspector, click Wrap in the Inspector to show the Wrap pane, and then click Object Causes Wrap.

The text wraps around the picture's right side. You can choose whether the picture appears at the left or right of the text object with the picture alignment buttons in the Wrap pane.

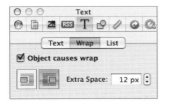

5   Click the Right Alignment button.

The picture moves to the right of the text object, and the text wraps around it on the left.

6   Drag the remaining performance picture from the Media Browser to the page, cut the picture to place it on the clipboard, place the insertion point at the end of the entry's text, and paste the picture.

7   Use the Text Inspector to wrap the text around the picture, and align the picture to the left.

Although there's no text remaining to wrap around the picture's right side, it's aligned with the left edge of the text object, creating a balanced layout.

Making a Blog Entry into a Video Podcast

In addition to the pictures taken at the 9:30 Club performance, the Brindley Brothers also had some video shot. That's worthy of a blog entry of its own.

1   In the entry list above the entry page, click the first entry you made in the blog, choose Edit > Duplicate, then rename the new entry *9:30 CLUB VIDEO* and set its date to *3/10/2007*.

2   Select the text in the entry's main content and delete it, then type *here's some video from our performance at the club.*

3   Drag the file **brindley brothers saturday night.mp4** from the **L15_Blog Assets** folder and drop it on the picture above the entry's title text object.

The video replaces the picture.

NOTE ▶ You can add video from the Media Browser or from files in the Finder, as you've done here. iWeb can handle most QuickTime files.

When you drag a video onto a blog entry's image placeholder, as you've done here, you've created a video podcast. You'll find out more about podcasts later in this lesson.

Creating a Text-Only Entry

Sometimes, less is more. You don't need pictures or video in a blog entry—in fact, the majority of blogs comprise text-only entries. One virtue of text is that it takes up very little storage space, which means it can be transferred over the Internet very quickly. The next blog entry you'll make is a text-only entry.

1   Duplicate the initial blog entry you made, then click its picture and press Delete.

The entry doesn't have a picture to go with the text. However, keep in mind that when you delete the placeholder picture object in an entry, there's no way of getting it back for that entry.

NOTE ▶ iWeb, as you've seen, can display the image in an entry's picture placeholder when it adds that entry to the main blog page. If the placeholder is deleted, iWeb won't show a picture on the main blog page, even if you added another picture to the entry at the same location as the deleted picture placeholder.

2   Shift-click to select the entry text object, the date text object, and the title text object, and move them up the page to reduce the now-empty space below the entry's header text object.

3   In the entry list, rename the new entry *LIVE AT BELMONT - LYNYRD SKYNYRD* and set its date to *9/9/2007*.

4   In the blog's entry text object, select the text and delete it.

5   In the Finder, drag the file **Blog 9-9-07.rtf** from the **L15_Blog Assets** folder into the entry text object in the iWeb window.

You now have a text-only blog entry, ready to be duplicated the next time you need to make a text-only entry.

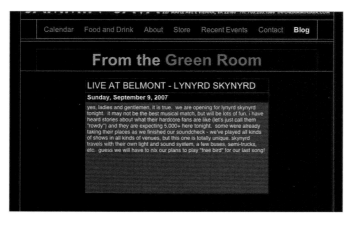

Reviewing and Refining the Blog's Layout

Although the From the Green Room blog is now ready for publication, you may want to review the main entry page to see if it looks the way you want, and to set any additional options for the blog. In this part of the exercise, you'll look at some of the available options.

1 In the sidebar, click Blog, and then double-click one of the entry summaries, making sure not to click any linked text in the summaries.

A Blog Summary panel appears. You can use this to show or hide pictures in the entry summaries, and to set the picture size, proportions, and placement in each summary. If you have a blog that is mostly text entries, for example, you might want to deselect the "Show photos" checkbox.

2 In the upper-right corner of the Blog Summary panel, click the round button with the *i* in it.

This displays the Blog & Podcast Inspector. You can use the Blog pane of this Inspector to set how many summaries to show on the page, to control the length of each summary, to display a blog search field so that visitors can search your blog, and to allow visitors to add comments and attachments, such as pictures, to your blog entries.

NOTE ▶ As was mentioned earlier in this lesson, if you allow visitors to make comments, you need to keep an eye on them so that you can swiftly act to delete comments that are inappropriate or offensive, or to remove attachments that you don't want on your entry.

The From the Green Room blog is now ready to be published with a single click of iWeb's Publish button.

Making a Podcast

What, exactly, is a podcast? In iWeb, it's any blog or podcast page that contains an audio or video file in the page's media placeholder. In practice, a podcast is the web equivalent of a radio or TV broadcast; a single podcast is called an *episode* and a group of them is called a *series*. People can subscribe to podcasts using a variety of applications, such as iTunes. In addition, with iWeb you can not only publish podcasts on your .Mac website, but you can submit them to the iTunes Store, where they can be made available to the few hundred million people who use iTunes.

You've already made one podcast in this lesson: the blog entry that contains the Brindley Brothers video clip from their 9:30 Club performance.

NOTE ▶ iWeb contains a podcast page template that you can use for a blog that consists primarily of podcast episodes. It includes a subscription link that allows visitors to your site to subscribe directly to your podcast series, so that every time you publish a new episode, the subscribers receive it automatically in their iTunes library. However, any blog page can be a podcast page if it has an audio or video media file in its media placeholder.

In this exercise, you'll take the podcast file you created with GarageBand in Lesson 12 and create a new podcast entry on the From the Green Room blog.

NOTE ▶ If you haven't worked through Lesson 12, just read through the next few steps. There's an alternate podcast file in the Lesson12 folder that you can use later in this exercise.

1   Open GarageBand, and then open the GarageBand podcast project that you created in Lesson 12.

2   Choose Share > Send Podcast to iWeb.

The Send Podcast to iWeb command in GarageBand is designed to send the podcast episode directly to a new entry in your site's blog. If your site has more than one blog or podcast, GarageBand first asks you which blog or podcast you want to receive the episode.

GarageBand then presents a sheet in which you choose how to prepare the episode for delivery to iWeb. You can choose whether GarageBand compresses the episode using MP3 (a widely used audio compression format) or AAC (a more advanced compression format used by devices such as the iPod). You can also choose how GarageBand optimizes the compression: for example, whether the episode should be compressed for best musical quality (which produces larger files), or for best spoken-word quality (which produces smaller episodes). If your GarageBand project is an enhanced podcast that contains pictures synchronized to the audio, you can also choose whether to put the pictures into a standard podcast size.

For the project created in Lesson 12, the default settings, shown here, are the ones you want.

Send your podcast to iWeb

Compress Using: AAC Encoder

Audio Settings: Musical Podcast

Ideal for enhanced podcasts with voice and music. Download times are moderate. Details: AAC, 128kbps, Stereo, optimized for music and complex audio. Estimated size: 7.0MB.

Publish Podcast: ☑ Set artwork to recommended size for podcasts (300 x 300 pixels) when exporting

Cancel   Share

3   Click Share.

GarageBand prepares the podcast episode for delivery, creating chapter markers if necessary, mixing the audio tracks together, and converting and compressing the audio. The process can take a few minutes depending on the length and complexity of the project, but a series of progress sheets appear to keep you informed about what GarageBand is currently doing.

When GarageBand finishes its work, it sends the episode to iWeb, which creates a new blog or podcast entry page to receive the finished goods.

As you can see, a problem arises if you've customized your blog or podcast pages from the template that iWeb provides: The podcast episode delivered by GarageBand ends up on a page that uses the uncustomized version of the template. That problem is easily solved with a few quick copy and paste maneuvers.

1 Select the text in the new entry's main text object and choose Edit > Copy (Command-C).

2 In the entry list at the top of the webpage canvas, select the first blog entry you made that includes a media placeholder, and choose Edit > Duplicate.

   The duplicate appears in the entry list and on the webpage canvas.

3 Select the text in the duplicate page's main text object and then choose Edit > Paste (Command-V).

4 Go back to the entry that GarageBand created, click the podcast in the media place-holder to select it, and choose Edit > Copy (Command-C).

5 Return to the entry you duplicated, select the current contents of the media place-holder, and choose Edit > Paste (Command-V).

6 Replace the text in the page's title text object with the podcast title.

7 In the entry list, select the now-unneeded entry created by GarageBand and click Delete Entry.

You now have the podcast on the customized From the Green Room blog page. It's ready to be published and for people to subscribe to it.

> **NOTE ▶** If you haven't created the podcast in Lesson 12, you can still create the podcast entry. First, perform step 2 above. Then replace the contents of the entry's main text object with a description of the podcast, and change the entry's title and date. Finally, in the Finder, drag the file **TLR_Brindley_Brothers.m4a** from the **L15_Blog Assets** folder into the entry's media placeholder in iWeb.

Adding the Podcast to iTunes

You can expand the potential audience for your podcast by submitting it to the iTunes Store, where it can be easily searched for and downloaded by the millions of iTunes users.

1   Bring up the Blog & Podcast Inspector and click Podcast to see the Inspector's podcast settings options.

The Blog & Podcast Inspector's Podcast pane has two sections: one for the entire blog, referred to in the pane as the Podcast Series, and one for the current blog entry, referred to as the Podcast Episode.

2   In the Podcast Series section of the Inspector, in the Series Artist field, provide the name of the author or artist responsible for the series, and then provide a contact email address in the Contact Email field.

The email address is not made public, but used only by Apple's iTunes Store staff so they can contact you.

3   Make sure Allow Podcast is checked in iTunes Store.

This checkbox applies to the entire blog. It must be selected for a podcast series to be submitted to the iTunes Store and for individual episodes in the series to be made available. You can also optionally indicate whether the series should have a Clean or Explicit label when it's listed among the Store's offerings by making a choice from the Parental Advisory pop-up menu.

4   In the Podcast Episode area, in the Episode Artist field, provide the name of the author or artist featured in the episode, and then click Allow Podcast in iTunes Store.

The Allow Podcast in iTunes Store checkbox in the Podcast Episode area can be selected or deselected for individual blog entries, which is necessary for a blog that contains a mix of entries, some of which are podcast episodes and some of which are not, such as the From the Green Room blog. You can also provide Parental Advisory ratings on an episode-by-episode basis.

5   Choose File > Submit Podcast to iTunes.

A sheet appears requesting some additional information about the podcast.

6 In the Copyright field, enter the copyright information for your podcast, and classify your podcast by choosing a category from the Category pop-up menu and an option from the subcategory pop-up menu to its right. Then click Publish and Submit.

iWeb publishes the site and opens iTunes. If this were your own site and your own podcast, you would then follow the instructions in the iTunes window to complete the podcast submission. When you submit a podcast, it may take a few days for Apple to approve it and for the podcast to appear in the iTunes Store.

With your site published and your podcast in the iTunes Store, fame and fortune surely await you.

Lesson Review

1. What is a blog?
2. What is the most important thing to remember about allowing comments on a photo page or blog?
3. What's the difference between a podcast page and a blog entry?
4. What's the most efficient way to create a new blog entry when you've customized the page template?
5. How can you add a text object below the photo grid on a photo page?
6. What happens when a visitor to a photo page subscribes to the page?
7. How can you add an image to a text object?
8. What are two consequences of deleting a blog entry's media placeholder?
9. What is the difference between a podcast on a page based on a blog template and one on a page based on a podcast template?
10. What is the difference between the blog archive page and the blog main page?

Answers

1. A blog is short for "Web log" and is a series of webpages, containing a set of entries that present personal observations, announcements, or insights, organized by date.
2. You must remember to monitor the comments frequently in order to delete inappropriate or offensive comments.

3. A podcast page is a blog entry that has audio or video material in the entry's media placeholder.

4. If you've customized a page template for your blog, you can make additional entries quickly by duplicating an existing entry and changing its content.

5. A photo grid dynamically resizes the page's content area, obscuring objects below it when new pictures are added or when visitors to the page view a picture's detail page—but you can put a text object in the page's footer area to keep the grid from appearing on top of the text object when it changes size.

6. When someone subscribes to a photo page, the photos on the page are added to an album in that person's iPhoto library, and subsequent changes to the page are reflected in that album.

7. To add a picture to a text object's contents, add that picture to the blog page, then copy the picture to the clipboard and paste it into the object's text, then optionally use the Text Inspector to control how text wraps around the picture.

8. When you delete a media placeholder in a blog entry, you can't associate a picture with that entry in the blog's main page, and you can't make that entry into a podcast entry.

9. When users subscribe to a podcast from a page based on a podcast template, new podcast episodes are downloaded directly into the subscribers' iTunes libraries.

10. The blog's main page lists summaries of only the most recent blog entries, whereas the archive page lists all of the blog's entries and doesn't provide a summary for each entry.

16

Lesson Files   iLife08_Book_Files > Lessons > Lesson16 > TDC_Ride

iLife08_Book_Files > Lessons > Lesson11 > Bike Ride Score FINAL.band

Time   This lesson takes approximately 90 minutes to complete.

Goals   Learn DVD concepts and terminology

Create an iDVD project

Modify the DVD menu screens

Add a slideshow to the DVD

Burn a DVD

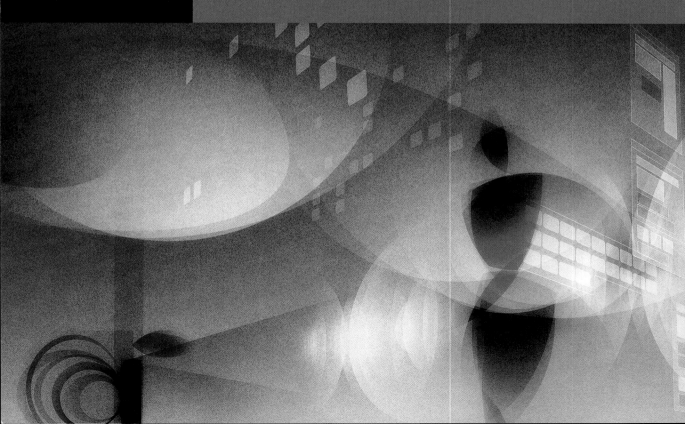

Making a DVD

A U.S. Senator once allegedly said, "A billion here, a billion there, and pretty soon you're talking real money." Substitute "capacity" for "money" and you could be talking about how many bytes it will take to store all the pictures, music, and movies you'd like to share.

As you've learned, iLife does make it pretty darn easy to take your songs and pictures and movies and put them on the web, but you've usually got to compress your songs and pictures and movies a fair amount to make that kind of sharing practical. What's more, it means that the people you share them with have to go online to enjoy them and, in the process, to suffer the unique joys of waiting for the download to finish. When it comes to a relaxing and engaging home entertainment experience, few things still beat popping a DVD in the player and curling up on the sofa with a bowl of popcorn and a remote control.

iDVD is the iLife application that puts you in touch with the couch potato lurking in all of us.

Exploring iDVD

At one time the acronym *DVD* stood for *Digital Versatile Disc* and in keeping with that original meaning, iDVD is certainly versatile. Making a DVD with iDVD can be a complex creative undertaking requiring a lot of time, thought, planning, and ingenuity—or it can be as simple as making a couple of menu choices, sticking a recordable DVD into your Mac's optical disc drive, and clicking a button.

The work you'll do in this lesson falls somewhere between a complex creative undertaking and the super-simple click-and-burn solution. Before you begin, though, it will help if you take just a few minutes and get to know some basic iDVD concepts, along with some of the names and functions of the tools that iDVD offers.

Although the purpose of using iDVD is to make a shiny DVD that you can play in your DVD player or on your Mac, what you are actually making as you work is an iDVD *project*. Each iDVD project is stored in its own *project file*, which you can store anywhere on your Mac. iDVD remembers the last project you worked on, and opens that project's project file when you launch iDVD.

If iDVD can't find the last project you worked on, it shows you this window when it launches, and it also displays this window when you close the project that you're currently working on:

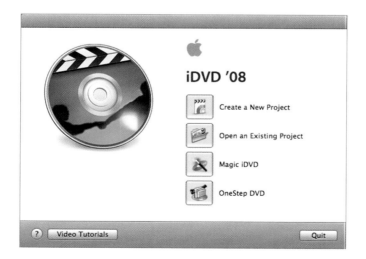

The functions of the first two buttons in the main pane of this window are obvious. Here are brief descriptions of what the other two buttons do.

Magic DVD

This button offers a quick way to create a DVD containing multiple movies and photo slideshows. You simply drag movies and sets of photos into the main iDVD screen, choose a design theme for the DVD, and click a button—at which point iDVD creates a complete project, ready for you to use to burn a DVD or to further customize. Magic DVD is a great way to get a running start when assembling a DVD project.

OneStep DVD

This is an even simpler way to use iDVD. Connect your video camera to your Mac, click this button, and iDVD takes the video from your camera and prepares a DVD from it.

Although you won't use either of these techniques in this lesson, the iDVD project that you'll create starts with a process just about as easy as the one that Magic DVD offers.

Exploring the iDVD Main Window

Nearly all the work you do when creating an iDVD project happens in the iDVD main window.

On the window's right side is a pane that displays various collections available to you as you build your projects. The first collection shown in this pane is a list of *theme families* that you can use as the basis for your project. These are similar in many ways to the themes that you use in iWeb when you design a site, or in iPhoto when you create a book, card, or calendar.

DVD Menus

On the window's left is the main area where you build your project. This area normally presents a DVD *menu*.

Unlike the menus you use in Mac applications, which drop down from a menu bar or pop up from a button on the screen, in DVD parlance a menu refers to the entire screen that the viewer of a DVD sees. On the other hand, DVD menus *are* like your Mac's menus in that they provide the viewer with a way to choose an item in order to cause something to happen: for example, starting the movie playing or showing a slideshow.

Menu Buttons

The items that DVD users interact with on a DVD menu are called *buttons*, even though they may not look like buttons.

Although they look like text labels,
these are DVD menu buttons

A DVD viewer typically uses the DVD player's remote control to move among the buttons on the DVD menu and to pick one—usually by clicking a real, physical button on the player's remote control. (If you use your Mac's DVD Player application to view a DVD on your Mac, you can navigate among the buttons on the DVD's menu with the simulated DVD remote control that DVD Player provides.)

The appearance of a DVD menu's buttons is set initially by the theme family that you choose when you create a DVD project. You can change a button's appearance with the Buttons pane, which you access by clicking Buttons below the pane on the right of the iDVD window. The Buttons pane contains a collection of button styles you can apply to DVD menu buttons.

Aspect Ratios

Many of the theme families you can use in iDVD come in two sizes: the 4:3 aspect ratio used by standard television sets, and the 16:9 widescreen aspect ratio used by modern HDTVs. You choose the aspect ratio for your project when you create it from scratch, though you can change it at any time. iDVD can also choose the appropriate aspect ratio for your project when you create it by sending a movie to iDVD from GarageBand, as you'll see later.

DVD Submenus

In addition to coming in two aspect ratios, many iDVD theme families offer three menu themes: one for the main menu, one for *chapters submenus*, and one for *extras submenus*.

Chapters submenus are used when a movie on the DVD is marked with chapter markers, as you did with GarageBand in an earlier lesson. Viewers use a chapters submenu to view the individual scenes in a movie.

Extras submenus are used when a DVD contains additional material, such as the behind-the-scenes production videos that many commercial DVDs offer in addition to the main feature.

Both extras submenus and chapters submenus appear onscreen when the person viewing the DVD chooses a menu button on the main DVD menu that links to those submenus. You establish those links when you construct your iDVD project.

Motion Menus

A number of iDVD themes provide animation, just like many commercial DVDs. Menus with animation are known as *motion menus*.

On a motion menu, a *playhead* appears in a *scrubber bar* at the bottom of the DVD menu in the iDVD window (it doesn't appear, of course, on the final DVD that you make).

You can position the playhead by dragging it left or right to see different parts of the animation. The shaded areas that may appear at the left and right of the scrubber bar indicate the presence of *intros* and *outros* in the animation. These are sequences of animation that appear respectively when the menu first appears on screen, and when the menu leaves the screen.

Drop Zones

Depending on the theme family, iDVD menus and submenus may also contain one or more *drop zones*.

Drop zones are sections of the DVD menu that contain an image, slideshow, or movie. Drop zones add visual interest to the menu, and frequently show small scenes taken from the content of the DVD itself. You can change the contents of a drop zone by dropping your own media into the drop zone as you build your project.

Motion Button

Finally, iDVD can play a motion menu's animation as you work. However, this can be distracting. You can stop and start the motion menu playback by clicking the Motion button at the bottom of the iDVD window.

Okay, enough preliminary information. Let's build something!

Building the Project

The project you're about to build you've seen before in a previous lesson: It's the film you scored in GarageBand.

1   Open the GarageBand project that contains the BikeRide movie you scored in an earlier lesson.

     If you didn't complete that lesson, the finished project can be found in the **Lesson11** folder inside the **Lessons** folder; it's called **Bike Ride Score FINAL.band**.

2   In GarageBand, choose Share > Send Movie to iDVD.

GarageBand displays a series of progress sheets as it prepares the movie for iDVD. When the preparation finishes, iDVD opens. After a few seconds, iDVD creates a new project containing the movie. Because chapter marks were added to the movie in GarageBand, iDVD automatically creates both a Play Movie menu button and a Scene Selection menu button. This last button links to a chapters submenu.

NOTE ▶ When you send iDVD a movie from GarageBand, iDVD chooses a default template and sets the aspect ratio based upon the dimensions of the movie it receives. You can change both of these in the project.

3   Quit GarageBand.

4   In the iDVD window, if the Play Movie menu button isn't selected, click it, then click the text inside the selected menu button.

The text inside the menu button is selected, and a formatting panel appears near the button. You can use the formatting panel to change the typeface, style, and size of the menu button's text.

NOTE ▶ Don't double-click a menu button to edit it—instead, click once to select, and then click a second time. Double-clicking a menu button causes iDVD to perform the action associated with that menu button. For example, double-clicking the Play Movie menu button causes iDVD to play the movie.

5   Change the button's text to read *Play the whole movie.*

6 Click the Scene Selection menu button once to select it, click it again to select its text, and then change the button text to read *Choose a scene*.

7 Double-click the text label above the menu buttons to select its text and change it from *BikeRide* to *Bike Ride*.

You can double-click text labels in the DVD menu to select their text because labels don't have any associated action. Notice that when you select the text of a label, it also displays a formatting panel.

Looking at the Navigation Map

Now that you have the main menu's text label and menu button labels squared away for the moment, you should take a look to see where each menu and menu button on the DVD currently leads.

1 At the bottom of the iDVD window, click the Map View button.

iDVD displays a navigation map of the project. In the map, the main menu, each sub-menu, and the movies they lead to are displayed as boxes with connecting lines so that you can see which ones are connected to which. For example, the Bike Ride menu (marked with a folder icon by its title) links to the movie you sent from GarageBand. It's labeled with the name of the menu button that leads to it, and is marked with a clapboard icon—the clapboard icon indicates that it is a movie. The main menu also connects to the chapters submenu, which is labeled "Scenes 1-4." This is not the label on the main menu's "Choose a scene" menu button, but the label that iDVD put on the submenu to which the "Choose a scene" menu button leads. The chapters submenu, in turn, links to four movies; the menu buttons on the chapters submenu are labeled with the names that the chapter markers were given in GarageBand.

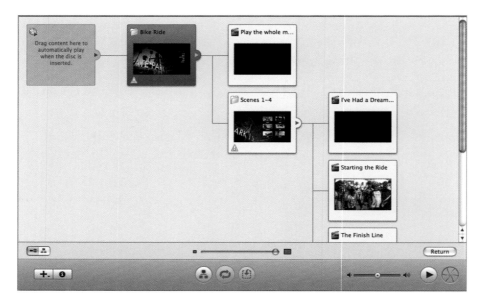

NOTE ▶ The four movies connected to the chapters submenu are actually one single movie. Each button on the chapters submenu points to a specific time in the movie. Clicking a chapters button plays the movie starting at that time.

2   Move your pointer over the warning icon at the bottom left of the Bike Ride box.

A help tag appears when the pointer hovers over the icon. iDVD marks menus in the navigation map with warning icons when it detects possible problems. In this case, iDVD has detected that the menu has empty drop zones.

3   Click the Bike Ride box in the navigation map. Then, at the bottom right of the navigation map, click Return.

The DVD's main menu appears in the iDVD window. When you select an item in the navigation menu, iDVD displays that item in its window when you click Return.

Switching Themes

When iDVD created the project, it chose a theme family for you, so next you'll change the theme family used by the project. Don't worry yet about the empty drop zone problem that iDVD pointed out on the navigation map. Because different themes have different drop zones, you can wait to deal with it until after you switch themes.

1   If the Themes collection isn't showing in the right pane of the iDVD window, click the Themes button in the window's lower-right.

2   Choose 7.0 Themes from the pop-up menu at the top of the pane, then scroll down the pane and click the Center Stage theme family.

A sheet appears telling you what happens when you switch a project's theme family: The theme for all menus in the project will change. If you like, you can click the disclosure triangle at the sheet's bottom-left to read additional information.

3   Click OK.

iDVD changes the theme of the menu shown in the window; it also changes the theme of any submenus in the project as well. As a result of this change, the menu buttons and text label have moved and changed appearance.

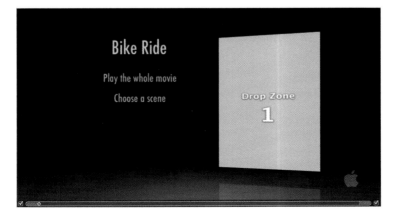

Editing Drop Zones

With the project's theme family swapped for a different one, you can now deal with the empty drop zone problem. But before you fill the drop zones, you first need the media with which you want to fill them.

1   In the Finder, open the **Lesson16** folder and drag the **TDC_Ride** folder inside into iPhoto to import the pictures it contains into your iPhoto library.

If iPhoto is in your Dock, you can simply drag the folder onto the iPhoto icon to import its pictures. Otherwise, open iPhoto and drag the folder onto the iPhoto window's main viewing area. When iPhoto finishes importing the pictures, you can, if you like, quit iPhoto.

2   At the bottom of the iDVD window, click the Drop Zone button.

The drop zone editor appears in the main pane of the iDVD window, listing all the drop zones on the current menu, as well as the menu itself along the bottom of the pane. In addition, the pane at the right of the iDVD window now displays the iLife Media Browsers. iDVD shows the Media Browsers automatically when you edit drop zones, because you usually fill drop zones with media from your various iLife Media Libraries.

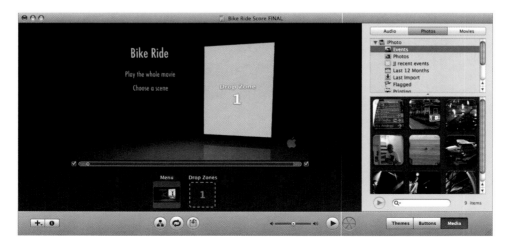

3   At the top of the iDVD window's right pane, click Photos, then click iPhoto in the list
    below, and type *bicycle* in the pane's search field.

    The Media Browser shows you a number of pictures that match the search term.

4   In the lower section of the Media Browser, find the picture titled "Bicycle_Ride 2" and
    drag it into the first (and only) drop zone shown in the iDVD drop zone editor.

    The drop zone in the editor shows a small version of the picture, and the main menu
    displayed above it shows a larger version of the same picture in the menu's drop zone.

NOTE ▶ Drop zones can contain either a movie, a single picture, or a group of pictures that are displayed as a slideshow.

5   At the bottom of the iDVD window, click the Drop Zone button again.

The drop zone editor goes away and the main menu again fills the left pane of the iDVD window.

Editing the Main Menu

Unlike the default main menu that iDVD picked when it created the project, the Center Stage main menu has no background audio. You'll add some and make some other minor adjustments as well.

1   At the bottom right of the iDVD window, click Media, then at the top of the Media Browser pane, click Audio.

Your iTunes and GarageBand collections appear at the top of the pane.

2   Click GarageBand at the top of the media collections list, and then select Bike Ride Score FINAL from the GarageBand folder in the Media Browser.

You'll use the first few seconds of the movie's score as the background music for the main menu.

NOTE ▶ If you haven't completed the lesson in which this was created, you won't find the score in your GarageBand music. In that case, pick any song from the GarageBand collection or any non–copy protected song from your iTunes library in the Media Browser instead.

3   Drag the song from the Media Browser to an unoccupied part of the main menu.

When the motion menu plays, it will play the complete soundtrack of the movie. You'll fix that next.

4   With nothing selected in the main menu, choose View > Show Inspector.

The semi-transparent Inspector window appears showing the Menu Info Inspector. The Inspector window will show a different inspector for each item you select in the current menu. When nothing is selected, the Inspector gives you options for modifying characteristics of the entire menu—in this case, the project's main menu. As you can see, the Loop Duration slider in the Inspector's Background section is set all the way to the end, meaning the entire audio file will play when the motion menu is playing.

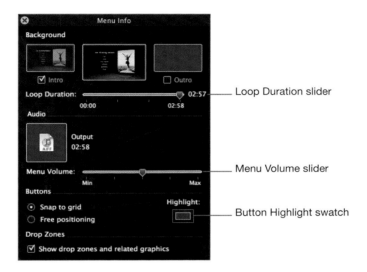

5   Drag the Loop Duration slider left to the 2-second mark.

As you drag, a help tag above the slider shows the current time setting of the slider. If your menu has movies in its drop zones, the slider also controls how long they will play. The duration slider shows the duration of the longest media in the menu, whether in a drop zone or background audio or movie.

6   In the Audio section of the Inspector, slide the main volume slider to the left until it's above the second tick mark.

You can choose to showcase the audio by raising the volume, which is better for complete songs, or to make it into something more like an ambient sound by lowering it, which is more suitable for short sound loops.

7   In the Buttons section of the Inspector, click the Highlight swatch.

A Colors window appears. The button highlight color shows the DVD viewer which menu button is currently selected; you can change the highlight color specified by the menu's theme to a different one.

8   Use the Colors window to pick a different menu button highlight color, such as a medium green.

9   Choose File > Save (Command-S).

It's always a good idea to save your work whenever you make changes to your iDVD project.

10   Close the Inspector and the Colors windows.

Previewing the DVD

Before moving on to the next design exercise, you can take a moment to use iDVD's preview feature to get an idea of how the DVD viewer will experience the DVD.

1   At the bottom of the iDVD window, click the round Play button.

The Play button turns the iDVD window into a preview window and brings up the iDVD remote control window so you can experience using the DVD as a viewer would.

2   Click the down arrow button on the remote control.

The "Choose a scene" menu button highlights.

3   On the remote control, click enter.

The preview window shows the outro animation for the DVD's main menu and then shows the Scenes 1-4 menu.

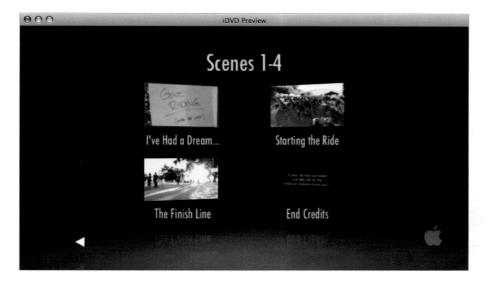

4   Use the remote control's arrow buttons to move to the Starting the Ride menu button and then click the control's enter button.

The Bike Ride movie begins playing, starting at the scene you picked.

NOTE ▶ You can also use your mouse to click the menu buttons directly in the preview window. However, using the control gives you a better sense of how viewers will experience the DVD.

5   On the remote control, click menu.

The Scenes 1-4 menu appears again in the preview window.

6   On the remote control, click title.

The DVD's main menu appears in the preview window.

7   On the remote control, click exit.

The remote control goes away and the iDVD window replaces the preview window.

Modifying Menu Buttons

Next you'll change the appearance of the menu buttons on the main menu to give them a thematic relationship to the movie's subject matter.

1   In the main menu, Shift-click to select both menu buttons.

2   At the bottom-right of the iDVD window, click Buttons.

The Buttons palette appears in the window's right pane. The menu at the top of the pane shows the extra highlight graphics that can be added to text-only menu buttons. The first item removes the highlight graphic from the selected buttons.

3   Choose Bullets from the pop-up menu at the top of the pane.

On this menu, the items above the line affect the button only when it's highlighted; items below the line change the button appearance at all times.

4   Scroll down the list of bullets in the palette and click the round bullet that has spokes inside.

This highlight bullet, though not specifically designed for the purpose, nicely carries the movie's biking theme over to the button highlight.

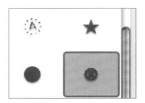

However, adding the bullet has caused the menu buttons to move to the right so they're partially hidden beneath the main menu's drop zone.

5   Choose View > Show Inspector.

The Inspector window shows the options for changing buttons, because buttons are the items that are selected on the main menu. The iDVD Inspector window is context-sensitive, showing the options for the currently selected objects.

NOTE ▶ As a shortcut, you can click the circled i button at the bottom-left of the iDVD window to show the Inspector window.

6   In the Inspector window, choose Left from the label pop-up and then slide the Size slider to the right until the bullets are as large as the rectangle that surrounds the menu button text.

When you choose Left, the menu buttons reposition themselves and the menu button text appears to the left of the bullet. The Size slider affects the bullets, not the text, which can be changed by adjusting its type size with the pop-up menu in the Inspector window's top-right.

7   Click the main menu to deselect the menu buttons.

The bullets disappear, because they're visible only when a button is highlighted.

Adding a Slideshow to the Project

DVDs are not just for video. You can also add slideshows of still images to your DVD. The pictures you use in the slideshow can come from anywhere on your Mac, but it's easiest to get them from your iPhoto library, which, as you've already seen, can be displayed in the iDVD Media Browser.

NOTE ▶ iDVD expects pictures for slideshows to have a 4:3 aspect ratio. It will scale pictures with wider aspect ratios to that aspect ratio. You can use iPhoto's Crop tool to crop pictures to the proper DVD aspect ratio.

You'll use the pictures in the TDC_Ride folder that you already imported into iPhoto to create the iDVD slideshow.

1   At the bottom-left of the iDVD window, click the + button.

A menu appears, offering items that you can add to the current menu.

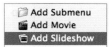

2   Choose Add Slideshow from the menu.

A new menu button appears on the main menu.

3   Using techniques you've learned earlier, add the same bullet highlight to this button that you added to the other two menu buttons and change the text of the menu button label to read *View bike ride slideshow*.

Remember to use the Inspector window to put the label to the left of the bullet, and to resize the bullet to match the other two menu buttons.

4   Double-click the slideshow menu button.

The iDVD slideshow editor appears in the left pane of the iDVD window, and the Media Browser's Photo collection appears in the right pane.

5   Type *bicycle* in the Media Browser's search field.

All the bicycle pictures that you imported appear in the bottom panel of the Media Browser.

6   Select all the bicycle pictures in the browser, then drag them to the left pane of the iDVD window.

iDVD lays the picture thumbnails out in the slideshow editor pane. A number appears at the bottom-right of each thumbnail to indicate its position in the slideshow.

7   At the upper-right of the slideshow editor pane, click the left side of the multi-segment slide layout button.

The slides now appear in a vertical list in the pane. The vertical list provides additional information about each slide, such as its file name, which can be useful when you build slideshows using several different collections of pictures.

8   Drag the Bicycle_Ride 1.jpg slide to the top of the list.

The slide you dragged is now the first one in the list. Rearranging the order of slides in an iDVD slideshow is a simple matter of dragging the slides into the order you prefer.

9   At the bottom-left of the slideshow editor, click the Slide Duration pop-up menu and choose 5 seconds, then click the Transition pop-up menu and choose Fade Through Black.

The top of the slideshow editor pane displays how long the slideshow will now take to play.

> 1 min, 15 sec (11 slides)

NOTE ▶ The Slide Duration menu offers a Fit to Audio choice that sets the length of each slide automatically so that the slideshow will last exactly as long as any music you add to the show. You can add a soundtrack to the slideshow by dragging an audio file from the Media Browser into the speaker well at the bottom of the editing pane. The Slide Duration menu also offers a Manual setting. When this is chosen, the slides won't advance automatically: instead, the DVD viewer uses the DVD remote control to move from one slide to another.

10 Click the preview button at the bottom of the iDVD window to view the slideshow.

The preview window replaces the iDVD window, the iDVD remote control appears, and the show begins playing. The show uses the timing and transition that you set. You can use the pause button on the remote to stop the show, and the left and right arrow buttons to move among the slides.

11 Click exit on the remote control window and then click Return at the bottom right of the slideshow editor.

The main menu of the iDVD project appears.

12 Choose File > Save (Command-S).

You are now ready to put your DVD into production.

Publishing the DVD

When your iDVD project looks the way you want, you can burn a DVD in your Mac's optical drive. But before you actually burn your iDVD project to a DVD, you should make a few final checks.

NOTE ▶ If your Mac doesn't have a drive that can burn DVDs, or if you don't happen to have a recordable DVD available, just read through this section.

1 Click the Map View button at the bottom of the iDVD window.

It's always good to take one last look at the map to see if there are any warning icons you need to deal with, and to make sure that the DVD menu structure is arranged the way you want it.

NOTE ▶ You can use the map orientation buttons at the bottom-left of the map to flip the map between horizontal and vertical orientations, and you can use the size slider beneath the map to change the size of the map's thumbnails so you can see more of the map.

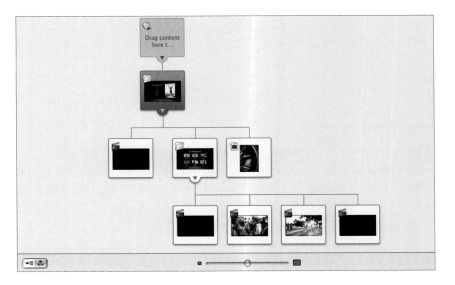

2 Click Return at the bottom right of the Navigation Map, and then choose Project > Project Info.

The Project Window appears. The bar near the top of the window shows you how much space on the DVD your project will take, and shows the amount of space taken by each kind of media in your project. You use the Media area at the bottom of this window to see which files iDVD will use when it creates the DVD, and to check whether they're all available. If a checkmark doesn't appear in the Status column for a particular file, it means that iDVD couldn't find the file. This can happen if the file has been moved or changed after you added it to the project. To fix this, you need to move the file back, or replace it in your project with a different file.

NOTE ▶ If you don't see the Media area, click the disclosure triangle at the bottom of the window.

You can also use the Project Info window to change the encoding method used for the DVD, to specify whether it's NTSC video (for US televisions) or PAL (European television systems), to change the project's aspect ratio, and to choose whether the DVD is to be burned on a single-layer or dual-layer DVD.

NOTE ▶ The encoding methods are Best Performance, High Quality, and Professional Quality. Best Performance is the fastest method, but it can fit less material on the DVD than the other two methods. When Best Performance is chosen, iDVD can encode your media (that is, convert it into the format used by DVDs) in the background as you work on your project; background encoding is not available for the other two methods.

3   Select the text in the Disc Name field and change it to *Bike Ride Movie*, and then close the Project Info window.

When you create a DVD by sending a movie to iDVD from GarageBand, iDVD automatically chooses a name for the disc you burn that's the same as the name of the GarageBand file. When you change the disc name, the name you specify is converted to upper-case when the disc is created. You can only use letters, numbers, and spaces in disc names (spaces are converted to underscores).

4   Get a recordable DVD disc and click the Burn button at the bottom of the iDVD window.

The button opens up to show the standard Mac disc-burning icon, and iDVD requests that you insert a blank disc.

Disc Insertion...
Insert a recordable DVD disc.

Cancel

5   Insert the blank disc into the Mac's optical disc drive.

After a few seconds, iDVD detects the disc and begins the disc-burning process. This process can take anywhere from a few minutes to several hours, depending on the amount of material you've included in the project and the encoding method you've chosen. A sheet appears to keep you apprised of the current stage of the disc-burning process, along with an estimate of how long it will take. You can cancel the process at any time, but canceling renders the recordable disc you inserted useless.

NOTE ▶ When iDVD finishes burning the DVD, it ejects the disc and gives you the opportunity to burn another copy. The second and subsequent copies may take less time to burn than the first because iDVD doesn't have to encode the material again.

TIP ▶ If you need to move your project to another Mac to burn it, or to give it to someone else to work on, you can choose File > Archive Project. This places all the media needed by the project into the archived project file.

Once the DVD is burned, you can quit iDVD, put the disc back into your Mac, and play it with your Mac's DVD Player application.

Or, even better, you can pop some popcorn, turn off your mobile phone, and enjoy your evening at the movies.

Lesson Review

1.   What is a OneStep DVD?

2.   What is a DVD menu?

3.   What aspect ratios does iDVD use for DVD projects?

4.   What is a submenu?

5.   What is a drop zone?

6.   How can you use the navigation map?

7.   What are intros and outros?

8.   Why is there a dividing line in the pop-up menu on the iDVD Buttons palette?

9.   Why might some of the pictures in a slideshow look squished?

Answers

1.   A OneStep DVD is a DVD created by hooking a video camera up to your Mac: iDVD burns the video recorded on the camera to a DVD in one step.

2.   A DVD menu is a screen that presents the DVD's viewers with buttons they can select using their DVD player's controls, to perform actions such as playing a movie, or presenting another menu.

3.   iDVD can create projects using the 4:3 aspect ratio used by standard television sets, and the 16:9 aspect ratio used by widescreen televisions.

4.   A submenu is a secondary menu screen, accessed from another menu. iDVD can create chapters submenus and extras submenus. Chapters submenus are used to present scene selections based on the chapter markers you set in a movie with another application such as GarageBand, and extras submenus can be used to offer viewers bonus material, such as slideshows or additional movies.

5.   Drop zones are areas on a DVD motion menu that present images, slideshows, or short video clips to provide visual interest; they have no other function.

6.   The navigation map shows where each menu leads in your iDVD project, and shows which media files are accessed from each menu, so you can see the path that a user

must follow to get to particular sections of the DVD. The map also displays icons that alert you to possible problems, such as menu buttons that have no media or menu associated with them, or drop zones that lack media.

7. An intro is a brief bit of animation that plays when a DVD menu first appears onscreen; an outro is animation that plays when the menu leaves the screen. Not all themes offer intros or outros.

8. The dividing line on the pop-up menu in the buttons palette separates items that only affect the appearance of a highlighted menu button from those that affect a menu button's overall appearance.

9. iDVD expects pictures used in a slideshow to have a 4:3 aspect ratio, and it will horizontally scale pictures wider than that to fit; you can use iPhoto's cropping tool to crop pictures to this aspect ratio and avoid having iDVD squish them onscreen.

Index

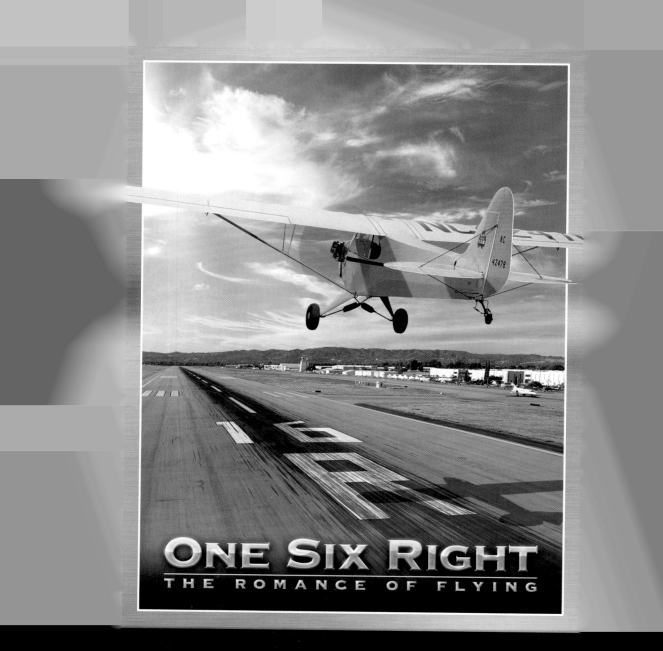

ONE SIX RIGHT
THE ROMANCE OF FLYING